AN APPROACH TO CHRISTIAN ETHICS
The Life, Contribution, and Thought of T. B. Maston

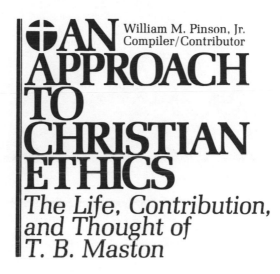

AN

William M. Pinson, Jr.
Compiler/Contributor

APPROACH TO CHRISTIAN ETHICS

The Life, Contribution, and Thought of
T. B. Maston

BROADMAN PRESS
Nashville, Tennessee

4261-20
ISBN: 0-8054-6120-5

Unless otherwise stated, all Scripture references are from the King James Version of the Bible.

Scripture references marked (RSV) are from the Revised Standard Version of the Bible, copyrighted 1946, 1952, © 1971, 1973.

Dewey Decimal Classification: B
Subject headings: MASTON, THOMAS BUFORD//CHRISTIAN ETHICS

Library of Congress Catalog Card Number: 78-71465
Printed in the United States of America.

Preface

Christian ethics brings together the various aspects of the Christian life and of biblical truth into a concentrated emphasis on doing the truth in daily life. No subject is more important, none more practical. An approach to Christian ethics which can be widely followed is needed—a model of how to live as well as teach Christian ethics, an example of a blend of scholarship and practicality. T. B. Maston in his life, teachings, and writings fills that need. This and future generations of churchmen and students will benefit from knowing the model T. B. Maston provides and by following his example.

These pages summarize an approach to Christian ethics as seen in the life and thought of T. B Maston. Christians from all denominations and theological persuasions will find them helpful even if they do not agree with all that Maston has done or said. Students of Christian ethics should know Maston, and should realize that his approach to ethics ought to be carefully and seriously analyzed, and follow his example of making Christian ethics not so much a discipline to be learned as a way of life to be followed.

A book about T. B. Maston is no simple project. Eighty years of life are difficult to compress into a few pages. A brilliant career as an ethicist, teacher, and writer can hardly be done justice in one book. A man whose life has literally touched millions cannot be pared down to fit neatly into a single volume.

Because T. B. Maston's life has been long and productive and because he has influenced many, it was felt that no one person could adequately summarize his life and teachings. Literally hundreds of persons could have contributed to this book—friends, former students, colleagues, editors, scholars, and Christian leaders from all over the world. After exploring several different possibilities, it was finally determined to have the book written by some of those who majored in Christian ethics under T. B. Maston while working toward their doctor's degree. The roll call of authors includes pastors, missionaries, denominational executives, seminary presidents, and college and seminary professors. The variety of persons who have written this book is symbolic of the wide influence Maston has had and the diversity of his areas of interest.

The book is in three sections. The first is a brief overview of the life of T. B. Maston. The second contains a series of statements about the varied and numerous contributions of Maston's life. He has made an impact not only by what he has written and taught but also by the way he has lived. The third section is made up of chapters summarizing Maston's thought on various subjects; none is a complete statement of his thought on the subject considered but rather each is a guidepost to further study. Taken as a whole the volume presents a model for doing Christian ethics.

Although I served as the coordinator of the project, many persons contributed to help make a dream become a reality. Jase Jones was particularly helpful in arranging for the financial underwriting to make the book possible. Mrs. Wanda Bundy served as a secretary for the project. Also assisting were Miss Bonnie Chappell and Mrs. Judy Harvey. Mr. Dan Ratliff assisted by reading through the manuscript in preparation for publication.

W. M. Pinson, Jr.
Golden Gate Baptist Theological Seminary
Mill Valley, California
Fall, 1978

Contributors

Jimmy R. Allen, pastor, First Baptist Church, San Antonio, Texas.

Wayne Barnes, pastor, First Baptist Church, Zachary, Louisiana.

Julian C. Bridges, professor and head of the Department of Sociology and Social Work, Hardin-Simmons University, Abilene, Texas.

C. W. Brister, professor of pastoral ministry, Southwestern Baptist Theological Seminary, Fort Worth, Texas.

James M. Dunn, director of the Christian Life Commission, Baptist General Convention of Texas, Dallas, Texas.

Thurmon E. Bryant, secretary for Eastern South America, Foreign Mission Board of the Southern Baptist Convention, Richmond, Virginia.

James E. Giles, president, International Baptist Theological Seminary, Cali, Colombia.

Felix M. Gresham, seminary chaplain and director of student aid, Southwestern Baptist Theological Seminary, Fort Worth, Texas.

John C. Howell, academic dean and professor of Christian Ethics, Midwestern Baptist Theological Seminary, Kansas City, Missouri.

A. Jase Jones, area missionary director, department of interfaith witness, Home Mission Board of the Southern Baptist Convention, Atlanta, Georgia.

Tom J. Logue, director of student department, Arkansas Baptist State Convention, Little Rock, Arkansas.

W. Randall Lolley, president, Southeastern Baptist Theological Seminary, Wake Forest, North Carolina.

Charles E. Myers, pastor, Alta Woods Baptist Church, Jackson, Mississippi.

Ralph Phelps, pastor, Virginia Hill Baptist Church, Athens, Texas.

Lee Porter, consultant, Adult work, The Sunday School Board of the Southern Baptist Convention, Nashville, Tennessee.

C. W. Scudder, administrator of internal affairs, Midwestern Baptist Theological Seminary, Kansas City, Missouri.

Ebbie Smith, associate professor of Christian ethics, Southwestern Baptist Theological Seminary, Fort Worth, Texas.

Cecil L. Thompson, book editor and theological textbook coordinator, Baptist Spanish Publishing House, El Paso, Texas.

Joe E. Trull, pastor, Calvary Baptist Church, Garland, Texas.

Foy Valentine, executive secretary-treasurer, the Christian Life Commission, Nashville, Tennessee.

Browning Ware, pastor, First Baptist Church, Austin, Texas.

Keith C. Wills, director of Fleming Library, Southwestern Baptist Theological Seminary, Fort Worth, Texas.

Marguerite Woodruff, professor of Sociology, Mercer University, Macon, Georgia.

Contents

I
THE LIFE OF T. B. MASTON

Thomas Buford Maston

1897   Born November 26, Jefferson County, Tennessee
1904   Entered elementary school at College Corners, Ohio
1911   Moved to Fountain City, Tennessee
1914   Baptized into the Smithwood Baptist Church; felt call into ministry
1916   Graduated from Central High School of Fountain City; licensed to preach; entered Carson-Newman College
1920   Graduated from Carson-Newman; entered Southwestern Baptist Theological Seminary
1921   Married Essie Mae McDonald, June 11
1922   Began teaching in the School of Religious Education at Southwestern Seminary
1923   Received master of religious education (M.R.E.) degree from Southwestern Seminary
1925   Received doctor of religious education (D.R.E.) degree from Southwestern Seminary; Thomas McDonald Maston born
1927   Received master of arts (M.A.) degree from Texas Christian University
1928   Harold Eugene Maston born
1932   Entered Yale University
1939   Received doctor of philosophy (Ph.D.) degree from Yale University
1943   Established the Department of Christian Social Ethics at Southwestern Seminary
1946   *Of One* published
1954   Went on speaking tour of mission work in Central and South America
1955   Taught as guest professor at Southern Baptist Theological Seminary
1957   *Christianity and World Issues* published
1959   Taught as guest professor at Southeastern Baptist Theological Seminary; traveled to the Orient speaking at American military bases
1963   Retired from Southwestern Seminary
1966   Taught at the Arab Baptist Seminary in Beirut, Lebanon
1969   Taught as guest professor at Golden Gate Baptist Theological Seminary
1974   *Why Live the Christian Life?* published
1978   *How to Face Grief* published

13

Biography

William M. Pinson, Jr.

Born in a log house in Jefferson County, Tennessee, across the French Broad River from the Great Smoky Mountains, Thomas Buford Maston spent his earliest years in a land still scarred by the American Civil War. His father, Samuel Houston Maston, a raw-boned, East Tennessee hillbilly with an eighth-grade education and a profound interest in his church, family, and current events, worked hard as a farmer and railroad section hand to support his family. Tom's mother, Sarah Rosella Sellers, who married when she was only sixteen, was a quiet woman, devoted to her family. Having only a limited formal education, she tended to withdraw from church activity, discussions about religion, and deliberation about world affairs in order to major on feeding and clothing her husband and children. The youngest of four children, Tom grew up with his sister Nora and his brother Charles Henderson, better known as Red because of the color of his hair. The older sister in the family died when she was about two years old.

Although very poor, the Maston family enjoyed stability and warmth. Hard work was part of the daily routine but so was fun. Tom's dad romped with the children, playing baseball and croquet with them. On cold winter nights, the entire family often played games together. Although not a musical family, the parents and children sometimes spent evenings singing together, off key but with zest and joy. Mother and Dad Maston never argued in front of the children. They had an understanding that if one of them, in a cross and irritable mood, said something which could be the basis for an argument, the other would not reply. Tom's dad often said, "It takes two to fuss." Neither did the parents display affection for each other in the presence of the children, both being rather reserved.

Life had its perils for young Maston. Hit in the head accidentally by his brother with an ax, Tom received a life-long scar. The accident almost cost him his life. Another accident had more of a long-range effect. One summer while playing under the bed kicking the straw mattress, a wheat beard fell into Tom's right eye. Not being able to locate the beard his parents took Tom to a doctor who cut around the muscles of the eye searching for the beard but could not locate it. He told Tom's parents that Tom would likely

14

never open his eye again. As the months passed the eye became more and more swollen. Soon both eyes were closed. One morning, four months after the accident, Tom's mother was feeding him—he could not see to feed himself—when she saw something sticking out of his right eye. She pulled out the object and discovered it was the wheat beard in the shape of the eye ball. For years the right eye remained half closed; later many would note a Maston hallmark—a twitch or wink of his right eye. A weakness in sight beginning with this childhood experience continued to plague him.

Frequently on the move, the Maston family changed locations as Mr. Maston sought better work opportunities and settings for the development of the children. When Tom was a child, the family never had its roots down very deep anywhere.

Mr. Maston's work as a farmer and section hand on the railroad brought in little cash. Only when a union was organized that covered section hands did he make as much as $1.50 a day from the railroad job. All the members of the Maston family worked to help supplement the father's income and stretch the family's resources as far as possible. Work played a big part in Tom's life from the time he was a small boy. Each child had definite responsibilities and chores. Every afternoon after school, Tom and Red cut crossties from the railroad for firewood. As the boys grew older, the saw grew larger. Starting out with a four-foot-long cross saw they finally graduated to a saw measuring six feet in length. Their mother would frequently help by sitting on the crossties while the boys sawed them.

Gardening also was an important part of the chores. Big and strong, Dad Maston could have cared for the garden himself, but he used it as an educational tool for the boys. A large, heavy garden plow was attached to a rope with a stick through the end of it. Tom and Red got on each end of the stick and pulled while their dad guided the plow behind them. What they didn't know was that he was pushing harder than both of them were pulling. Farm work filled out home responsibilities. In addition to working in their own family, the Maston boys also worked for others. When he was nine, Tom was busy chopping corn for fifty cents a day. A year later he and his brother began working for a nursery for seventy-five cents a day. Tom also worked for two women on Saturday cleaning chicken houses and doing odd jobs. By the time he was fourteen, he was working on a farm and earning adult wages—$1.50 a day. With his earnings, Tom bought all of his own clothes.

Although education played a big role in Maston's life, his school career began on a negative note. At the age of seven, he entered the first grade. A small, timid child, he wailed and begged to stay home, but his mother forced him to go. Gradually he began to excel in his studies. Bright and alert, he usually led his class academically. This pleased his father who valued education highly. Although his academic achievements at Central High School in Fountain City, Tennessee, were not as high as in elementary school, he remained a superior student. Much of his time was devoted to athletics, playing varsity football and second-team baseball. In his senior year he was elected as captain of the football team.

While in high school, two of the most important experiences of Maston's life occurred—his conversion and his call to Christian ministry. Mr. and Mrs. Maston were Southern Baptists, his father very active in the church and his mother less so. Although the family did not observe thanks before meals, have Bible study, or share devotional times (possibly because Mr. Maston felt these might become mere religious forms), Christian influence was present in conversation and life-style. There were no Baptist churches in College Corner, Ohio, where the Mastons lived for ten years so the Maston children attended a Methodist church and a Presbyterian church. When Tom was fourteen, the family moved back to Tennessee so that they could be near a Southern Baptist church. His dad, mother, and sister joined the Smithwood Baptist Church. Red began to drift away from the church and seldom attended. Tom attended Sunday School only occasionally until under the influence of Nora, his sister, he began to go regularly. Nora and several other young people pled with him to become a Christian, but he felt no urge to make any commitment.

In the fall of his sixteenth year, during a football game in Asheville, North Carolina, one of the members of the team suffered a serious injury. On the train returning home, Tom struggled with a feeling that he was not ready for death and that he could have been the one seriously injured instead of "Stinky" Davis. The next week Tom's mathematics professor, also the pastor of the Smithwood Baptist Church, preached a revival. Each night as Tom came in from football practice, having walked two miles home, his dad or sister would ask him to go with them to the revival. Each night he gave an excuse for not attending. On Friday he ran out of excuses and went with his dad. Years later Maston described what happened:

I do not remember anything the pastor said that night. But I do know that when he gave the invitation, they started to sing the grand old invitation hymn, "Just as I am, without one plea." I also know that I was broken up quite a bit and my head fell over on the pew in front of me and I was weeping. A friend of mine who was not too good a Christian, but who knew enough to know what to do, put his arm around me and asked me what was wrong. I said, "I wish I could accept the pastor's invitation." He simply said to me, "You can if you will." If I interpret it correctly, what happened to me that night was that back behind those pews in the old Smithwood Church I said, "I will," and when one says, "I will" to God, he surrenders his will to the Lord's will. I got up and went to the front. And when I turned around, my daddy was seated over to the right and I saw him crying and laughing at the same time.

As an adult Maston often referred to this experience. He frequently would tell young people, "I've doubted practically everything about the Christian faith as I've gone along through the years except this one experience that I had."

Shortly after his conversion and baptism into the Smithwood Baptist Church, Tom began to experience a sense of special calling to Christian ministry. Concerning this significant event in his Christian pilgrimage Maston recalls:

I was seated in church one day and our pastor said that he had been praying that the Lord would lay His hand on some of the young people in the church and call them into His service. Something hit me almost just like a voice had spoken and said that I was one of those. It was something that I could not get away from. I struggled with it only for a few weeks. One night during the B.Y.P.U., I felt like I would just have to tell somebody or I would burst. During the church service, I was seated back close to one of the two stoves that we had in the auditorium. When the pastor gave the invitation that night, I went up to the front and told him that I felt that I was called to preach. He turned to the congregation, "Tom has something that he wants to say." I stood up and told them that I felt that the Lord was calling me to preach. Again my daddy was over to the right, and I saw him crying and laughing at the same time.

The statement to the congregation was the beginning of a long struggle concerning what kind of church related work he was to do. He talked the matter over with his dad, explaining that he somehow did not feel that he was supposed to be a pastor. At that time few churches had any staff member other than a pastor, and there was little else a person could do in vocational church work other than pastor. However, his dad told him that as long as he felt the way he did, he should not be ordained. Although Tom was licensed to preach, following his father's advice he was never ordained. He preached his first sermon before going to college and continued to supply and preach at churches, but he never felt that pastoring was the right vocational choice for him. Through the next few years the conviction grew in young Maston that he was not to pastor but rather to teach. As he gained experience in teaching in Sunday School and in other places, he began to believe that teaching might be God's will for his life.

Outstanding in both academics and athletics, Tom graduated from Central

High School of Fountain City in 1916. Faced with the decision about which
college to attend he decided almost at the last minute to enter Carson-
Newman College, a Baptist school in Jefferson City, Tennessee. His father,
a profound influence on him during his teen years, continued to influence
him through college and beyond. Later, while studying for his Ph.D. at
Yale, Maston wrote his father, "Your influence in my life has been greater
than anyone who has touched it. I have said many times that you are the
best man I have ever known." In the letter Maston referred to specific
incidents in his life related to his father. These say a great deal about the
home life of young Tom Maston and the special relationship he had with
his father:

> I've thanked the Lord many, many times that he gave me the opportunity of
> working with you those years on the farm. I learned more Bible and doctrine from
> you during those years than from any teacher I have had since in college or seminary.
> And in what was more important I think I caught something of your spirit. I never
> can forget or get away from the influence of those chats we used to have at the
> end of the corn rows, when we talked about the most serious problems of the universe
> and the deepest possible religious problems. I've always thought I knew you better
> than anyone except mother.
>
> I remember how happy you were the night I was converted and how much encour-
> agement and help you were to me after I decided to go into religious work. Well
> do I remember the time just before I went to Carson-Newman to college when
> you told me while we were digging potatoes just back of the woods about the prayer
> you prayed when I was only about two years old that the Lord would take one of
> your boys in your place. I have lived since that time in the conviction, ever growing
> deeper, that God had called me. And that call was not only to my own task but I
> was to try to do for God what you wanted to do but was prevented.

Part of Maston's drive to accomplish significant tasks can be attributed
to the fact that his father had asked God to take one of his boys into
Christian ministry in his place when he concluded that he could not support
his growing family and serve in the kind of churches which would call him
as pastor with his limited education. Further, Tom's sister had felt called
into vocational Christian work but had not responded. His brother, Red,
until late in life was not a Christian. Maston seemed to feel that he was
living out God's purpose for mission not only for himself but also for his
father and sister and that in some way this would help to bring his brother
into the family of God. When he left home for college, therefore, he went
with a sense of purpose beyond that of the average college student.

Although plagued by financial difficulty and by poor eyesight, Maston
had an outstanding career at Carson-Newman College. He arrived on the

campus with $12.40 in his pocket. By sweeping floors, waiting on tables, serving as dorm manager, and working in the summers, he managed to pay his way through school. At one time he was so short of money that he had to borrow the stamp from his football coach to mail a letter home to tell his dad and mother that he was broke. The financial difficulty became a means of spiritual growth. Maston recalls the following incident:

After being there about two months I was behind with my rent and with everything else. I had been fretting and worrying about it. One evening I came in from prayer meeting at the First Baptist Church and that night as I prayed I said something like this, "Lord, I'm here because I think you want me to be here. I have been worrying about being in debt. I'm going to leave it up to you now." The next morning after I had turned the thing over to the Lord, I was in the library and one of the fellows came to me and said, "I just saw your brother Red downtown and he is looking for you." I started out of the building and met him on the front porch of the administration building. The first thing he said to me was, "Tom, I have just been by the bank and deposited some money for you." He had not heard that I was up against it and it could be as some suggest that this was just happenstance, but I did not think so then and I do not think so now. It was the only time my brother ever gave me any money.

At Carson-Newman Maston played football, basketball, and baseball. He was active in a number of clubs and organizations, serving frequently as an officer. This activity did not keep him from achieving a splendid academic record. When the United States entered World War I, Maston was drafted into the army, the possibility of volunteering having been ruled out by the government. As a part of the Student Army, he did not go on active duty.

Perhaps the most significant event in Maston's life at college was meeting Essie Mae McDonald. A very timid boy in high school, Tom had never dated. During his first months in college he only casually visited with girls and did not date. Yet from the time he was a freshman he prayed almost every day that the Lord would lead him to the girl he was to marry. Tom met Essie Mae through campus religious organizations. As they visited informally Tom began to have a strong conviction that she was the person God wanted him to be with as a life's companion. He describes the way they began to merge their lives toward marriage:

On a Sunday afternoon on the campus of Carson-Newman, sitting on a sled that had been left out following some of the snows of the winter, I asked her if she would not like for us to plan our lives together with the Lord. Her reply was in the affirmative. I've been grateful through the years that before having that date that day, I got down on my knees in my room in Davis Hall and asked the Lord that His will might be done. I knew that I was going to ask her that afternoon.

After she gave me her reply and I had shared with her my experiences before I left the dormitory, she shared with me that she likewise had prayed in a special way before we had the date. She knew that I was getting serious and had the feeling that a proposal might come that afternoon.

Engaged during their junior year, Tom and Essie Mae told no one of their engagement. They graduated from Carson-Newman in 1920, and after serious prayer for direction they both entered Southwestern Seminary in Fort Worth, Texas. After a year, they married. Following their marriage each completed their M.R.E. programs. Essie Mae taught two years in the School of Religious Education at Southwestern Seminary and then the Mastons decided it was time to start a family. Hoping to have a large family of six children, difficulties with two pregnancies led them to accept a family of two boys. The first child, Thomas McDonald Maston, was injured at birth and has been an invalid all of his life. The second son, Harold Eugene, was born in 1928 following another difficult pregnancy in which Mrs. Maston almost died. The Mastons decided that it was better to have two children and a live mother than for them to endeavor to have more children and risk their being orphans.

Through the years "Mommie," as Maston affectionately calls his wife, has remained a strength and stabilizing factor. A quiet, strong woman, she has cared unflinchingly for an invalid son, has helped a man destined for greatness to pursue what he sensed to be God's will, and has served faithfully in her church. A highly intelligent person, she could have taught at Southwestern Seminary but chose rather to major on being a wife and mother. Her strong constitution enabled her to survive two difficult pregnancies, several major surgeries, and a number of other illnesses without loss of strength or stamina. Because of Mrs. Maston's choices and character, Maston was able to devote his energy to his calling which turned out to be teaching.

One of the turning points in Maston's life came when he was a junior at Carson-Newman. W. D. Hudgins, state Sunday School and Baptist Young People's Union (B.Y.P.U.) Secretary of the Tennessee Baptist Convention, visited the campus recruiting students to work in a summer program of conducting leadership training schools in rural churches. Maston asked to be part of the program—the only time he ever made such a direct request for himself. Hudgins agreed, and for five summers as a college and later as a seminary student Maston worked in small churches throughout Tennessee. These experiences helped him discover his ability was in teaching, not preaching, and aided him in overcoming his shyness and timidity. Hudgins told the young people working with him, "Whether you have a houseful or a handful, give them the best you have." Maston followed that advice all of his life.

When Maston arrived at Southwestern Seminary he was still not sure whether he should be a pastor or go into some other phase of vocational religious work. Uncertain as to whether he should enroll in the School of Theology or in the School of Religious Education, he sought the counsel of seminary leadership. President Scarborough indicated he should enroll in the School of Theology. J. M. Price insisted he should go into religious education. In describing how he made the decision, Maston says, "I went to my room in Fort Worth Hall and asked the Lord again to give me the sense of leading that I needed. I had the impression that I should go the religious education route and hence I did enroll for an M.R.E." He began teaching on a part-time basis while working toward the degree. After receiving his M.R.E. in 1923, he began to teach full time on the faculty and to work toward the D.R.E. at Southwestern. He was the first to earn that degree from Southwestern.

Although he had an earned doctor's degree and was teaching at Southwestern Seminary, Maston did not feel that he had adequate preparation for a teaching career. Because he more and more sensed that God wanted him to teach at either a college or seminary, he continued to pursue graduate study. By 1927 he had earned his M.A. from Texas Christian University in sociology. One summer he studied sociology at the University of North Carolina and another summer he studied at the University of Chicago. Convinced that his teaching area was to be in the field of Christian ethics, he entered Yale University in 1932 to pursue a Ph.D. in Christian ethics. While a Yale, he almost died from pneumonia and consequently it was not until 1939 that he received the Ph.D. from Yale.

Completing the Ph.D. from Yale during the depression of the 1930s reveals a great deal about Maston's dedication to excellence and his determination to follow what he believed to be God's will regardless of the cost. Southwestern Seminary granted him a leave of absence, but some of the professors discouraged him from going to Yale. Jeff Ray, professor of preaching, said, "I have always had a lot of confidence in your business judgment, but I declare I do not see how you are going up there with your family and support them adequately." The discouraging word was not without basis in fact. During one year Maston received from the seminary only $1026.00, and much of that was in the form of services rather than money. While at Yale, his salary from the seminary during the first fall averaged $90.00 a month. He worked in the library at Yale for his fees and wrote for the Baptist Sunday School Board for rent and food money. A month in the hospital with pneumonia left him far behind in his academic schedule and weak in health. A summer of work and sun on a Tennessee farm aided him in recovering his health. When he returned to Southwestern Seminary,

Jeff Ray saw him, looked him over, and said, "Tom, if it did not sound sacrilegious I would say that we wasted a lot of praying on you."

Although Maston began his teaching career in religious education, offering classes in almost every phase of religious education, he experienced a growing interest in the field of Christian ethics. J. M. Price, head of the School of Religious Education, had taught a course in Christian ethics but gradually turned it over to Maston. For several years the Christian ethics courses were in the School of Religious Education. More and more Maston felt that the Christian ethics courses should be shifted to the School of Theology. He felt that pastors needed these courses. He also felt that ethics was more of a theological than a religious education discipline. Before going to Yale in 1936 to complete his work there, Maston developed an agreement that he would continue to teach in the School of Religious Education but that the ethics part of his load would be in the School of Theology. In 1943 Maston began to teach all of his courses in the Department of Christian Social Ethics in the School of Theology. A doctor of theology (Th.D.) program in Christian ethics was developed; the first two graduates were Charles Johnson and Charles Myers.

As the ethics department grew, Ralph Phelps, a Th.D. graduate under Maston, was added to the teaching staff. At first he taught both Old Testament and Christian ethics, but eventually he taught entirely in the Department of Christian Social Ethics. When Phelps left to become president of Ouachita Baptist College, C. W. Scudder became a professor in the Department of Christian Social Ethics, working hand in hand with Maston offering work on the diploma, master, and doctorate level until Maston's retirement in 1963.

During his years at Southwestern Seminary, Maston had many opportunities to accept other positions. The Tennessee Baptist Convention asked him to serve on its staff. Baylor University approached him about teaching in the field of religion at Baylor. Both Southeastern Seminary and Southern Seminary invited him to become a member of their faculties. Maston gave the invitation from Southern Seminary serious and careful consideration. He visited the campus, talked with members of Southern's faculty, consulted with close friends such as J. Howard Williams and W. R. White, prayed with his wife, and reflected for some time before declining.

The only time Maston definitely felt he should leave Southwestern Seminary, the opportunity did not materialize. Charles Maddry, in a chapel address at Southwestern Seminary, mentioned that the Foreign Mission Board (SBC) was looking for someone to head its new education department. As Maddry spoke, Maston had a very clear impression that he should do the job. At one time Maston had thought he should be a foreign missionary, but God turned him in a different direction. Nevertheless his interest in foreign missions remained strong during his career and thus this opportunity particularly gripped him. He could hardly sleep for thinking about the possibilities of the position. He discussed the matter with close friends. Although Maddry was aware of Maston's interest, the invitation to come to the Board never developed. Maston remained convinced that he should have gone. Out of this experience he developed two important insights. One is that doing the will of God is sometimes dependent upon the willingness of others for us to do that will. The second was that if we are willing to do the Lord's will and it does not work out for us, we can be assured that God will take care of us.

In working through these various decisions, Maston developed some basic guidelines to follow when considering a vocational move. One is that if you are convinced God has led you where you are, the burden of proof should be on moving, not staying. Another is that if your head tells you one thing and your heart tells you another, you should do whatever it seems your heart is leading you to do. A third guideline is that through prayer and a willing heart God will guide his children.

As a professor, Maston placed a top priority on his relationship to students and on his classroom work. Although he served his denomination, wrote extensively, spoke in many parts of the world, and worked in his home church, he majored on his teaching and upon the development of his students. Students were impressed not only with his knowledge of Christian ethics but with his interest in them as persons. Frequently he and Mrs. Maston would invite students into their home. When students were having difficulty, they often went to Maston for counsel. He seldom gave direct advice, but he always had a sympathetic, listening ear.

Maston related well to his colleagues on the faculty. His excellence as a teaching professor can partly be attributed to his colleagues. Those with whom he worked and taught were an outstanding collection of scholars and writers: H. E. Dana, W. T. Conner, W. W. Barnes, B. A. Copass, J. M. Price, Jeff Ray, and S. A. Newman. Although not much for small talk or time in the faculty lounge, Maston did take time to be a warm, open friend to those with whom he worked.

The most serious difficulty within the faculty occurred while E. D. Head was president of the seminary. Following the presidency of L. R. Scarborough, Head came from a successful pastorate at the First Baptist Church, Houston, to the seminary. The dissatisfaction among the faculty with the administration of the school became so intense that meetings were held to discuss what to do. No one questioned Head's Christian commitment, personal goodness, or preaching abilities. The difficulty revolved around his approach to administration. In the faculty discussions, it was agreed that Maston would talk with the president. The other faculty members felt that as spokesman for the group, he could calmly lay the faculty grievances before Head, whereas the others would become too emotional. Although the difficulty led to several meetings of the faculty with representatives from the trustees, the relationship between Maston and Head remained warm and friendly. Partly as a result of the conflict, R. T. Daniel and S. A. Newman went to Southeastern Seminary to teach, and Earl Guinn left to become president of Louisiana College. Following President Head's retirement, J. Howard Williams became president of Southwestern, pulled the faculty together, and led the school in new growth and harmony.

Maston carried his convictions about the importance of Christian ethics beyond the classroom to the denomination. While serving on the committee of the Southern Baptist Convention for the denominational calendar, Maston suggested that the Convention observe a race relations Sunday—a suggestion that was squelched quickly and somewhat rudely. He also served on the Social Service Commission which was later changed to the Christian Life Commission (SBC).

One of Maston's most significant contributions to his denomination was the development of the Christian Life Commission of the Baptist General Convention of Texas. J. Howard Williams, then executive secretary of the Baptist General Convention of Texas, became concerned about the lack of ethical emphasis at the annual meeting of the Convention. Under his influence, a committee of three was appointed—W. R. White, A. C. Miller, and T. B. Maston—to bring a recommendation to the annual convention for action. The three men recommended that a committee of seven be appointed to study the matter for the establishment of some kind of commission to emphasize Christian ethics. Wallace Bassett, serving as president of the convention, appointed Maston to be chairman of the committee of seven. The result of the committee's report was the establishment of the Christian Life Commission of the Baptist General Convention of Texas. The first chairman of the commission was Arthur Rutledge, then pastor of the First Baptist Church, Marshall, who later became the executive secretary of the Home Mission Board (SBC). Maston served for many years on the commission and was particularly influential in the development of a number of pamphlets and tracts dealing with various subjects in Christian ethics.

Serving as the first chairman of the Advisory Council of Southern Baptists for Work with Negroes, Maston helped to develop the constitution and bylaws of the group. Maston was also chairman of a subcommittee of a larger committee to develop a statement of Baptist ideals. Meeting with a group of Southern Baptist leaders over a period of months, the committee worked out a statement which was widely used by denominational agencies. In a more informal way, Maston influenced his denomination through a constant barrage of correspondence with denominational leaders as well as frequent speaking engagements at various Baptist meetings, such as the annual meetings of the Southern Baptist Convention and of state conventions, conferences at the Glorieta and Ridgecrest Baptist conference centers, and college focus weeks.

Perhaps more influential than his speaking has been his writing. Authoring both scholarly and popular books and articles, he sowed down the Southern Baptist Convention with ethical emphases and insights. Characterized by a deep commitment to the Bible as the basis for Christian ethics and by a commonsense practicality, his writing touched the lives of young and old. A frequent contributor to Sunday School lessons, Church Training programs, and scores of periodicals, he got his message across to the grass roots of Baptist life.

Through the lives of thousands of students whom he taught as well as the hundreds of books and articles he wrote, Maston extended his emphasis and influence far beyond the confines of his Fort Worth classroom. And because he majored on students and writing, that influence will remain strong for years.

Ethics was not Maston's only theme. Deeply interested in the spiritual growth of a Christian, much of his writing and teaching centered in Christian growth and development. Vitally concerned about missions, he highlighted missions not only in the classroom but also from the speaker's platform and the author's printed page. Aware of his interest, mission boards and agencies made frequent use of him as a speaker and writer. Maston's commitment to missions came early. He says:

"I remember the many times when down on my knees by my bed at night telling the Lord that I was willing to go anywhere he wanted me to go I went to bed knowing that I did not mean it. One night I prayed the same prayer and that time I knew that I meant it and I had a peace in my heart that I had not had for a long time."

The plans to go to a foreign mission field, probably Africa, did not materialize. Yet Maston influenced many mission fields both by his personal presence through assignments with the Foreign Mission Board and by the life he lived through his students, many who became foreign and home missionaries.

Maston's life in regard to missions makes it clear that God has more than one way to use our dedication, more than one avenue through which he can channel our interest and concern.

As a churchman, Maston excelled. Not only did he train persons for leadership in local churches, he was himself active in his church. Maston devoted large amounts of time to his church, the Gambrell Street Baptist Church in Fort Worth. Teaching a Sunday School class, visiting the sick and the unsaved, serving as a deacon, participating as a member of various committees, his church involvements were many and his contributions great. On one occasion he undertook an enormous task, visiting more than three hundred Gambrell Street church members who had become inactive to encourage them in their life and in their relationship to the Lord. During that time, he did a brief case study on each family. At the end of the eighteen-month visitation project, he analyzed what he had discovered. This venture demonstrates his concern for the kind of evangelism that leads to discipleship and faithfulness in the local church. At another time he was chairman of a mission action group that implemented a tape ministry to a large number of people who could not or would not attend church services. Lloyd Elder, Maston's pastor for seven years, said of the Mastons' churchmanship:

Dr. and Mrs. Maston and Tom Mc are beautifully faithful in their support of the life and ministry of Gambrell Street Baptist Church. They do this as acts of service as well as continuing personal discipleship. No part of the Gambrell Street Church has missed his encouraging hand.

One of the chief influences in Maston's life was Tom Mc. Mrs. Maston was not able to travel with her husband as much as wives of many other seminary professors because of the need for someone to stay home and take care of Tom Mc. She did this unselfishly and lovingly. Speaking of the relationship of the Mastons' to their invalid son, Lloyd Elder says:

Both of them had an amazing commitment to the support system needed by Tom Mc. They chose to keep him in their home through all these years, rather than placing him in an institution. With the loving hearts of parents, they have never gotten use to him being an invalid. They know he has a bright, though untrained mind. His inability to express his life in meaningful service is felt to be a great loss. When Dr. Maston looks at Tom Mc, he understands something of the passion of Jesus: "Pastor, I think I understand why in his earthly ministry Jesus touched some and healed them. Of all the spectacular gifts of the spirit I could wish for, it would be for the gift of healing. When I walk amidst the many like Tom Mc, I understand why Jesus would lift the heartbreak and sorrow by healing some."

In 1963 Maston retired as professor of Christian ethics at the seminary he had entered as a student forty-three years before. The primary impact of his retirement was that he no longer was a regular teacher in the classrooms of Southwestern Seminary. Most of his other activities he continued in high gear—speaking, writing, counseling, serving in denominational life, and contributing to world missions. Through correspondence, telephone calls, and personal visits, he keeps up with the large number of students who had been influenced by his teaching ministry. He remains particularly close to those who had majored in Christian ethics in their doctoral studies.

From his office in the library at Southwestern, he carried on an extensive writing ministry. Operating from two desks, he used one for scholarly, academic writing and the other for more popular writing. He has written more books following retirement than he had written prior to leaving the classroom. He authored two series of articles for denominational papers and continues to write for various denominational publications, including four series for the *Adult Teacher*. To this office former colleagues, former students, and students often made their way for visits, consultation, and suggestions.

Retirement did not end his teaching. He served as a visiting teacher at several institutions including Golden Gate Seminary in California and Midwestern Baptist Theological Seminary in Missouri. He also taught overseas at the Baptist seminary in Beirut, Lebanon. He returned to his alma mater, Carson-Newman College, for teaching assignments. Frequently a guest teacher at the journeyman training center for the Foreign Mission Board and for the orientation for career missionaries under appointment by the Foreign Mission Board, his influence through missionaries continued to spread throughout the world. David Gooch, who was influenced by Maston in the training program for journeymen, wrote about him:

> In these days
> We have watched you
> We have seen
> A man
> Who walks with God
> Responsibly as he demands
> And we pray
> That when we reach
> "Maturity" we will have walked
> Along the cutting edge of life
> As you, old man.

The discipline and balance which had characterized his life as a professor has carried through into his years in retirement. He carefully watched his diet, exercised, and rested during the middle of the day following lunch. He rose early in the morning to take care of Tom Mc, participated in family worship at breakfast, worked regularly in his yard and garden, and remained home on Friday afternoons to care for correspondence and allow Mrs. Maston time to be away from the house. Such a schedule was one reason why he could accomplish much and yet never appear to be in a hurry. He believed his body was the temple of the Holy Spirit and cared for it; this may in part explain the number of years in his life span. All of the other members of his immediate family died relatively young.

Those who heard Maston speak several times or who read a number of his writings usually noted certain key emphases and themes. While not necessarily unique, they were distinctive. One was his teaching concerning tension in relation to change. Frequently he illustrated his point with a rubber band around his hands. Holding one hand over the other, first he would show that unless the higher hand is moved up, producing tension in the band, the lower hand does not move upward. Next he would demonstrate that by moving the upper hand higher tension is produced which pulls the lower hand upward. Suddenly he would move his upper hand high causing the band to break and the lower hand to fall. Then he would point out that while too little pressure brings no change, too much tension ruptures a relation and is nonproductive or counterproductive. What is needed is for a change agent to keep the right amount of tension on persons, leading neither to apathy nor broken relations but to progress. He endeavors to follow this model in his own teaching, speaking, and writing.

Another distinctive feature is an emphasis on the ethics of the cross. Basically Maston emphasized that the cross-kind-of-life is the way of a Christian. This involves voluntary suffering in the will of God out of love for someone to help them. Emphasizing the cross of the Christian, as well as the cross of Christ, he would call people to the life of a servant—suffering, taking up their crosses, following Jesus. A key in his ethic was, therefore, the will of God.

Being thoroughly biblical is another Maston distinctive. Familiar with philosophical and theological ethics, sociology and anthropology, he nevertheless made his approach to ethics basically biblical. A feature of his teaching and speaking has been a large, well-worn Bible referred to by him frequently as he lectured. With vigor he punched home his ethical points with biblical quotations. No one who heard him could miss his obvious reverence and love for the Bible.

Few men have been as widely known or as deeply loved as T. B. Maston. Few have blended ethics and evangelism, scholarship and pietism, a conservative theological outlook and a progressive social concern as well as he. Frequently the object of attack because of his stand on controversial social issues, he never reacted with anger or vindictiveness. His quiet spirit and obvious dedication to Jesus Christ and the Bible won the respect of those who knew him even when they disagreed with his stand. His influence has been enormous but seldom direct. Some persons seem to believe that Maston had a master plan to capture the Southern Baptist Convention and perhaps all of evangelical Christianity for a particular viewpoint. Although some of his former students achieved positions of influence within the Southern Baptist Convention, never did he direct any kind of master plan. In fact, unless asked, he did not offer advice.

Maston's influence has penetrated like salt and leaven. He has never been flamboyant, aggressive, or pushy. Quiet and humble in spirit, he prevails where others either burned out or antagonized those around them. He speaks often of the ethics of the cross, a willingness to suffer as a servant for the benefit of others. He lives out what he taught and in so living he influenced a multitude for Christ. A dedicated scholar, he can communicate with and relate to the humblest person. A white man from the deep South, he loves and champions the cause of oppressed minorities. A disciplined man with high standards, he can show compassion for persons guilty of irresponsibility and immorality. A hard taskmaster in the classroom, he understood the plight of the overworked student. Frequently criticized, he is almost never critical of others.

Those who have known T. B. Maston well do not claim that his life is one of perfection, but they do know that he approaches as close to Christlikeness as anyone they have known. Superior teacher, dedicated Christian, involved churchman, devoted family member, understanding friend, prolific author, disciplined human being, friend of students, outstanding scholar, servant of Jesus Christ—that is how a multitude of persons remember T. B. Maston.

II
THE CONTRIBUTION OF T. B. MASTON

To the Local Church

Felix Gresham

My conviction has always been that any member of a local church should accept the responsibility that that entails. My life has revolved around three institutions and they are within about two or three blocks of one another: my home, my church, and the seminary. I think I am honest when I say that I have attempted to be a good church member.

This statement by T. B. Maston reflects the view of a man who has ministered to churches around the world but has not neglected the responsibility of ministry in and through the local church where he has been a member. Central in his theology is the supreme importance of the local church in the advancement of God's kingdom on this earth. He has both lived and taught this conviction. He has done this primarily by his dedicated service as a member of such a body.

As we look at the contribution T. B. Maston has made to the local church, it will be helpful for us to examine the influence of local churches on his early life. While he was born in East Tennessee, he spent ten years of his life from four to fourteen in Ohio. A major reason for the family's return to East Tennessee was the need his father felt for a local Baptist church where he and his family could worship and serve in harmony with their personal convictions.

The first church that really made a significant contribution to his spiritual development was the Smithwood Baptist Church near Knoxville, Tennessee. Maston attended Sunday School there for some time after the family returned to East Tennessee. It was in that church that Tom Maston yielded his heart and life to the Lord Jesus Christ as his Savior during a revival meeting. He lacked only a few days of being seventeen years of age when this occurred. It was in that church that he first stood on his feet to speak in the B.Y.P.U. and he first led in public prayer. It was in that church that he felt the call of the Lord to vocational Christian service.

In his lifetime, Maston has been a member of five churches:

Smithwood Baptist Church, Knoxville, Tennessee, from 1914 to 1916.
First Baptist Church, Jefferson City, Tennessee, from 1916 to 1920.

33

This was his church while in college at Carson-Newman.

Gambrell Street Baptist Church, Fort Worth, Texas, from 1920 to the present, except for brief times in two other churches.

First Baptist Church, New Haven, Connecticut, from 1932 to 1933 and from 1936 to 1937. He was a member of this church on these two occasions while completing his Ph.D. at Yale University.

College Avenue Baptist Church, Fort Worth, Texas, from 1935 to 1936. He served this church for one year as their part-time minister of education.

As noted above, Maston has been a member of Gambrell Street Baptist Church for fifty-five years. His major contribution to the local church has been related to his work and service in this fellowship. He speaks of this church as follows:

I have said on many occasions that Gambrell Street Baptist Church is one of the best churches I know. I have also said that I think a child of God should rather be with his church family than anywhere else except with his own personal family. I really think that next to my family at the corner of Broadus and James, I love Gambrell Street Church more than anything else. The church has meant a great deal, not just to me personally, but also to my family.

Maston has served in nearly every position of leadership in the local church except that of pastor and music director. His earliest place of service was that of Bible readers leader in the B.Y.P.U. He has held many offices in the Training Union. For several years he was the director of the Training Union at Gambrell Street Church. Probably his major ministry through these years has been as a Sunday School teacher. He taught a boy's class while a student in Carson-Newman College. He taught teenage boys when he first came to Fort Worth and did so for several years. He taught a Sunday School class regularly during the two years he was in New Haven, Connecticut. For many years he was a teacher of adult men at Gambrell Street Church.

A major area of service in his local church has been as a deacon. Maston does not recall the exact date of his ordination as a deacon, but it was approximately fifty years ago. He has been regular in attending the meetings of the deacons each month and in the developing programs of ministry carried out by the deacon body of his church. By his own choice he was never elected chairman of the deacons. It was his conviction that the chairman should not be connected with the seminary. He was recently elected as a life member of the deacon body and is no longer expected to be active in the monthly meetings.

Maston has served on nearly every committee in Gambrell Street Church.

For several years he alternated as chairman of the finance committee with C. M. King, the business manager of Southwestern Seminary. He was chairman of a special committee that worked out the present committee structure of his church.

Maston has been active through the years in the visitation program of his church. He visited regularly as a Sunday School teacher during the years he served in that position. After Maston's retirement from the seminary in 1963, he began a systematic visitation program of inactive church members and in more recent years of shut-ins. Mrs. Maston has shared with him through these years in his visitation ministry as she has in all phases of work in the local church. In the most recent years they have concentrated on visiting lonely and neglected people, both members and nonmembers.

Maston has served two churches in an employed staff position. He served for one year as the part-time minister of education at College Avenue Baptist Church in Fort Worth, Texas. This was in 1935-1936, during the depression years. He also served Gambrell Street Church for a short time during the depression years as part-time minister of education and youth director. While he was never a regular pastor of a church, he has supplied as preacher in many churches and has also served as interim pastor. The longest interim pastorate was for two months at the First Baptist Church of Jasper, Texas.

In addition to the preceding, he has had a varied and extensive ministry in many other local churches. He says that he has probably been in more churches for family week emphases than for any other type of engagement. Another major emphasis has been the teaching of study courses. While still a college student, he was employed by the Tennessee Baptist Convention during the summer months to teach study courses in rural and village churches. This continued for five years. He has written some books to be used primarily for study course purposes. His first two books, *Handbook for Church Recreation Leaders* and *Of One* were written for this purpose. *The Bible and Race* was adopted as a study course book by the Woman's Missionary Union.

Maston has ministered to local churches on several mission fields. He has visited in Mexico on seven different occasions, speaking in a number of local churches in connection with these visits. He has toured the mission fields in Central and South America and spent several weeks in Beirut, Lebanon, teaching in the Arab Baptist Seminary. He had the opportunity to speak in a number of Arab churches. On a military sponsored mission to chaplains in Korea, Japan, and Okinawa, he was a speaker at the dedication of the Tokyo Baptist Church. He also had opportunity to speak in churches in Korea and Okinawa.

Maston has been a supporter of his pastor, and in the sixty-four years since he became a Christian, he has had many pastors. He has not always agreed with them but he has tried to be constructive in such disagreements. When the church adopted a program, he supported it. When Gambrell Street Church made plans to construct a new, modern building, Maston was troubled over the necessity to reduce the percentage of giving to the Cooperative Program. The church had worshiped for many years in an inadequate frame building which had been moved from the seminary campus where it had been used as a temporary classroom building. It could no longer serve the needs of the growing church. For many years the church had given 50 percent of its income to outside mission causes. It grieved Maston to adopt a policy of spending a larger percentage of its income on local causes. But for the church to grow, this was necessary. Maston supported the program and came to realize that the growing church was giving a far larger amount in total funds to mission causes than it had when the percentage was larger.

Maston has often been a wise counselor to his pastors. Most of them have sought his counsel. Arthur Travis was pastor of Gambrell Street Church for thirteen years and was Maston's pastor for the longest period of time. In speaking of his relationship to Maston, he speaks for others who have served in this relationship:

Dr. Maston was a deacon who supported his pastor. He was not averse to counseling with his pastor, and if he felt it necessary, of differing from his pastor's views, yet all the time, his interests were in the welfare of his church. He was not afraid of taking a stand, even when he knew it to be contrary to other church leaders.

. . . .

Although at times I found Dr. Maston rather slow in coming to approve of something suggested for the church, when once he was convinced that it was a good thing, he supported it wholeheartedly. Since I am somewhat conservative in my own personal views and practices, Dr. Maston and I usually saw "eye to eye" on most matters associated with our church. I learned a great deal from him, and shall always cherish my thirteen years as his pastor.

Bernes K. Selph was pastor at Gambrell Street Church for five and one half years and was the pastor during the time of the building program mentioned above. Selph also speaks with warmest regards of the support given to him by T. B. Maston:

During the five and one half years I served as pastor of Gambrell Street, I found him loyal and cooperative in the total program of the church. Well do I remember how he led out in a tithing-financing program after I made an appeal to the Budget

Committee of which he was a member. Cautious and conservative, he provided strength and counsel for both pastor and people. He carried tremendous influence among the membership but I never found him using this in any way but in what he thought to be the best interest of the church and the glory of God. I loved and respected him.

What has been T. B. Maston's greatest contribution to the local church? Surely it is in the matter of his being a faithful, active, consistent church member who has set an example that all Christians may well follow.

To His Denomination

Jimmy R. Allen

Setting on my desk is a picture of the officers elected by the Southern Baptist Convention in Kansas City, Missouri in 1977. The president, vice-president, and secretary are persons who earned doctorates in the field of Christian ethics under Professor T. B. Maston. The picture symbolizes the contribution to the life of the denomination made by this quiet, scholarly deacon.

His contribution is far broader than the work of his students. It is also fashioned by his own participation in denominational affairs. He has helped change the atmosphere of Southern Baptist life on racial attitudes, participation in community life, and responsible ethical action. His writings have helped set the agenda for Southern Baptist life for several decades. He has been the catalyst for shaping the principles of the gospel to life. He has contributed to the atmosphere of concern for the world mission cause. He has been a voice to the conscience of Southern Baptists at critical decision-making times. He has helped Southern Baptists toward strengthening family life.

Few persons would argue with the observation that Southern Baptists have matured into a responsible and responsive body of Christians concerned with impacting society. When a process that complex takes place, there are many factors in shaping it. A major factor is leadership. No description of that process of change in Southern Baptist life could be complete without the name of T. B. Maston.

Role of Catalyst for Shaping Structures

While some may mark the major contribution of T. B. Maston to denominational life to be his scholarly writings or his classroom nurture of future leaders, I believe it to be his role in shaping the formation of the Christian Life Commission (SBC).

Any examination of the denomination's directions over the past thirty years will reveal the key role of the various Christian life commissions in shaping conscience and programs. The Christian Life Commission (SBC) has had a phenomenal growth in its size of staff, budget, and sphere of influence. The times have demanded such an emphasis. It has furnished the rallying point for a continuing emphasis on critical issues confronting this increasingly influential denomination.

In 1949 a committee of seven members was fashioned by the Baptist General Convention of Texas to study the way to bring greater influence to bear on Christian behavior and on society. Executive Secretary J. Howard Williams, who was later to become president of Southwestern Seminary where Maston taught through the years, had had a heart attack which felled him during the annual session of the Convention. Williams said later that he was pleased with all that he heard out of the sessions about growth in numbers but was burdened by how little those numbers were counting in impacting our world and its value systems. Conferring with Maston and others, Williams issued the call for a study. The Committee of Seven had distinguished names such as A. B. Rutledge, later to be executive director of the Home Mission Board. Maston also served on the committee. It recommended the formation of a structure to be called the Christian Life Commission. Maston served on the commission from its inception. The document analyzing the issues and calling for the formation of the organization was authored by the group in an editing process but was largely the work of Maston. The first executive for the fledgling commission was A. C. Miller. Miller went to accept the leadership of the Social Service Commission (SBC) in 1953. He led the national body to change the name of their structure to the Christian Life Commission.

Maston helped to shape the policies of the Christian Life Commission in Texas toward responsible scholarship in developing a body of popularly written pamphlets on key issues of Christian behavior. He assisted the commission with his time and energy. The successor to A. C. Miller as the executive of the Texas commission was one of Maston's first students to earn the newly authorized doctorate in the field of Christian ethics, Foy Valentine. In 1960 Valentine succeeded Miller as the leader of the Christian Life Commission (SBC). Other states began forming commissions, standing committees, or other similar structures to carry this emphasis on ethics.

It is significant that the Texas Christian Life Commission, on which Maston served several rotating terms, has had to this day as its executive leaders men who earned their doctorates under T. B. Maston.

Role of Counselor to Leaders

A less visible but crucial role through which Maston has shaped denominational life has been that of counselor to people in places of influence. Some of these have been his former students. He has had a pastoral spirit toward his graduate students which caused him to keep track of each one. He prays regularly for them and stays in communication with them. Since they scattered into all levels of denominational life as well as community life, his alert concern for them has placed him in a position to counsel them.

The unusual esprit de corps of these men who were imbued with concern for making their denomination's influence relevant to society's needs has sometimes created an erroneous impression. It became a matter of amusement to his graduate students that some participants in the denomination's political processes viewed Maston as consciously strategizing to manipulate denominational decisions. While lecturing about the responsibility to participate in political processes both in the community and in the denomination, Maston's skill for the political is simply not one of his gifts. He often repeats the refrain that the privilege of a professor is to observe his students doing things of which he himself is not capable. That thesis is proven in his role as a denominational politician. Oriented to issues, his political judgments on processes and personalities often are far wide of the mark.

His contribution as counselor to those in denominational leadership is all the more valuable because of his lack of political aspiration. He can see issues clearly and help beleaguered and busy leaders analyze the issues in the light of Christian conscience.

While his counsel has been welcomed by many leaders, one should be especially noted. No more powerful Baptist figure existed in the decade of the 1960s than E. S. James, editor of the *Baptist Standard* of Texas. As editor of the largest religious weekly paper in the nation, he used the platform with unusual forcefulness. He influenced not only Baptists but the very course of some national events. James had not attended a seminary. He was keenly conscious of that fact though not intimidated by it. He did seek the counsel and insight of several trusted people. There were times when he used trusted advisers as sounding boards for his editorials before allowing them to be printed. He told me on numerous occasions that some of the most valuable assistance he ever received came from T. B. Maston.

Vivid in my memory was a day during a convention of Baptists in Texas while I was serving as executive of the Texas Christian Life Commission. We were in a heated controversy on policies concerning religious liberty and separation of church and state. I was in a quandary about my role in the discussion. As an employee of the convention, I felt certain restraints about expressing my views. Yet I also knew that my voice could very well tilt the scales of decision making on the issue. Personal friendships as well as relationships to those in the power structure of my organization were involved. Just before the session, I was undecided about my role in the discussion. I had spent most of the night before in a prayerful search for guidance. Just before the session, I sat down by Dr. Maston. He reminded me that we were not talking about a policy but about a direction for the denomination's life. I became acutely aware that I could live without my job or with people misunderstanding my decision, but I could not live with myself if I did not follow my conscience in line with my established pattern of openness in my position on issues. I did speak that day. The separation principle carried. I lived with the scars of the battle far better than I could have with regrets over not taking a stand.

Role of Gadfly

There are times when a conscientious person with issue orientation in his life-style will play the role of gadfly. Maston has surfaced uncomfortable questions in his denomination's life. He thus has contributed to its well-being by sensitizing conscience even when his efforts to affect policy have failed.

I do not view his role in calling us to change our racially prejudiced policies as that of gadfly. While he was at the task early in Southern Baptist experience and often sounded like a voice crying in the wilderness, he was to live to see his positions become policies. The tides of truth, as well as of history, were on the side of his position. I remember well the tense moment of decision making in the 1954 Southern Baptist Convention immediately after the United States Supreme Court decision on school integration. Maston's voice along with J. B. Weatherspoon called us to responsible support of racial justice. They prevailed. That was not gadfly.

His gadfly role is demonstrated in his dealing with issues of war and peace, economics, and affluence. During World War II it was not popular for Southern Baptists to defend conscientious objection to war. T. B. Maston did so. His position was not officially adopted by Southern Baptists. Our conscientious objectors had to stand the onus of being cared for by Quakers instead of by their own fellowship. T. B. Maston raised his voice in defense of the right of Christian conscience to dissent to war even when feelings were running high in favor of war.

Maston's concerns about our affluence are very real and very unpopular. Two instances illustrate it. When Southwestern Seminary trustees decided to build a president's home, the original plans seemed too plush to Maston. In characteristic forthrightness, he wrote a letter to the trustees saying so. Since a number of others had similar opinions and expressed them publicly, a controversy followed. The house was built with slightly altered plans. Maston's concern for the salaries of denominational executives and especially for the fact that there was difficulty in discovering the rate of their pay is another instance of his gadfly role. He wrote a letter to each executive asking for his salary. The matter became a matter of Convention discussion. Instructions to give the salary figure were given to the agencies by the Convention. No changes in denominational salaries have resulted, but a great deal of controversy has been created by the discussion.

The columns Maston submits to Baptist state papers often raise crucial issues. Thus his role of gadfly is a sensitizing process toward ethical demands of Christ in practical behavior.

Conclusion

By combining a deeply sensitive devotional life, a serious respect for biblical authority, an active commitment to the local church, an unreserved concern for world missions, a disciplined scholarship, and an urgent calling to bring the reign of God into the affairs of men, T. B. Maston uniquely met the criteria for Southern Baptist leadership. He struck the notes to which Baptists hearts are tuned. He, therefore, has become an instrument of God in the process of a dynamic denomination fulfilling its role in a tangled world.

To Seminary Education

W. Randall Lolley

A Christian must be both a declaring and a demonstrating person, one whose words act, whose deeds speak. The ethical force which flows from such a rhythm of life blends personal piety with social concern. This has been T. B. Maston's life-style throughout a career which spans more than half a century.

Maston's primary contribution to seminary education has come through his seminary teaching. He began teaching at Southwestern Seminary in the fall of 1922, the last year of his undergraduate study. He received his M.R.E. in 1923. In 1925, he earned the first D.R.E. in Southwestern Seminary's history. His thesis was entitled: "The Play Program of the Church." Interestingly, the first of his more than twenty books was on church recreation.

Since the course offerings were rather small, Maston taught all over the map in the School of Religious Education. In addition to courses in ethics, he taught student work, social work, adolescent psychology, adolescent religious education, and church recreation.

He was elected as the student speaker at his commencement. On that occasion during a walk with President Scarborough from the old chapel, which was a frame building at the time, to Fort Worth Hall to have a picture made, Scarborough took hold of his arm and said, "Tom, it looks like we are going to need you here."

During those early years Maston had a soul struggle whether he should teach on the college or the seminary level. During a conversation with Scarborough on this matter, the president again made a life-changing statement. He quoted B. H. Carroll, the founding president at Southwestern, to remind Maston: "If you definitely feel that the Lord has led you here, then the burden of proof should be that you should leave."

In 1928 Maston attended a summer session at the University of North Carolina, Chapel Hill, where he met Ernest R. Groves, the early pioneer in family sociology. They talked about the decision Maston was facing, and Groves counseled him to remain in seminary education.

From the beginning of his seminary teaching, Maston felt that Christian ethics ought to be in the School of Theology rather than in the School of

Religious Education. He believed that the impact on preachers and laypersons would be enhanced by the transfer. In 1930 he presented President Scarborough with a paper outlining the reasons why he thought the shift should be made. It took a while to work out details, but before he went to Yale the second time, in 1936, an understanding was reached that certain courses he had been teaching would remain in the School of Religious Education and that others would be transferred to the School of Theology. Price, the head of the School of Religious Education, would have preferred that the course on the family remain in the School of Religious Education. However, it too was transferred.

Influenced profoundly at Yale by H. Richard Niebuhr, Roland H. Bainton, and D. C. Macintosh, Maston returned to Southwestern Seminary in 1937 determined that the focus of his teaching career would be Christian ethics. For six years he taught in both the School of Theology and the School of Religious Education. In 1943 Christian Social Ethics was made a department in Southwestern's School of Theology. Maston transferred to this department and headed it until his retirement in 1963.

He was a member of the graduate studies committee most of the years he was in the School of Theology. On two different occasions he was chairman of a committee to study and restructure the curriculum in the School of Theology. His teaching career spanned the administrations of all the presidents of Southwestern Seminary except B. H. Carroll, the first one.

Beginning at Southern Seminary in the summer of 1955, Maston taught in all six of the Southern Baptist seminaries except New Orleans Baptist Theological Seminary. He has been on the New Orleans campus many times for other engagements.

Maston had the opportunity to join the faculty at Southern Seminary and also at Southeastern Seminary. He made a trip to Louisville to talk with President McCall and members of the faculty about teaching at Southern Seminary. While there he visited with J. B. Weatherspoon who, along with Olin Binkley and Maston, is regarded as a seminal thinker among Southern Baptists in the area of Christian ethics. After the conversation with Weatherspoon, Maston went to see W. O. Carver, retired teacher of missions and outstanding denominational statesman. Carver met Maston at the door and in his rather gruff way asked, "What are you doing here?" Maston explained that sooner or later he would know that he had an invitation to join the faculty and had made the trip to see whether he could sense the leading of the Lord.

Carver said something to him which made a lasting impression while it assisted him immensely in the immediate decision he faced. His counsel was: "I'll tell you what I have told many young people through the years—after you have thought through a thing from every possible viewpoint, if your head tells you one thing and your heart tells you something else, you had better follow your heart." Reflecting on that event, Maston has said, "My head told me to leave Southwestern but I could not get the consent of my heart."

For forty-one years as a teacher at Southwestern Seminary, Maston made a direct personal impact upon seminary education. During that time he became the dean of Southern Baptist ethicists. He came to Baptists as they were becoming the largest evangelical denomination in the United States. With unusual balance he synthesized a foundational, East Tennessee, Christian experience with strong biblical emphases, personal evangelism, and social concern.

From his Fort Worth outpost at the largest theological training base in the Christian world, Maston visited college campuses, considering himself more than a teacher at Southwestern Seminary. He represented theological education in general. He frequently collected student requests for materials from the other seminaries. He readily sent the requests to the other schools. His counsel to seminary-bound college students was twofold: If you are going to work among Southern Baptists, get basic theological training in a Southern Baptist seminary; whichever seminary you attend, you will be glad you went. In 1954 he made an eight-week trip to Latin America on the campuses of seven Bible schools and seminaries. He also taught a term at the Arab Baptist Seminary, Beirut, Lebanon, in 1966.

Above all, T. B. Maston prefers to be remembered as a good teacher. This has been his mission, his response to God's love.

Maston's long and influential ministry has been entirely within the context of seminary education. His own thorough preparation attests to his serious commitment to excellence in theological studies. His teaching, writing, and lecturing have demonstrated the same commitment. His major books and published articles reveal a wide and diverse knowledge of the primary theological and ethical sources. He has lived a lifetime of continuing theological education.

His continuing impact focuses in several thousand "Maston alumni" throughout the world. Through his students his ethical methodology and thought have been disseminated in churches, schools, seminaries, and mission stations everywhere. His students have been influenced by essentially the same classroom techniques throughout his career. He has presented various options which a Christian might have on an issue, then led his students to think through the options and reach their own conclusions. This has also been his method with graduate students.

A 1978 list of Christian ethics majors at Southwestern Seminary includes sixty-three names along with three others deceased. Forty-nine of these majored personally with Maston. All the others have been profoundly influenced by him through the ethics teachers at Southwestern, all of whom were his majors. For years he has kept a small book in his pocket. It contains the names of every one of his ethics majors. They constitute his prayer list.

Through the continuing impact of persons such as these, Maston has led two generations of Southern Baptists to apply Christian ethical norms to contemporary life. During 1977-1978 three top elected officials of the Southern Baptist Convention—Jimmy R. Allen, Olan H. Runnels, and Lee Porter—were "Maston alumni." At present four of the six presidents of Southern Baptist seminaries are former students of his: William M. Pinson, Jr., Russell Dilday, Milton Ferguson, and W. Randall Lolley.

T. B. Maston has lived and worked during a revolutionary age. Three-quarters of the twentieth century with their devastating wars, economic boom and bust, social, racial, educational, and technological cataclysms have given rise in his thinking and writing to an ethical motif noted for its basis in the Scriptures along with a radical application of biblical principles to contemporary personal and social situations. Throughout, his method has been developmental. Beginning in his own personal Christian experience, it has ranged through a matrix of biblical, theological-sociological themes and ethical strategies issuing in numerous practical applications.

Maston's enduring impact on seminary education centers in his great contribution toward making Christian ethics a theological discipline. His basic course in the seminary was biblical ethics. In his elective courses and seminars, he continually dealt with a variety of moral issues always applying biblical norms. It may be a gap in his scholarship that he did not address many of the technical critical questions in biblical studies. He failed to develop a precise, consistent, and critical biblical hermeneutic.

He was continually confronted by the notion that social action was the antithesis of evangelism. He answered by demonstrating the biblical basis for social concern. Consequently he has exerted an enormous influence upon the developing social conscience of Southern Baptists and other denominations. Because he has loved Southern Baptists, Maston's critique has ranged from cheerleader to umpire. Always working within the structures for change, he has been a pioneer and a prophet among his people. Henlee H. Barnette says, "Dr. Maston has awakened the social consciousness of Southern Baptists more than any other seminary teacher." He has lived and taught only one gospel which is both personal and social.

To Christian Ethics

Foy Valentine

T. B. Maston and Christian ethics. The two are "joined together in a lasting union," to use one of his favorite phrases. I first felt the impact of that union in the fall of 1944 when I enrolled in his basic biblical ethics course at Southwestern Seminary. Others had already begun to feel that impact through the power and moral energy of his inspired teaching. Multitudes, probably multiplied millions, would be feeling that impact in the next few decades as his teaching, writing, speaking, and personal impact expanded at first from his own direct involvement and then from the involvement of students and a broad cross section of other learners whose lives he touched.

The term *Christian ethics* was practically unknown among Southern Baptists four decades ago when Maston responded to God's call to bear this standard as his lifework. In those early days, some were using the term *Christian sociology* while others spoke of *applied Christianity*. *Social ethics* was the term Maston used most frequently, however, as he began to build the sturdy platform on which he would stand for the next four decades. Then over a period of many years *Christian ethics* gradually evolved as the nomenclature most generally accepted to refer to the discipline to which he was called and uniquely committed. He helped effect that change so that the term *Christian ethics*, as it is now generally used, is both descriptive of his lifework and is in some part a trophy of his personal mind and heart and commitment and energy and life.

The contribution of Maston to Christian ethics has been made primarily through his teaching. The teaching of Christian ethics has been his special calling from God, a calling which he has pursued with singleness of mind and unswerving commitment. Never faltering in his clear understanding of what the Lord wanted him to do, he taught Christian ethics year in and year out, decade in and decade out, with a supreme passion. So strong was his own feeling at this point that he found it very hard to understand why anybody in his right mind who had an opportunity to teach Christian ethics would not plunge into it head over heels and never look back. (It was only because of an almost psychotic conviction that I should march to the beat

47

of a different drummer that I personally resisted his importunings to be a seminary teacher of Christian ethics.) It was in order to teach Christian ethics well that he trained himself exceptionally, studied carefully, read voraciously, and prayed faithfully. He disciplined himself to give his students accurate, up-to-date, relevant Christian ethics material every time he entered the classroom. Resisting the calls to go out and expend his energies in extracurricular activities that might have produced more immediate returns, he stayed by the stuff of teaching Christian ethics in the belief that his impact for the biblical ideal of righteousness would ultimately be greater through his students than it ever could be through any personal ministries or outside engagements which he might pursue. It has been my impression that this may have been one of the reasons he never chose to be ordained by the church as a preacher, preferring rather to cling to his understanding that God had ordained him to be a teacher of Christian ethics. Looking now across the entire Baptist denomination and around the world at his students and at his students' students who are involved in Christian ethics through preaching, pastoring, teaching, public service, and denominational activity at many levels, the judgment he made early in life to major on teaching Christian ethics seems to have been eminently justified for him, altogether right for Baptists, and of genuine significance for the kingdom of God.

Maston's teaching has always gone beyond the formal presentation of Christian ethics lectures to his generally crowded classes. His goal has been to teach Christian ethics to students. His concern has been not only the content of a very broad range of Christian ethics courses but also the practical ways in which students could be most effectively equipped to communicate that content to their churches, their communities, and their groups and power structures with which they could be expected to have some influence. He was also concerned that Christian ethics should become a vital part of the daily life of his students. He often said in the biblical ethics course, "I have failed as a teacher if you are not better men and women when you have finished this course."

When I studied with Maston, he was never too busy to take the time to talk with me, to reason with me, to explain to me, and to give me the correcting and prodding and shaping and molding which he felt would ultimately enable me to make some useful contribution to Christian ethics in particular and to the Lord's work in general. If in this presentation of Maston's contribution "To Christian Ethics," the ideas flow with some smoothness, if the commas are in the right places, and if the sentence structure approaches some measure of clarity, it is primarily because of that personal teaching, over and above the classroom involvement, which he invested in me.

Moreover, I believe Maston always viewed his family life conferences, his Christian life conferences, his foreign mission assignments, and his other outside engagements as legitimate extensions of his seminary teaching of Christian ethics. Using teaching as his basic tool, he communicated Christian ethics in such a way as to put the stamp of his insights, his vision, and his deep convictions on the whole discipline of Christian ethics as it is now perceived and subscribed to by Southern Baptists. With a gift almost unique in our generation, T. B. Maston has multiplied his ministry in Christian ethics over and over and over again in the lives of his students.

Maston has never viewed writing in the field of Christian ethics as his special gift. Writing has been, rather, something of a burden which he has borne resolutely through the years because there were not enough others on the scene who were willing to assume the hard discipline involved in writing so as to use this important medium to communicate Christian ethics. Some of Maston's prolific writing in Christian ethics has been designed to reach the academic community, an outstanding example being *Christianity and World Issues* published by Macmillan and called by some an ideal example of what a seminary textbook in Christian ethics ought to be. Most of his Christian ethic writings, however, have been designed to communicate to pastors and church members about race such as *Of One*, moral decision making such as *Right or Wrong?*, daily cross bearing on behalf of the kingdom of God such as *Why Live the Christian Life?*, and many, many others. Probably his most influential writing on behalf of Christian ethics has been his prolific output of brief articles on dozens of special Christian ethics issues, articles he prepared through the years for the millions of readers of state Baptist weekly publications.

From the beginning of his long and distinguished career in Christian ethics, Maston has been convinced that Christian ethics has as its source of authority the will of God. Elaborating on this deep conviction about the will of God has been one of his long suits in his teaching and in his writing. Many generations of seminary students and untold readers and conference participants have understood his forceful and convincing defense of the will of God as the Christian's absolute summum bonum in life. He has been equally convinced that the kingdom of God is central to all proper understanding and practice of Christian ethics. He has seen love as the main virtue of Christian ethics and has clearly perceived and plainly taught that justice is the natural, required outgrowth of self-giving love.

A favorite figure of Maston's has been the two-dimensional cross as the ideal symbol for Christian ethics, with the perpendicular piece symbolizing every human being's right relationship to God and the horizontal piece representing every human being's right relationship to other human beings. The most significant emphasis he has made regarding the characteristics of Christian ethics has been his never changing, never compromised theological orientation for this discipline. While some practitioners of Christian ethics have become enamored with social fads and have developed a sociological or humanistic orientation for their concerns, Maston has held a steady focus on theology as this discipline's only adequate orientation. His depth of reading in and understanding of the theologians of the present as well as of the past have astounded many of his teaching colleagues both in Christian ethics and in other theological seminary disciplines. The Bible has always had a very special place in the life, thought, and work of this Christian ethicist. Few men and women in the field of Christian ethics in his lifetime have maintained a higher view of the Scriptures or have gone more faithfully and consistently to the Bible in careful study and scholarly exposition of the biblical material, including the original Hebrew and Greek, than has T. B. Maston.

So great has been Maston's lifelong commitment to Christian ethics that he early sought avenues in addition to teaching and writing and speaking through which he might disseminate to the Southern Baptist constituency his God-given understanding that Christianity has profound meaning in everyday life and in all society. He joined other Baptist leaders of vision and courage in shaping and projecting the work of the state and national Christian life commissions. He helped to settle on ways to communicate the meaning of Christian ethics to rank-and-file Baptists by hammering out the divisions which would enable most church members better to understand what Christian ethics is all about so that family, race, citizenship, economics, daily work, and special moral concerns are now general divisions widely used throughout Southern Baptist life and beyond to deal with the whole field of Christian ethics. Moreover, the stamp of Maston's influence is clearly evident in the personalities and the programs of the Christian ethics agencies of the various state Baptist conventions which have established such work.

One of T. B. Maston's special gifts has been the ability to maintain an uncompromisingly strong prophetic witness without abandoning a compassionate sympathy for those with whom he found himself in disagreement. This pastoral spirit, closely akin to his calling as a teacher, has often enabled him to win to his cause those who started out thinking they were his implacable foes. In the area of race relations throughout the 1940s and 1950s, he kept teaching and writing the good news that in Jesus Christ the dividing wall of hostility between whites and blacks has been broken down once and for all. His was one of the most influential voices (I think the most influential voice) among Southern Baptists in effecting change for God and for good at the point of race relations. Time and again he has discerned the social and moral issues about to emerge as critically important and has moved in ahead of many opportunists to declare the whole counsel of God with the effective combination of prophetic and pastoral qualities which has characterized him as a leading change agent among Southern Baptists.

T. B. Maston is an authentic Christian. He is a faithful churchman. He is a loyal Baptist. He is a consistent citizen. He is a superb teacher. He practices what he preaches. No Christian ethicist in Southern Baptist history comes close to having exerted the influence for good that he has exerted. Christian ethics, both as an academic discipline and as a major emphasis in Southern Baptist life and work, bears the mark of T. B. Maston's special genius. Only eternity will tell what profoundly significant results will yet come from his continuing impact on behalf of Christian ethics.

To Colleagues

C. W. Brister

A quarter century ago when T. B. Maston became my mentor in ethics, he had already been teaching at Southwestern Seminary for thirty-one years. His name was listed among seventeen theology school members in the 1953 catalog when I enrolled at Southwestern Seminary. Church historian W. W. Barnes had retired and theologian W. T. Conner had died in May 1952. Only the late E. Leslie Carlson and L. R. Elliott were listed in the faculty roster ahead of Maston. He was a senior professor, Ph.D. graduate from Yale University, well-established scholar, and influential denominational statesman when I became his doctoral student in 1953 and faculty colleague in 1957.

How shall we clarify Maston's contributions to his colleagues until we first understand the concept of colleagueship? Webster defines *colleague*, from the Latin *collega*, as "an associate in a profession." Thomas Buford Maston has been associated with distinguished colleagues on the Southwestern Seminary faculty and across the United States. I recall planning a trip to Union Theological Seminary, New York City, in the fall of 1955. It was my purpose to research the life and work of Harry Emerson Fosdick, the noted pastor of Riverside Church. In a typical gesture of helpfulness, Maston addressed a letter to President John C. Bennett of Union Seminary, requesting that full privileges as a visiting scholar be accorded me there. Maston and Bennett knew of each other professionally, not personally; yet, the New Yorker extended me a most gracious welcome. I lived in "the prophet's chamber" at Union, attended classes of notables like Reinhold Niebuhr, and joined the faculty for mealtime fellowship precisely because of T. B. Maston's colleagueship and John Bennett's kindness.

Like filings drawn to a powerful magnet, men and women from across the United States came to Southwestern Seminary, at least in part, to learn from Maston. His discipline has focused on the cutting edge of life: economics, personal morality, war and peace, race relations, church and state, Communism, world tensions, and the family and its future. He has possessed a solid biblical foundation for his wide-ranging ethical impulse, plus a love for persons that has been contagious.

A vital personal quality, noted by students and faculty friends alike, has been T. B. Maston's gracious Christian spirit. The native of East Tennessee has brought a warm, caring quality to his interpersonal relations. Though a layman, ordained as a deacon not as a minister, his pastoral capacities have abounded in sensitivity, insight, and supportive concern. He was never trained in a formal or clinical way to do counseling, yet students, administrative staff, and faculty friends relied upon his wise guidance.

He and Essie Mae, his companion of the years, have been "given to hospitality," as the Bible recommends for all of God's people. His graduate students became something of an extended family over the earth. The Mastons have been tempered by sorrow in caring for their multiple handicapped son, Tom Mc. They discovered early that Tom Mc had been seriously injured at birth. They took him to many doctors and several hospitals in search of help. Their hearts were saddened as doctor after doctor said: "We do not know anything that can be done for him. All you can do is take him home and give him the best possible care." They have done that for more than half a century.

The Mastons are convinced that God speaks through tragedy. They have discovered some profound spiritual gifts through suffering: understanding, obedience, patience, high values, humility, deepened fellowship with God, a capacity to wait for him and to pray "nevertheless," while placing their lives in God's hands. Because of their profound confidence in divine providence, the Mastons have both been resourceful helpers with faculty and student families where special children were involved.

From the moment of our first meeting in 1952, T. B. Maston and I were attracted to each other. Though years apart in age, we found ourselves brothers in spirit and substantival concerns. The transition in our relationship—from student to faculty friend—was gradual and unbroken. I had served as pastor of an active suburban congregation during and following my doctoral studies, yet my teacher always had time for a meaningful visit when I was on campus. Largely through his encouragement and initiative, along with support from other faculty friends, I was invited to join the School of Theology faculty. Because I had gained pastoral experience, done clinical pastoral education, and minored in pastoral care and preaching, I was offered a post in the Department of Pastoral Ministry. Our fields were related; there was a proper overlap in our disciplines.

Given that background, here are some major contributions which T. B. Maston has made to his colleagues and friends.

First, he has brought the example of a highly disciplined life to each task and relationship. Maston did not settle for a set of dated lecture notes from the 1920s as he taught through exciting epochs of human history. He updated his lectures and read the published works of leading theological scholars—knew their positions, weaknesses, and major contributions. The Baptist ethicist remains an authority in his own right. His spirit has been one of openness to truth—to God's revealing light—wherever he has found it. The fact that he continues to read, travel, speak, and write evidences his remarkable desire for knowledge.

In his eightieth year, Maston reminded some of his faculty friends that he had published as many books since retirement, fifteen years before, as during his active professorship. He has authored seventeen books and countless articles, many of them aimed at a lay, rather than a professional, audience.

Second, T. B. Maston's discipline has related to his churchmanship and devotion to Christ. His has been an unwavering faith in God. One of his colleagues, who once was interim pastor of Gambrell Street Baptist Church, noted that Maston had served that congregation as a deacon for many years. "He was always at deacons' meeting, active in the life and work of his church, and befriended me numerous times during that interim pastoral period," said Robert A. Baker.

Maston has reflected an unashamed confidence in prayer and practiced daily devotion to Jesus Christ. We who have labored at his side have sensed that he remains on good speaking terms with God. He has viewed himself as somewhat mystical in religious expression. I recall the time when he related an experience of a "vision of God" during a critical personal illness. He and his family were in New Haven, where he was completing doctoral work at Yale University. He contracted pneumonia in a prepenicillin era. Without the aid of antibiotic miracle drugs, he went through a life-or-death crisis period when medical personnel could not help. He envisioned himself balanced on a fence, where he might have fallen one way into death, another into life. He felt God moving him toward life and, thereafter, never doubted the grace that claimed him.

Third, Maston has had a readiness to practice what he has taught. He has been an encourager of his faculty brethren. A letter came shortly after I had begun teaching at Southwestern Seminary. "Just a note to tell you that I appreciated your recent article in the *Baptist Standard* and hope that you will keep on writing . . . . I do not think there is any better training for more serious writing than to write some for denominational publications." He modeled a role of unimpeachable integrity. In faculty meetings he most frequently championed the cause of the students. They were underdogs in the institutional power system; he became their advocate on many occasions.

His word was his bond. His promises, while prudently made, were faithfully kept.

As a faculty member, Maston was concerned for the financial support and healthy family relations of professional associates. A fiscal conservative, he wanted his faculty friends to live within their means. It bothered him when they plunged precipitously into debt for a new house or automobile. Also, he felt that the gap between ample provisions for educational administrators and the modest salaries paid to faculty members was too great.

Fourth, T. B. Maston has been a committed critic of Baptists and other denominational groups. There has been a prophetic quality to his vision which has created constructive tension towards divine ideals in life. Whatever the issue, he has possessed the tutored conscience of a Christian. His criticism was reflected in occasional chapel addresses, like: "The Heresy of Orthodoxy." Articles in state Baptist papers needled consciences toward correcting error or constructive action. His correctives were salutary and constructive, with commitment to Christ and Baptist causes.

Excerpts from a letter I wrote to the Mastons, upon the occasion of his retirement in 1963, express a young colleague's appreciation for his mentor and friend.

Gloria and I are particularly grateful for the influence of your obedience to Christ and openness to truth, for your parental example of steadfast love in the home, for the unspoken influence of having attained to highest academic excellence, for sharing your knowledge with wisdom, for the devoted ministry of writing, for the strength of your love for persons of all races and classes, for the deep missionary burden of your hearts, world-encompassing vision of your concern, the practice of good churchmanship through a local Baptist fellowship, the prophetic dimension of your lives under the Spirit of God, and for the promise of years unfolding in future ministry.

Since those words were written, God has granted Maston fifteen additional years of usefulness. He has continued to lecture, write, travel, counsel, and inspire countless individuals across the world. He has enjoyed the friendship of many colleagues and lived to see his ministry multiplied a thousandfold through lives like those who honor him in this book.

To Students

Tom Logue

T. B. Maston is and always has been a student. Thus he has been able to relate to students in a remarkable way, despite any age or philosophical or theological difference. During a teaching experience at Carson-Newman College when he was in his late 70s, he found it hard to realize that he was four times as old as some of his students.

But, to many, he also seems always to have been a professor. Browning Ware of First Baptist Church in Austin, Texas, tells of his own chagrin as Maston told him of a dream he had had of Browning on a trip Maston had made overseas. In the dream Maston had already returned home and Ware had waved and yelled, "Welcome home, T. B." Just hearing Maston tell the experience embarrassed Ware, who confessed, "If I live to be seventy and he hangs around, then perhaps I'll call him 'T. B.' "

The only student I ever knew who called Maston by his first name was Agnes Durant Pylant, for many years with the Baptist Sunday School Board, and this incident was in friendly retaliation. Earlier Maston had spoken at Wayland College while Agnes was teaching there. In his chapel address Maston said nice things about several faculty members in the audience who had formerly been his students. Then Maston looked at Agnes on the front row and with a puzzled look said, "Now there is Grandma Pylant. I can't remember whether I taught her or she taught me." Later Agnes was at the seminary and returned the courtesy. One morning she opened Maston's office door and said, "Hi, Tom, how are you today?" and quickly closed the door and went her merry way.

A conservative estimate of the number of seminary students that Maston has taught is eight to ten thousand. Even more college students have had brief, but profound, relationships with him at over a dozen religious focus weeks at both Baptist and state college campuses, at his ten appearances at Student Week at Ridgecrest and Glorieta, and at many local and state Baptist Student Union conventions and retreats.

Jerrell McCracken of Word, Inc., first met Maston at Baylor during a religious focus week. Because Maston was honest and forthright in talking about social and personal problem areas, Jerrell says Maston probably reached more unchurched students than anyone on a religious focus week team during his student years at Baylor.

Maston had great pride in the ethics department of the seminary and the quality of instruction in that department. But he did not have illusions about the basis of the Christian faith. He knew that theology, what God had done in history, was basic and that Christian ethics, what man should do in the light of what God had done, was derivative. Charles Petty of the Christian Life Council of North Carolina remembers some advice Maston gave him just prior to his departure for North Carolina.

Charles, don't let people ever question your theology. Let the work you are in be controversial because of the ethical application rather than the theological foundations. Keep your ethics tied closely to the Bible and you'll be all right.

As well prepared as Maston has always been for assignments, always with fresh notes in hand—totally illegible, by the way, to anyone but himself—he has probably been more successful by roles he has modeled than by thoughts he has expressed in the classroom.

Maston's roles as appreciative husband and caring father have been noticed by countless numbers of students. The affection he displays as he speaks lovingly of Mrs. Maston and their care for Tom Mc's needs have been profound lessons to others.

Robert Dale, professor at Southeastern Seminary, recalls Maston being asked at the end of a graduate seminar who had been the most influential person in his life. Dale's imagination flipped through a list of teachers and leaders who had molded Maston's thought. Maston mentioned none of these but stated that the person was Tom Mc.

Then he told how his son had been brain damaged at birth, had never spoken or walked, and had to be fed and cared for every moment. Maston didn't identify the lesson in his statement. My guess? That love gives people life! I imagine his and Mrs. Maston's love have kept Tom Mc alive.

Invitations to the Maston home for a meal or time of fellowship and refreshment remain in the minds of many former students when details of classroom discussions have often faded. Probably no seminary professor's wife has had as many students as guests in the home as has Mrs. Maston.

Sam Fort, director of student work for the Northwest Baptist Convention, had a series of family tragedies in 1963. Sam had to make some difficult decisions in order to direct his father's estate toward helping in the care of his mother and sister. Instead of an office appointment, Maston invited Fort to the house where Sam says Maston revealed "the matchless combination of keen ethical insight and deep piety that had made me respect him so much in the classroom and was so appreciated in my time of need."

Maston has also modeled well the roles of professor, scholar, and author. Albert McClellan of Nashville, Tennessee, speaks of Maston being the best friend he had among seminary professors. "He gave me the impression of seeing me," McClellan writes. Joshua Grijalva of San Antonio says that ethics was his favorite course at the seminary but that it was not the material but the personality and Christian experience of the teacher that attracted him. Guy Greenfield of Los Alamos, New Mexico, says, "Maston did not just teach ethics; he taught students."

Maston not only had a remarkable memory of names but could recall, years after students left the seminary, where in the classroom they had sat. Howard Bramlette, editor of *The Student*, says this memory also held true for books in his library. Maston sent Bramlette after a book one day. "It is the third one from the right on the second shelf from the bottom." The book was exactly where Maston had said it was.

Maston always set the standard high for students, and sometimes they did not understand this until the first test. When Nell Magee, now of National Student Ministries Department of the Baptist Sunday School Board, finished her first test, she went immediately to the school library and found most of her classmates at the same place and with the same realization of how little they knew of contemporary affairs.

Phil Card, for many years director of student work for the Colorado Baptist Convention, is noted for his drawings of people who have made lasting impressions on him. Several years ago he featured Maston in the *Rocky Mountain Baptist*. In the drawing Phil had inadvertently put two *f*s in the word *professor*. When Maston called the mistake to Phil's attention, Phil answered that he had received so many *f*s in Maston's classes that he thought there were at least two *f*s in *professor*.

Warren Hultgren of Tulsa remembers a paper he hurriedly put together on a Monday following a weekend revival: "He saw me in the hall some weeks later and said to me, after suitable prefacing remarks, that I was capable of better than that and that it is unworthy of a servant of God to do less than ones best, which I obviously had done."

Nor would Maston allow a student to be too proud about a good grade or action. As Maston returned a paper with a rare *A* on it to student Cal Guy, now missions professor at Southwestern, he warned, "You'd better frame that one."

Jase Jones, now with the Home Mission Board, remembers telling Maston of incidents on his church field which he felt he had handled well. Maston would reply with something like, "Well, that is all right, as long as you did it in the right spirit."

James Musgrave, Jr., who teaches in the Baptist seminary in Rio, attributes to Maston the insight and patience to see him back to the mission field after coming home before completing his first term. "Church discipline and the authority given to pastors and denominational leaders made it possible for me to make the same kind of demands on others that I was making upon myself, driving us all up the wall," Musgrave says. Maston quietly told him that his enthusiasm for zealous ethical demands sounded like Judaism and legalism. Musgrave says that it was not until ten years later the truth really soaked in.

Many former students recall his encouragement to them to write. For some it was the finishing of the thesis. Cleve Horne of the Christian Civic Foundation of Saint Louis fears that without the encouraging phone calls from Maston that he would never have completed the thesis. James Carter, of Fort Worth, recalls Maston telling him that if Southern Baptists' doctoral graduates do not write, we will have few writers. This challenge, Carter says, has inspired his attempts to write. Each time they meet, Maston inquires about what Carter is writing.

Cecil Sherman recalls that in 1955 Maston said he expected to have another ten or twelve active years and that if he were going to write, he would have to get about it. Sherman says he watched with amazement as five or six books came forth, "the best of T. B. Maston, ample witness to a man's resolve to use all of his talents."

Those majoring in ethics have had such a pride in the department that others may feel ethics majors didn't know there were other departments around. Jerry Self, Christian Life Consultant for Tennessee Baptists took his three-year-old son, Jay Mark, with him to the library one day. They met Maston and Self introduced his son to his professor. Later Jerry was leaving their seminary apartment and told his son he was going to study. "You mean over in Dr. Maston's school?" Jay Mark asked.

Maston's role as churchman was obvious to students, even to those who did not attend Gambrell Street Baptist Church where the Mastons and their two sons, Gene and Tom Mc, worshiped. Mike McCrocklin of Des Moines, Iowa, remembers a hot day in August, "when the wind wraps you up like an electric blanket." Maston knocked on Mike's door, welcomed him to Fort Worth, simply introduced himself as a member of the church, and invited him to visit the church. "While at the seminary I observed the constancy in his commitment to his local church, rarely matched by even paid staff members," Mike says.

The most mentioned quality of Maston's life, as former students reflect upon the subject, is his compassion. Clark Scanlon, of the Foreign Mission Board, recalls being out of town in a revival during his wife's recovery following the birth of their second child. Each night Maston, a patient in the hospital himself, would call Mrs. Scanlon: "I know Clark is out of town, but it is now fathers' visiting hours, and I just wanted to check on you since Clark can't."

Marguerite Woodruff of Mercer University changed majors at Southwestern Seminary in her doctoral program. As she began her first seminar work, the second-year students frightened her when they discussed subjects and authors so knowledgeably.

I began to feel totally inadequate and in typical female fashion I found my way to his office, sat down, and cried. He was so reassuring, I dried my tears and decided if he had that much confidence in me, then surely I must have the same confidence in myself . . . . He was the most approachable man I ever met.

Joe Trull of Garland, Texas, recalls a seminary student and his wife being killed in a train-car accident as they traveled to their church field. Maston stopped his planned lectures and spent the week talking about evil and suffering.

Eddie Rickenbaker recalls how very nervous he was during his oral examination for his Th.D. After five or ten minutes of preliminaries, Maston announced that he had to go to the bathroom. Later Maston explained to Eddie that he had done this to relieve the student's tension. "It certainly helped," Rickenbaker says. Bill Sherman of Nashville, Tennessee, recalls Maston coming to his defense in his oral examination when Bill and a questioning professor were in debate about a matter. "Maston was always our friend and our supporter," Sherman says.

Maston has always felt a real loyalty to his students, especially to those who majored with him. Three of these have died, and Maston keeps close tab on their widows, Mrs. Charles Johnson of Ottawa, Kansas; Mrs. Harold Basden of Richmond, Virginia; and Mrs. Woodrow Phelps of Nashville, Tennessee.

Jean (Mrs. Cecil) Thompson of El Paso was one of Maston's secretaries. The seminary was paying only sixty cents an hour in those days, but most businesses paid at least a dollar an hour. Maston explained to Jean that he did not think the salary was fair and that he would pay her another forty cents an hour himself.

The last illustration of Maston's concern for others is existential. When collecting material for this chapter, Maston warned me not to write to too many former students lest I get more material than I could use and some, whose contributions weren't used, feel slighted. As usual, Maston was prophetic—at least partially so, right now.

I did!

But please, you who answered, don't feel slighted.

To Race Relations

Jase Jones

The indebtedness of Southern Baptists to Maston for his pioneer leadership in the development of Christian race relations cannot be measured. His leadership has been exercised through classroom teaching, writing and speaking, denominational and community organizations, his local church, and personal encounter. Behind all that he does are deep convictions that the Christian gospel is to be applied in the area of race, that Christian treatment of minority racial groups had not been based on Christian ethical principles, and that he must be directly involved in the struggle for racial justice.

Maston has taught about the race problem in five Southern Baptist seminaries. In all but Southwestern Seminary, race was just a part of a course covering a broader subject. He taught his first course in Christian ethics at Southwestern Seminary in 1922. From that time on, he taught all that Southwestern Seminary offered in ethics until the Christian ethics faculty was enlarged in 1948. An increased emphasis on race came in 1938 when Maston offered a new course, Social Problems of the South, half of which dealt with the race problem. A full course on race, The Church and the Race Problem, began in 1944. In this course, distinguished black leaders addressed the class. The students were taken on a field trip through the Fort Worth black community. "I always thought that the field trips would be the things they would remember most about the course," says Maston. Another feature of the course was an individual student field study and report on a selected racial problem in Fort Worth, such as the provision for blacks in the public school system.

His first published writing on race (pamphlet) bore the title *Racial Revelations*, and was published by Woman's Missionary Union in 1927. *Integration*, a pamphlet published by the Christian Life Commission (SBC), was first prepared in 1956 at the request of the Advisory Council of Southern Baptists for Work with Negroes to be read at its annual meeting. Another booklet, *Interracial Marriage*, was published by the Christian Life Commission in 1963. The Brotherhood Commission of the Southern Baptist Convention published *The Christian and Race Relations* (pamphlet) in the same year.

In 1932, Maston wrote a Training Union monthly program series on the social teachings of the Bible. Race and class was the subject of one month's program. Another Training Union program on race appeared in November, 1941. Maston wrote the *Graded Lessons Sunday School for Sixteen Year Pupils* in the thirties, with one quarter's lessons on social problems. Another Sunday School lesson in 1943 was entitled "Christianity Crosses Racial Lines."

An early periodical article on race appeared in *Home and Foreign Fields* in 1929. Other publications for which Maston wrote on race were *The Baptist Student, The Commission, The Brotherhood Journal,* and Baptist state papers.

Of Maston's many books, the following dealt solely with the subject of race: *Of One* (1946), *The Bible and Race* (1959), and *Segregation and Desegregation* (1959). Race was dealt with in parts of six other Maston books. Maston considers *Segregation and Desegregation* to be his major scholarly work on race. He thinks that *The Bible and Race* has been his most influential book on race. Woman's Missionary Union chose it as a study book in 1962, and Broadman Press published over 50,000 copies.

Maston did a considerable amount of important writing on race which did not appear under his name.

The speech which Maston made before the Southern Baptist Convention in Kansas City in 1956 drew more reaction and was probably more influential than any other that he made on the race issue. Carried by the Associated Press, it was widely reported in secular and religious publications. Coming as it did not long after the United States Supreme Court decision in *Brown v. Board of Education,* it is of historical significance. The speech contained specific suggestions as to valid Christian attitudes and actions in racial matters. It provided timely guidance for Southern Baptists striving to help their communities adjust to the Court's decision.

When Dallas, Texas, was ordered to desegregate its school system, the Baptist pastors of Dallas asked Maston to speak to them on the subject, "A Pastor in a Community Facing Desegregation." His speech was reported in word and picture by the secular press, and it caused a reaction next in size to the Kansas City speech.

Maston spoke quite often before interracial meetings of pastors and laymen in a number of states. He often participated in religious focus week at colleges. Frank Leavell, Southern Baptist student work leader, called upon him to speak many times, usually on the race issue. Carson-Newman College in Tennessee invited him to speak on race at its faculty conference. Maston spoke several times at conferences of Southern Baptist workers with Negroes. After he had spoken about love at one of these, a young black worker asked a question that Maston says he has never been able to get away from. "Isn't there a real danger that one may make love a substitute for justice, a mere sentimentality?" Maston answered, "Not genuine Christian love. It is inclusive of justice."

There were other messages at Ridgecrest Baptist conference center at the annual meetings of the Social Service Commission and the Christian Life Commission (SBC) and to the North Carolina Brotherhood.

Maston participated in a variety of denominational and community organizations. He was one of the principal founders, along with J. Howard Williams, A. C. Miller, and W. R. White, of the Christian Life Commission of Texas. The race issue has been a major concern of the commission since its founding. Maston played a key role in the preparation of the commission's literature, particularly in its early years, and served on the commission for almost twenty years.

Southwestern Seminary opened its regular classes to blacks in 1951. Maston had urged it for many years. In a faculty meeting, he said to President Scarborough, "If we would do what we should, we would open up our classes to them." Scarborough replied, "Well, we might be further along on this than you think." He then asked each faculty member, "Would you object to this?" Only one objected.

Maston was a member of the Christian Life Commission (SBC) for six years, becoming associated with it first in the 1940s when it was the Social Service Commission.

The Advisory Council of Southern Baptists for Work with Negroes was another organization in which Maston served. He was its first chairman and was reelected chairman several times. The council performed a valuable service for leaders of the Baptist boards and agencies represented on the council by keeping them abreast of the issues, concepts, and developments in the race struggle. Other groups to which Maston belonged were the National Association for the Advancement of Colored People, the local Urban League (serving on the Executive Committee), and the Southern Regional Council.

The Mastons are members of Gambrell Street Baptist Church, Fort Worth, where Maston is a deacon. A black man once called Maston when the Gambrell Street pastor was out of town and said, "We're looking for a church home, and my pastor suggested I call you." Maston invited him to visit the church that Wednesday night. He met him on the sidewalk and escorted him into the church, where the visitor was warmly welcomed. A fellow deacon later said, "Here's the fellow [Maston] more responsible than anybody else for the church's open-door membership policy." This statement reminds one of a remark made by Theodore F. Adams after Maston's speech in Kansas City. "The progress that we have made among Southern Baptists on this matter of race is due to men like you and O. T. Binkley."

Maston developed strong personal relationships in the black community. He describes the "real kinship of spirit" which exists between himself and J. M. Ellison, longtime chancellor of Virginia Union University and editor of *The Religious Herald,* and tells of visiting in the Ellison home. Ellison calls Maston his "very real friend." He tells of being a guest at the Maston table, of being an overnight guest in the home, and of sharing "the full meaning of their fellowship and thinking as we had devotional moments together."

The black students of Southwestern Seminary were Maston's friends. One of these, Clarence Lucas, now pastor in Louisville, Kentucky, said, " 'At a time when I wasn't even allowed to live in dormitories, Maston would come and talk with me. He offered some direction, then let me as a proud human being struggle with it myself . . . . I personally prefer this to any paternalism.' "[1]

Maston has extensive files of correspondence which came as a result of his writing and speaking. The letters of support and condemnation were about equal. He never failed to reply when the person identified himself as a Southern Baptist. A perusal of the files reveals that his answers were polite, factual, kind, and noncondemnatory, even to the most vicious letters. To a young colleague troubled by the ugly letters, Maston said, "If we are right, the Lord and time are on our side."

To those aspiring to be active in the racial struggle, Maston said, "Don't go into this if you have to be accepted by everybody." Colleagues said that two keys to his effectiveness were that he knew when to act and when to wait and that he refused to let anyone make him angry.

Maston continues to be involved in the racial problem as a writer and speaker and as adviser to Baptist leaders. The Christian Life Commission (SBC) elected him as an official consultant in 1977. He continues to serve as a member of the Texas Christian Life Commission.

Black-white relations has been the area of the race problem in which Maston has been directly involved. His influence in relation to other minority groups has been more indirect than direct. Because of the basic ethical principles enunciated in all his work, that influence is formidable.

Maston says of the future, "Of course, I don't think the race issue is settled by any means. There are plenty of things that still need to be done."

Note

1. Chris Evans, "Race Relations: Black and White Liaison," *Home Missions,* 43 (November, 1973), p. 37.

To Evangelism and World Missions

Thurmon Bryant

While speaking to a group of missionaries of the Foreign Mission Board meeting in a missions conference in Salvador, Bahia of Brazil, in 1963, Maston related his experience of God's call to the foreign mission field while a student in college and his acceptance of that call. However, during his seminary days he came to experience a deepening conviction that the Lord did not want him to go as a foreign missionary. Why? Maston has also asked this question. He noted that among the fifty-five missionaries present at the conference in Salvador thirty of them had been his students. At that point of his ministry nine of his students who had done graduate work in Christian ethics had gone to the foreign mission field. He had been informed at that time by one from the personnel department of the Foreign Mission Board that more missionaries were serving on the mission field with doctor's degrees in Christian Ethics from Southwestern than from any other department in any other Southern Baptist seminary.

Many believe that one of his greatest monuments will be the extension of his life and ministry through his students found around the world. Doubtless, this helps to explain why God did not want him to go personally as a foreign missionary. Having taught for so many years at Southwestern Seminary, his contribution to evangelism and world missions has been much wider and probably more significant than it would have been otherwise.

God's plan for the distinguished teacher did not mean that he would never reach the foreign fields. On the contrary, at the request of the missionaries, he has been invited many times by the Foreign Mission Board to go overseas to serve and stand with missionaries and nationals alike who have been called to preach Christ to the nations.

While Mrs. Maston was on a trip to the Baptist World Alliance meeting at Stockholm, she wrote to her husband that she wanted him to go to the next meeting in London. He replied by stating his preference to visit the foreign mission work. This became a reality in 1954, when Maston embarked upon his first extensive mission trip. It took him to Latin America and lasted for eight weeks. Seven of those weeks were spent lecturing and teaching either in a Bible school or seminary.

Besides this trip, which began in Guatemala and terminated in Brazil, Maston has spoken in regional conferences of missionaries in Brazil and South and Central Spanish fields in Latin America. The fact that the missionaries believe that he always has something fresh, vital, and relative to say is evident by the seven invitations he has received to return to Mexico. Twice he went to speak at pastors' retreats or conferences, twice to be the speaker at mission meetings. Twice he was lecturer at the seminary in Torreón and once was the speaker at a youth conference.

He has spoken in mission meetings in the Middle East, Guatemala, Honduras, Venezuela, Colombia, Ecuador, and Peru. He taught at the Arab Baptist Theological Seminary in Beirut, Lebanon and has visited some of the mission work in Jordan, Israel, Europe, Korea, and Japan. Accompanied by Mrs. Maston and Tom Mc, he made an extensive trip in 1965 which carried them to South America, Europe, and the Middle East. These travels help to account for the statement made by David Lockard, director of the Missionary Orientation Center of the Foreign Mission Board, that, other than the folk of the Foreign Mission Board, Maston has spent more time overseas than any other Southern Baptist.

The missionary orientation for new appointees is held twice a year in Georgia. Maston has been with each group except the one when he had to cancel because of illness. Among those speakers who have received high ratings as to their effectiveness by the appointees, Maston always stands near the top.

Not all of Maston's overseas activities have been related entirely to missionaries. At the invitation of the chief of chaplains of the army, Maston has made a distinctive contribution to world missions and evangelism. He was given the opportunity to serve as speaker at various chaplain's retreats in the Orient, to lead seminars for navy chaplains in Norfolk and Pensacola and, more recently, to participate, along with a Roman Catholic and a rabbi, in a seminar on ethics for the chaplains of the Matériel Command. Rear Admiral James W. Kelly, Chief of Chaplains of the United States Navy, confirmed the significance of Maston's labor of this nature when he stated to him: "Your dedication and sense of purpose were reflected throughout the entire proceedings; therefore, your service to the mission of Navy Chaplains will long be remembered."[1]

It appears that Maston's concern about evangelism and world missions reached its peak concurrently with his becoming aware of our emerging world in search of a path or direction. He is perceptive in his observation that the missionaries of today "go to their fields with the same Christ in their hearts and the same basic message on their lips as their predecessors, but they go to a drastically different world."[2] It is this world which he describes as "a world in travail."[3]

Both in the classroom and throughout the world where he has gone, Maston has sought to alert future missionaries and those already on the field that this changing, revolutionary world may demand new strategies and different methods than those formerly used. It is worthy to note that most of the missions of the Foreign Mission Board are presently involved in a reevaluation of our missionary enterprise and that Maston's former students are often found leading out in such endeavors.

He has helped our missionaries understand that the integrating centers of the cultures where they serve have been disturbed, if not destroyed, by their contact with and competition from the basic values of Western civilization which, presently, is experiencing the inner decay of its own integrating center. He has helped them see that their task has become intensely complicated in this world in travail and that "they dare not continue to do business as usual or they will be left beside the road."[4]

The new strategies being mapped out today will probably reflect Maston's suggestions that there needs to be an acceleration of our work by using more effectively improved means of transportation and communication, while at the same time avoiding removal and isolation from the masses which otherwise would make our approach more impersonal.

As missions strategist, Maston has helped a number of our missionaries to understand the masses where they labor. Their attention has been called to the fact that the restless masses of the contemporary world seek four things: more of the good things of life (food included), freedom, respect, and a sense of purpose. He believes that it is tremendously important for the missionary to maintain a good rapport with the restless masses, for they represent in a very real sense the wave of the future.

His contact and involvement with missionaries in their overseas setting has made him aware of their temptation at this point, against which they must be on constant guard. "Because of his desire for peace and for law and order, the missionary, if he is not careful, will find himself supporting traditional regimes that are set against the masses and their legitimate demands."[5] Maston understands that such regimes are destined to fall. "We and our missionaries, who are identified with an affluent society, must guard against the temptation, in a revolutionary world, to become defenders of a status quo that is crumbling at our feet."[6] "If our Christian forces are to have an effective voice in shaping the future, they must maintain an effective witness to the masses."[7]

Maston has observed that the pallid type of religion found in many of our churches and individual lives is inadequate for the kind of world in which we live. He, therefore, warns the missionary that if he is to meet the challenges facing him, he must not simply transport to the mission field an anemic religion to which he may have been accustomed. Rather, he must attain fresh vitality in his Christian faith until it becomes in him the dynamite of God. "He must remain open and responsive to the leadership of the divine Spirit, recognizing that the Spirit may lead in previously untrodden paths."[8]

Overseas assignments have frequently placed Maston in strategic conferences in which both national leaders and missionaries have participated. His ability to analyze and size up the situation, along with his moral courage and forthrightness, have enabled him to serve as a catalyst in some potentially disruptive situations. He has been quick to perceive that in some mission fields the most complex and delicate problems faced by the missionary is the growing self-assertiveness of national leadership. In such cases he has helped the missionaries to see that ultimately the work will be that of the nationals, that the missionary will likely work under national leadership, and that the missionary's work is largely to supplement and strengthen the work of the nationals. At the same time he has not been reluctant to remind the nationals that problems may arise when, under the impact of extreme nationalism, they push too vigorously or prematurely for complete control of the work.

Another matter on which Maston has provided sound catalytic orientation for both missionaries going to the field and those already in service has been the need for the missionaries to maintain a wholesome perspective in reference to the political order where they serve. During these recent years of so much political upheavel and turmoil throughout the world, Maston has had occasion to say to hundreds of missionaries now serving with the Foreign Mission Board that "while we may be strong believers in democratic government, we cannot expect the revolution in many of the new nations to express itself in democratic processes such as we have grown accustomed to in the United States."[9] He knows that one cannot expect people who have had no experience in self-government to be democratic as we interpret democracy. Missionary Albert W. Gammage, Jr. of the Philippines has appreciated the point which Maston makes on the essential relationship which exists between Christianity and culture. Extensive use has been made of his books, *Christianity and World Issues*[10] and *The Christian, the Church, and Contemporary Problems*,[11] to teach theological students how to relate the gospel in mission field cultures. It is perhaps at this point that Maston has most effectively served as catalyst in the missionary context.

Maston's biblical approach to ethics has received the attention of many missionaries as they have faced the necessity of interpreting the Christian message which speaks to social issues in a foreign context which may present some peculiar aspects hitherto unmet by the Western missionary. Missionary Stanley P. Howard, Jr. of Japan affirms that this emphasis on God's Word, rather than on traditional sociological patterns, has been highly beneficial as he tries to provide the Christian response to strange social situations.

Especially in countries where race differences are not too prominent, Maston has often served as catalyst by becoming a corrective in the midst of race discrimination in the United States. Missionary Burley Cader of Brazil remembers how Maston's stand on race was supportive to him as he tried to interpret to his Brazilian brethren the attitude of Southern Baptists who were the senders of missionaries to Brazil. He recalls that when Brazilian Christians were perplexed by the attitude of white Southern Baptist churches towards the black, "It was a real blessing to us to be able to quote Dr. Maston's solid stand."

These are only some of the many ways that Maston has served as a catalyst in helping the missionary not to become a mere exporter of Western civilization but to accept a foreign culture for what it is and wisely let the Christian message speak to it.

Research in preparation for this chapter included a study of responses to a questionnaire sent to former students of Maston who presently serve with the Foreign Mission Board. The thing which most impressed me as I read their responses was that, hardly without exception, they mentioned how Maston had been an encourager to them in their missionary ministry. The missionaries throughout the world affirm that the Mastons have tremendously helped them to react properly and as a Christian to their own suffering. The suffering of a missionary is similar to that which many others endure— a physically or mentally handicapped child, absence of loved ones, loneliness, personal illness, being misunderstood, rebellion of children—but his suffering is usually compounded by virtue of the exigencies placed upon him because of living in a foreign culture. Whenever he reacts adversely to suffering, more than likely his missionary ministry will be greatly curtailed, even if he is able to continue on the field. Therefore, the example of the Mastons has been and still is a source of encouragement and strength which has enabled a large number of missionaries to find the grace of Christ sufficient for them to stay on the field and continue in effective missionary service.

While serving in Israel in 1965, the Dwight Bakers, now missionaries in India, had the privilege of hosting the Mastons. Observing their ministry among them and the way Maston identified with the missionaries, Baker wrote:

> Missionaries love to have him visit their field. He gives them, or opens up to them, new and hidden resources to do their jobs more effectively and joyfully. The beauty of his life instills in them to desire to be more like him and his Lord. I would say that Dr. Maston has a unique ability and gift to sharpen other men and women to the point of their greatest effectiveness. He is not a missionary, nor does he claim to be, but he produces great missionaries.

One means by which Maston has encouraged missionaries has been by writing letters. "We have derived much encouragement and support from him through correspondence. He has often written us a personal letter in response to our circular letter, always with a personal touch that lets us know that he does remember us, pray for us, and support us." This testimony of James Bartley of Uruguay is frequently that of other missionaries around the world to whom Maston has written.

Many have felt at liberty to receive counsel from him because, as one puts it, "He has always assured us of his blessing and gives us the freedom to make the decision without pressure." It may well be that when Maston's contributions to world evangelism have been perfectly assessed that his role as an encourager of others will be his greatest.

An attempt to summarize T. B. Maston's contribution to world missions and evangelism is made by the use of a biblical phrase. In Acts 13:36 the statement is made that David, king of Israel, served his own generation. The same can be said of Maston. He has disciplined himself to understand the world in which he lives in order to serve it. In the context of this understanding and upon basic theological and ethical precepts which he found taught in the Bible, he has proceeded to apply biblical ethical teachings, which are universally and abidingly relevant, to man and society in such a way that they are placed in a state of tension which moves both man and his social order closer to Christ and closer to his ideals for mankind.

Notes

1. Rear Admiral James W. Kelly to T. B. Maston, October 18, 1968.
2. T. B. Maston, "This Revolutionary World" (A background paper presented at the Missions Consultation, Miami Beach, Florida, June 30-July 3, 1965).
3. T. B. Maston, *A World in Travail* (Nashville: Broadman Press, 1954).

4. Maston, "This Revolutionary World."

5. Ibid.   6. Ibid.

7. Ibid.   8. Ibid.

9. Ibid.

10. T. B. Maston, *Christianity and World Issues* (New York: The Macmillan Company, 1957).

11. T. B. Maston, *The Christian, the Church, and Contemporary Problems* (Waco: Word Books, 1968).

Through Personal Example

Lee Porter

"T. B. Maston is the ideal personification of the gospel he taught" commented a denominational leader who had studied at Southwestern Seminary more than two decades ago. Another former student said: "In him, you saw the gospel come to life. The Christian way was not just a wonderful theory. It was lived out in his day-by-day experiences." Individual after individual gave similar expression regarding the personal example of Maston.

"He is contagious Christianity in daily action."

"I remember him as a Christian gentleman."

"He has genuine Christian character that runs deep in his soul, his life, and his spirit."

"I found him to be an authentic Christian with a solid core of true religion."

"He is the most down-to-earth Christian I've ever known. I found him at home with the Christian gospel. When I read the statement that Jesus made in the Sermon on the Mount concerning the salt of the earth, I always think of Dr. Maston."

"He is a strong, consistent practitioner of Christian ethics."

"As I studied his life, I found one who practiced a personal Christian life-style."

"Dr. Maston does not just write carefully worked out pronouncements on ethics; he makes Christian ethics his personal life-style. I see the quality of Jesus surface in his life more than in the life of any man I know."

"He is a saint in our midst."

Undoubtedly, Maston will be greatly embarrassed when he reads these comments others have made about him because he is a humble individual. Those who know him best have never known him to be self-seeking. He is not a status-seeking individual. No one that I talked to could ever remember having known him to be pompous. In every kind of occasion, he has the demeanor of a humble man. A seminary professor probably expressed it best when he said, "He has a refreshing, genuine humility."

Maston probably will respond to the statements concerning himself with some witty comment, for he has an active sense of humor. Many students have seen that mischievous twinkle in his eye followed by a sharp witty comment. A colleague describes him as "a happy man totally at peace with himself." He enjoys life. He has a wholesome sense of humor.

An underlying tenet of many of Maston's ethical positions is the value of every individual person. Probably in no area does he teach this truth more eloquently than in his own personal relationships with individuals. He loves and cares about people—not just people in the mass but people as individuals. He has a genuine interest in persons. Persons are important to him. He sees persons as persons. He has a gracious way of dealing with persons. Individuals always feel comfortable with him. Again and again, individuals seek him out. He always seems to have time for everyone who wants to talk to him. He seizes the moment and makes it a very important one in the life of an individual. He is alert to people and to their needs and to their hurts. You sense that he has a gentle feeling towards persons and that he really cares. Whether he was dealing with a student or with another professor, he always respected his personhood. He is not an individual who will put another individual down. He does not talk down to a person or try to intimidate him. His approach and mood always show consideration for others. In the classroom or in personal conversation, he always is very careful in his responses so as not to hurt an individual. During many interviews, individuals frequently responded by saying that Maston treats people as Jesus did.

Through the years, he has had an unusual love and appreciation for students. Students of every generation have returned that love and appreciation. Students and colleagues alike have sought him out for counsel and just to talk to him. Being around him is a joy. One is never the same after having spent some time with him. He has the capacity to inspire and to make people want to do better. He reinforces the desires of purity and decency within individuals. A pastor expressed it this way: "When I'm with him, I feel I've been in the presence of a godly man. At times, I even feel I've been in the presence of Jesus. Although we did not talk about my sins and failures, I became conscious of them and wanted to live a purer, holier life after having talked with him. I feel that this is the way Jesus affected people with whom he came in contact."

Whether dealing with individuals or with a group, Maston always seemed to be so human. As one colleague noted, "He was never one to hide behind academic robes or his degrees." Although he was a competent scholar with a deep biblical grasp of truth, his ideas or opinions were not forced on others. One Baptist Student Union (BSU) president stated: "His degrees never weighted him down. He talked to us right where we lived."

As Maston moves through a busy and often hectic life, he demonstrates a serenity of soul that is obvious to all those around him. He seems always to live for the moment. A calmness and a quiet depth permeate all that he does. One is impressed that Maston knows who he is and what he is about. He seems to savor the importance of every moment and lives it to its fullest. This serenity of soul allows him to be the same all the time. You sense that he is a gentleman full of love and compassion. He is gracious and has a spirit of kindness. His every act and word is warm and considerate of those around him.

Students knew him as a very congenial, open individual. A student who had only one class with him declared: "I always enjoyed meeting him in the hall. He always had a twinkle in his eye, and he would speak to you with a slight grin on his face. He always looked at you as a real human being. You just knew that you counted with him. I was always impressed that he treated every student as a real person."

One cannot be in Maston's presence long without coming to the conclusion that one of the driving concerns of his life is that all Christians truly live the Christian life. He enjoys teaching. He enjoys sharing his faith with others. Through the years, he is still learning and constantly eager to learn. At the same time, he is always the teacher, encouraging others to learn, to grow, to develop, and to become what Jesus wants them to become.

He has a strong belief in Christian ethics mixed with an intensity of spirit. He wants to share his beliefs with all around him. He not only teaches his beliefs but he also lives his beliefs. He is secure in what he believes. He can state biblical truth without being arrogant. He is secure in his own faith and relationship with God, and he wants others to share in that experience. He is not a person to strike back or to be obnoxious. He knows how to disagree without being disagreeable. In quiet gentle tones, he always is ready to share the realities of the Christian life. He has too much respect for an individual to try to force his beliefs on someone else, but he is always ready to share. He constantly trusts the power of God and the power of the Word to change individuals.

Merely by living the Christian life before thousands of students, Maston has greatly affected their lives. Students saw him as a godly man who had spent time with Jesus. He was seen as standing before his class with total integrity. His life is a constant demonstration that he tries to practice what he teaches. He knows biblical truth, and he puts into daily practice what he believes. His prayers are sincere and childlike as he comes into the presence of his holy Father. Student after student sensed that here was a genuine Christian spirit.

When around Maston, one feels that here is a clean man. In his relationship with Jesus, his life is made clean. He is decent. He never is involved in off-colored jokes and never refers to sex in any cheap or flippant terms. He is clean in his language and in his thought.

Although he has a great concern for social issues, he lives out his beliefs in a personal morality that is different from the ordinary. You know that he is real and genuine in his personal morality.

Again and again in his teachings, Maston emphasizes that the end never justifies the means. He says that to do the right thing in the right way is to receive the blessings of God. I remember an occasion when a number of students were involved in some political action trying to influence the Convention on a crucial issue. The group had met and made detailed plans. They decided to receive the counsel of Maston, probably hoping to receive his blessings because they were going to be involved in trying to change Convention action.

Maston listened carefully to all the plans that had been made and then reminded the group that what they were trying to accomplish would come to naught unless they did it in the right spirit. Maston definitely wanted that action to take place at the Convention, but he was unwilling to compromise his principles to bring the action about. This was another occasion when a group of activistic students learned from his life as from his words. He often warned his students that even though they espouse a right cause, they could compromise that cause by going about it in the wrong spirit or attitude. He saw this as an ever-present danger and temptation to those who were activists in the field of Christian ethics.

Maston has made numerous contributions to the lives of his students through his own personal example and life-style. He is a disciplined individual who always makes use of his time. Through the years, he has developed a schedule. He is not a slave to a schedule, however, and is not so rigid that he would not change it. But his schedule allows him to live a full and meaningful life. He believes that a balance should exist between work and rest and that one should care for his health. A regular part of his routine is rest each day for a few moments after the noon meal. He then returns to his afternoon responsibilities refreshed. During the week, he follows a set pattern that allows time for family responsibilities in caring for Tom Mc and a systematic time for study and growth. Friday afternoon and Saturday always seem to be times away from academic pursuits. On these days, tennis and his garden consume much of his time and vitality. He finds tennis and gardening renewing and revitalizing.

Maston's schedule allows time for individuals. He can be interrupted and never make an individual feel guilty for having interrupted him. Those who know him best are amazed at the amount of work he can turn out. Through the years, he has not only occupied his office that is open to students but also he has maintained a carrel in the library where he can study and write. To find him writing on two different levels is not unusual. His study carrel contains two desks, one for more academic and theological writing and the other desk is for lighter or more popular writing. He has so disciplined himself that he seems to be able to move at ease from one of these desks to the other. He obviously has disciplined himself to study hard, to work hard, and to relax completely.

Maston also eloquently teaches the value of the local church through his own personal example. Sunday after Sunday through all the years, he and his family have been faithful in attendance at the Gambrell Street Baptist Church. Saturday afternoon often is used as a time to visit and to invite people to the church. His faithful commitment to his own local church as a seminary professor often says to many young persons training for the ministry that the local church is where the action is.

I personally feel that one of the greatest contributions Maston has made for the lives of thousands of students is in his relationship to his own family. Early in his teaching career, he instituted a course on the family as a part of the curriculum at Southwestern Seminary. His course on biblical ethics had much to say in regard to the family. I am convinced that his greatest contribution to family life is not in his courses but in his own personal example regarding his own family. One student who roomed with the Mastons during seminary days expressed it this way, "I learned more about the Christian family by watching how he operated in his own family than I did in taking his courses."

One cannot be around T. B. Maston very long without sensing a real and genuine devotion to his family. His example as a loving and caring father has influenced many students throughout the years, and students come to know of his special love and concern as he cares for Tom Mc's personal needs. They are compelled to reexamine their own family relationships. Engagements often are accepted or rejected as to how they will affect Tom Mc and Mrs. Maston. He has never been known to grumble or to feel sorry for himself because of his responsibility for Tom Mc.

The relationship between Dr. and Mrs. Maston also has affected the relationship of numerous families. In personal conversation or in the teaching situation, he often speaks lovingly of Mrs. Maston. He speaks of love growing more deeper and having more meaning through the years in a way that causes many a young seminary student to want to develop that kind of relationship within his own family. During his lectures on the family, Maston often referred to the relationship of husband and wife as like the relationship between a fiddle and the bow. Then with a twinkle in his eye, he says that "Mommie" would remind him of the example that marriage was also like the relationship between a baseball and a bat. The very way that he would give that illustration, you knew that he and "Mommie" had a very special relationship.

One student reports that the only example he remembers was when Dr. Maston was teaching about the importance of the husband-wife relationship. Maston explained that a husband and wife didn't have to touch or be in verbal communication to relate. He said that he could be working out in the garden and Mrs. Maston could be standing at the kitchen sink and the exchange of a look or a smile between them would let each know that the other one cared and that they loved each other.

This young married student said that he walked out of the class that day determined to try to build that kind of relationship with his own wife. He said that during all of the years, he has been striving to develop the kind of experience Maston had described in class that day. Through the years, many students have learned about the real meaning of family life through the personal example of Maston as well as through the classes he has taught.

Through the years, thousands of students have been in Maston's classes. One often hears the old statement, "What you are and the way you live speak so loudly that I cannot hear what you say." Quite the contrary has been true in Maston's life. This godly Christian man in his day-by-day actions and life style gives genuine validity to the gospel that he teaches by the way he lives. I along with so many others dearly love this man because of the many, many things he's taught me, not only through his writings and in the classroom but also through his personal example. For me and for many others, he has become the personification of Jesus in my world.

Through Writing

Keith Wills

Writing has occupied a major role in the ministry of T. B. Maston. Early in his career he realized the importance of sharing with a larger reading audience those insights and truths that he shared with many others in the classroom, in retreats, and in conferences. He has often recalled saying to his wife, "Next to teaching, the thing I'd rather do than anything else is write." This statement was made before he had written any book.

Since 1937 Maston's writing ministry has been and continues to be prolific and fruitful, as evidenced by the publication of nineteen printed books, four mimeographed books, and booklets for the Brotherhood Commission and the Christian Life Commission (SBC). At least five of these books and portions of others have been translated into other languages, including Arabic, Chinese, German, Indonesian, Korean, Portuguese, and Spanish. If all of his articles published in journals and denominational periodicals were simply listed, it would require more than eleven typed pages.

The subject range of his writings has been as broad as the fields of Christian ethics and religious education, including such varied topics as abortion, alcohol, church recreation, marriage and family, capital punishment, civil disobedience, evangelism, pornography, poverty and wealth, and war and peace.

Maston's authorship has been directed toward two different types of reading audiences and, consequently, has employed two different writing styles. His more scholarly works, such as *Christianity and World Issues* and *Biblical Ethics*, were intended primarily for well-trained pastors, college and seminary students, teachers, and well-informed laymen. His less formal works were produced for the general Christian reading audience, especially Southern Baptists. These stress personal issues in ethics and Christian living. This is the characteristic quality of his writings for the Baptist state papers and explains the widespread appeal of such books as *Right or Wrong?* and *God's Will and Your Life.*

Early in his experience at Southwestern Seminary, Maston became involved in a writing career. In February, 1925, he became the ex-student editor for the *Southwestern Evangel,* a monthly publication of the school. Soon the managing editor of this publication, L. A. Myers, was encouraging Maston to submit articles based upon messages he had delivered at prayer meetings or in chapel. Such articles included "Play in the Home" (March, 1926), "Some Trends in Family Life" (May, 1928), "Ten Temptations of Theologs" (February, 1929), reflecting his diversified interests.

Maston's five years of experience as a summer field-worker for the B.Y.P.U in Tennessee, his experience as a religious education professor at Southwestern Seminary, and his friendship with Jerry Lambdin, who was secretary (1929-1959) for the Baptist Young People's Department (changed to Training Union Department in 1934) brought invitations to write curriculum materials and assembly programs for that organization. His writings include the lesson quarterlies for the Senior B.Y.P.U. for January, 1930, April-June, 1932, and July, 1934, as well as the general assembly program for each month of 1930-1932.

The Baptist Sunday School Board also asked Maston to prepare a series of graded Bible lessons for sixteen-year-old pupils (both the pupils quarterly and the teachers book) on the general theme, the young Christian and social problems. These were first used October 1932 through September 1933. Vance Kirkpatrick, in researching this series for his dissertation "The Ethical Thought of T. B. Maston" (Fort Worth, Southwestern Seminary, 1972) was amazed to discover the depth and breadth of the insights into such issues as race, war, poverty, economics, marriage, sex, and world order in these lessons. He said, "It's all there," referring to ethical issues that were coming into focus in Southern Baptist circles some thirty or forty years later. The Baptist Sunday School Board continued to draw on the writing talents of Maston during the succeeding years. At the latest count he had written approximately 275 lessons for its publications and still is receiving assignments.

Maston's first published book, *Handbook for Church Recreation Leaders* (1937) was an outgrowth of a course he taught at Southwestern Seminary. A study course book for the Training Union Department of the Sunday School Board, it was widely used because it met a real need among Southern Baptist churches and later was translated into Spanish for use in Latin America.

These early writings gave opportunity for the development of creative talents and the sharing of convictions on ethical issues. They also supplied needed financial support during the lean years of the Great Depression when seminary salaries were low and often delayed or unpaid. In some of the depression years of the 1930s his income from his writings exceeded his salary payments from Southwestern Seminary. In reference to his experience while on sabbatical leave at Yale University in 1932, he says, "I still don't know how we got by except that I was doing some Sunday School lesson writing then."

Maston has always sought to direct a large portion of his writing toward the general level of Christian readership. He has endeavored to write to the needs of the layman in the local church, the student in high school and college, to local pastors and others facing troubling questions in ethical areas. He has tried to make people sensitive to ethical issues that are often ignored or even unrecognized in everyday Christian living.

His short articles printed in Baptist state papers probably have given him the broadest readership and exerted the greatest influence among Southern Baptists regarding ethical questions. His series "Problems in the Christian Life," containing 104 articles distributed through the Baptist Press in 1968-1969, was published regularly in at least seventeen Baptist state papers. Many letters to the editor were received by the Baptist state papers in response to Maston's articles—many with a favorable tone but a great many others were critical. Like Elijah in the Old Testament, Maston was often accused of being "he that troubleth Israel," especially when he wrote on the race issue in the 1950s. His effort was always to maintain a proper tension on these issues that would stimulate the readers to think through the matters with a proper Christian perspective.

A subsequent series of 104 articles entitled "Bible Nuggets" was also distributed to the Baptist state papers but was not used as widely as the earlier series. His series of seven articles "Trends to Watch" was distributed through the Southwestern Seminary Public Relations Office.

Maston wrote extensively about race relations in the 1940s and 1950s, feeling this was one of the most challenging ethical issues facing Southern Baptists in those years. He says that *Of One*, published by the Home Mission Board in 1946 and widely used by the Woman's Missionary Union as a study text, created the most controversy of any of his writings. This book, written over eight years before the May 17, 1954, United States Supreme Court ruling that racial segregation in the public schools was unconstitutional and was to be ended "with all deliberate speed," was a prophetic voice speaking long before a day of general acceptance but anticipating many of the future developments in race relations. Two additional books published in 1959, *The Bible and Race* by Broadman and *Segregation and Desegregation: A Christian Approach* by Macmillan, also provided timely guidance in this sensitive area. The Woman's Missionary Union distributed 50,000 copies of *The Bible and Race* among its members.

The two most popular and widely translated books, *Right or Wrong?* (1952) and *God's Will and Your Life* (1964), resulted from questions raised by young people in conferences and through the mail. Maston says that these two manuscripts were the easiest of any of his writings—they flowed from his experiences in meeting with this age group over a period of years. A revised edition of *Right or Wrong?* with William M. Pinson, Jr. as coauthor, was published by Broadman in 1971.

Although the response to his writings for a general level of Christian readership has been very satisfying to Maston, he has gained even more personal satisfaction from his writing in a more scholarly vein. This required more research, more time, more rewriting than the other writings. *Christianity and World Issues* (Macmillan, 1957) which was selected as book-of-the-month by the Pastor's Book Club, was almost completely rewritten three times before publication.

Biblical Ethics: A Biblical Survey (World Publishing Company, 1967) was intended primarily to be a textbook for college and seminary students. This particular title was not promoted adequately by the original publisher, so the publishing rights were transferred to Word Books in 1969. There continues to be a steady demand for this book as a text.

Isaac Backus: Pioneer of Religious Liberty (James Clark, 1962) is a reworking of part of Maston's Ph.D. dissertation, "The Ethical and Social Attitudes of Isaac Backus," approved by Yale University in 1939. Maston so earnestly desired the publication of this volume that he did something for it that he never did for any other book—he subsidized its printing. Most of his investment was recovered; a few copies are still available for sale at Fleming Library, Southwestern Seminary.

A World in Travail: A Study of the Contemporary World Crisis (Broadman, 1954), *The Christian, The Church, and Contemporary Problems* (Word Books, 1968), and *Why Live the Christian Life?* (T. Nelson, 1974) should also be included in this category of scholarly writings.

Maston has been a frequent contributor to numerous journals over the years, including *Interpretation, Journal of Church and State, Quarterly Review, Review and Expositor, Social Science, Southwestern Journal of Theology, Eternity,* and *Family Life.* He has also written many book reviews for these journals, although most of this was done before his retirement as a professor in 1963. However, he still reviews books regularly for the *Journal of Church and State.*

Maston looked forward to retirement from most of his classroom responsibilities because it would allow him more time for his writing projects. He had many of these in the back of his mind. It is to be noted that he has had ten major books published since his official retirement in 1963. This is a production of one book about every eighteen months—a remarkable record.

He seems always to have a manuscript in some stage of progress. At the time of the writing of this chapter, at the age of eighty, he is preparing a manuscript for an adult teacher's quarterly for the Baptist Sunday School Board's Life and Work Curriculum. The creative juices continue to flow, keeping fresh this production for his reading audience. As the Friends would say, "He speaks to the condition of his readers." The Maston pen writes on, and readers around the world, Southern Baptists particularly but also a host of others, are continually in his debt for wise spiritual guidance, for a pricking of the conscience, for a calling to the higher levels of Christian living and Christian responsibility.

Bibliography of T. B. Maston's Published Books

1937   *Handbook for Church Recreation Leaders.* Nashville: Southern Baptist Convention Sunday School Board.

1946   *Of One.* Atlanta: Southern Baptist Convention Home Mission Board.

1952   *The Christian in the Modern World.* Nashville: Broadman.

1954   *A World in Travail.* Nashville: Broadman.

1955   *Right or Wrong?* Nashville: Broadman.

1957   *Christianity and World Issues.* New York: Macmillan.

1959   *The Bible and Race.* Nashville: Broadman.

———   *Segregation and Desegregation: A Christian Approach.* New York: Macmillan.

1962   *Isaac Backus: Pioneer of Religious Liberty.* London: James Clark.

1964   *God's Will and Your Life.* Nashville: Broadman.

1967   *Biblical Ethics: A Biblical Survey.* Cleveland: World. (Published by Word Books since 1969)

———   *Suffering: A Personal Perspective.* Nashville: Broadman.

1968   *The Christian, the Church, and Contemporary Problems.* Waco, Texas: Word Books.

1971   *The Conscience of a Christian.* Waco, Texas: Word Books.

———   *Right or Wrong?* Nashville: Broadman. (Revised edition co-authored with William H. Pinson, Jr.)

1974   *Real Life in Christ.* Nashville: Broadman.

1974   *Why Live the Christian Life?* Nashville: T. Nelson.

1977   *God Speaks Through Suffering.* Waco, Texas: Word Books.

1978   *How to Face Grief.* Waco, Texas: Word Books.

Chapters in Other Books

1960   "The Master Needs Men" and "The Minister's Preaching Ministry" in *Messages for Men.* Compiled by H. C. Brown, Jr. Grand Rapids, Zondervan.

—— "The Heresy of Orthodoxy" in *Southwestern Sermons*. Compiled and edited by H. C. Brown, Jr. Nashville: Broadman.

1963 "The Husband and Father" in *J. Howard Williams*. Compiled and edited by H. C. Brown, Jr. and Charles P. Johnson. San Antonio: Naylor Company.

1966 "Reflections Regarding Democracy" in *Chapel Messages*. Compiled and edited by H. C. Brown, Jr. and Charles P. Johnson. Grand Rapids: Baker Book House.

1969 "Interracial Marriage" in *The Cutting Edge: Critical Questions for Contemporary Christians*. Compiled by H. C. Brown, Jr. Waco: Word Books.

1976 "Running a Good Race" in *The Ministers Manual for 1976*. Edited by Charles L. Wallis. New York: Harper & Row.

1977 "The Fairness of God" and "Branded for Jesus" in *The Ministers Manual for 1977*. Edited by Charles L. Wallis. New York: Harper & Row.

—— "Six Tough Adjustments" in *Plain Talk About Growing Old*. Compiled by George W. Knight and John W. Steen. Nashville: Convention Press.

Through Teaching

Wayne Barnes

"I am just a teacher." Thus did T. B. Maston identify himself to those gathered for the inauguration of one of his former students, William Pinson, as president of Golden Gate Seminary in April of 1978. Early in his life Maston came to understand that God's call for him was to teach. During his lifetime he has made great contributions in many areas, but his most significant has been through the classroom, always his priority.

"Just a teacher"—but what a teacher. Maston is the teacher whom Warren Hultgren, pastor of the First Baptist Church, Tulsa, Oklahoma, calls "the greatest product of Southwestern Seminary." His thought has had great impact on many who do not know his name. Numerous knowledgeable leaders feel Maston has affected the life of Southern Baptists more than any other man in the last fifty years. Charles Trentham, pastor of the First Baptist Church of Washington D.C., states, "In the Convention at large Maston has been the source of much of our best thought and work in applying the Christian gospel to life." Francis DuBose of Golden Gate Seminary says, "If Southern Baptists have produced a prophet in this twentieth century, it is T. B. Maston." Kenneth Chafin, pastor of the South Main Baptist Church in Houston, clearly expresses the view of many when he says, "I think when we come to that day when we see everything, we will probably decide that T. B. Maston had more to do with the character and integrity of the mission of our churches than any other human being."

Maston's teaching ministry greatly contributed to the development of a biblical social ethic among Southern Baptists within the context of conservative theology and fervent evangelism. He created ethical awareness by making Baptists conscious of the ethical nature of the biblical revelation and thereby developed a keen sensitivity to the ethical application of the gospel. He helped Baptists become alert to the modern moral and social problems. He was a prophet in the classroom, pointing out inconsistences in the world long before they became public issues, creating social consciousness. Not stopping with stating the problems, Maston challenged Baptists to become involved in answers, thus stressing moral responsibility. Milton Ferguson, president of Midwestern Seminary, points out that "Maston's most significant contribution was the bringing together of the biblical material and life situation problems in a creative and productive way by his emphasis on creative tension."

Maston's teaching content was totally new territory for most students. Few had ever considered that moral issues went beyond dancing, smoking, or drinking. Bruce McIver, pastor of the Wilshire Baptist Church in Dallas, gives testimony typical of Maston's students.

Few people have had the influence on my life that T. B. Maston has had. I enrolled in one of his basic classes at Southwestern Seminary. A whole new world opened up to me. I had some understanding about the personal nature of salvation but little understanding of the practical application of this to daily living. Maston made me aware that the gospel touches all areas of life including economic matters, moral and ethical issues, family relationships, political involvements, and racial and ethnic concerns. Each of these practical and contemporary problems confronting the Christian was approached from a thoroughly biblical basis. Through the influence of this teacher I came to see that the Lord is concerned about the total man and all of the problems that confront man in his daily existence.

One issue in which Maston contributed to significant change was race relations. Clyde Fant, pastor of the First Baptist Church of Richardson, Texas, says, "The greatest contribution Maston made to many of us was his consistent Christian position concerning the race issue." Keith Parks, director with the Foreign Mission Board says, "He was one of the first clear voices calling for Christian application in the field of race relations, and he did more than any other person to turn the tide of racism in our Convention."

The substance of Maston's contribution came from the biblical and personal nature of his teaching. These two factors account for the degree of acceptance that his ethical teachings received, even when they were upsetting.

Maston is a biblical ethicist, upholding the authority of the Bible and believing in its power. A recurring statement to his students was, "Make sure that everything you do is tied to the Bible." He believes "that when your teaching, preaching, and action is grounded in the Scripture, there is a conviction that you do not have otherwise." He holds that "the Bible will put a little iron and backbone in fellows."

Maston's teaching was undergirded by direct biblical principles. He used sound hermeneutics, and while aware of critical problems, he did not emphasize them. He required his classes to do extensive exegesis of biblical passages. Many would agree with William Tanner, executive director of the Home Mission Board, who says, "I learned more about the Bible and gained a deeper appreciation for the Bible from Maston's classes than from any others."

Maston was right in his conviction that this biblical emphasis gave his teaching the power to affect change. Frank Pollard, pastor of the First Baptist Church of Jackson, Mississippi, concurs in stating, "Maston's teaching has contributed to much change for good simply because he approached what many thought to be 'liberal' subjects (social issues) with a thoroughly 'conservative' biblical application."

Maston's contribution was significantly heightened by the personal nature of his teaching. One of the main things students received in Maston's classes was the man—Maston—and that was worth getting. Presnall Wood, editor of the Baptist Standard of Texas, says, "While the source material was there and excellent, Maston the man was even better." Gene Garrison, Pastor of the First Baptist Church of Oklahoma City, reflects, "The inspiration of his life was as influential on me as any particular aspect of his teaching." The content of his teaching and the contact with the teacher were inseparable dimensions of his teaching ministry. The content had a changing impact on Baptist life, but the acceptance of the ethical teaching was made more readily by the appreciation for the teacher. His teachings gave the insight and his person gave the inspiration.

Students respected the qualities of genuineness, gentleness, and caring shown by Maston. Most would agree with Charles Petty of the governor's office in North Carolina, when he says, "He was a man who knew God well and knew God's expectations of his children and who personally lived out these expectations. I figured he had put it together as well as any human being could, in terms of knowing and doing God's will." Frank Means, former secretary for Eastern South America of the Foreign Mission Board, states, "Maston, more than anyone I have ever known sought earnestly and diligently to know and do the Lord's will, and I owe him more than I can ever acknowledge."

Maston took a deep personal interest in every student, receiving him into a circle of love and allowing him to participate in the personal warmth of his life. More than a few graduate students majored in ethics because of Maston's intense personal interest. This interest carried far beyond the classroom. Albert McClellan, associate executive secretary of the Southern Baptist Convention Executive Board, states:

More than any other teacher in the Seminary Maston took personal interest in his students. Once he made a friend in these classes he never let him go. No matter where or what in the years afterwards he seemed always to be interested in what the person was doing.

Because of the gentle manner of sharing his knowledge, it was almost a discovery to realize how much of a scholar Maston was; however, he was a master of his subject and a master in the art of teaching. Elaine Dickson of the Baptist Sunday School Board says, "Maston was a superb teacher and I learned from him as a model." His teaching was informal, practical, simple, and presented warmly and with humor. Hardy Clemons, pastor of the Second Baptist Church of Lubbock, Texas, says, "Maston was one of those rare people who could go deep and come up clear." He had the ability to take scriptural truth, translate it into practicality, and apply it to life in a way that motivated a person to see the truth of what he was teaching. Maston was most effective in combining lecturing with class discussion. He was skilled in handling questions, usually responding in a way designed to compel the questioner to think more deeply into the matter for himself.

In a disarmingly gentle way, Maston dealt with controversial issues. Throughout a disagreement, he maintained a kind relationship with his students. Julian Bridges of Hardin-Simmons University recalls, "No matter how controversial the subject, Maston was a gentleman in the manner with which he patiently responded, never compromising, but always expressing himself in a spirit of love."

Though gentle in presentation, Maston was a thorough and demanding teacher. He expected his students to work hard, feeling that they would not, he said, "have appreciation for a course unless it required something." Pressure came not so much from Maston but from the students' desire to measure up to Maston's expectations.

Southwestern Seminary had ethics as part of the curriculum from the beginning, but Maston was responsible for developing the Christian Ethics Department in this the world's largest seminary. He first taught a course in ethics, Christian Sociology, at Southwestern in 1922 at twenty-four years of age and for the next thirty years was the only teacher of ethics.

Maston considered Biblical Ethics 31 and Theological Ethics 32 to be the foundation courses. The purpose of the biblical ethics course was to give insight into the ethical content of the Bible. The theological ethics course was to deal with the question, Why live the Christian life? A course on the family was the most popular, and the one on race the most significant for the times. He developed and taught courses on world crisis, Communism, moral issues, labor relations, ism, and church-state relations.

Maston taught much more than ethics. His classroom was an arena of life, dealing with practical matters such as personal discipline, church work, relating to people, handling difficulties, knowing the will of God, and decision making. Endless are the personal testimonies of the influence of Maston's teaching ministry in terms of personal inspiration and understanding. Richard Jackson, pastor of the North Phoenix Baptist Church in Arizona, acknowledges that "Maston's counsel on the will of God has helped me over and over and had a significant direction on my ministry." So many can echo the sentiment of Archie Brown, pastor of the First Baptist Church, Vandalia, Illinois, in declaring that "the entire course of my life was changed because of Maston's influence."

Karl Barth indicated that great Christian teaching is distinguished by two things. First, it stays close to the Bible. Second, it stays close to people. It is not easy, but very necessary, to know both what the Bible says and also how to apply it to life.[1] At this, Maston was a master.

Note

1. Karl Barth, *Final Testimonies,* ed. Eherhard Busch, trans. Geoffry W. Bromiley (Grand Rapids: William B. Eerdmans, 1977), p. 43.

Through Graduates

James Dunn

T. B. Maston was and is a master teacher. Early in life he discovered his gift of teaching and cultivated it. The fruit of his labor has benefited his students, Southern Baptists, and the world. The forty-nine students who received their Th.D.s with Maston offer a distinctive reflection of the man. They are an extension of his thought and personality. Among those who did graduate work with Maston are many professors in the six Southern Baptist seminaries. They teach practically every field of study in the seminary curriculum. They often approach these subjects with the particular ethical perspective of T. B. Maston. In addition to his doctoral graduates T. B. Maston taught from 8,000 to 10,000 other seminarians from 1922 to 1963. He taught as many who received Th.M. and D.R.E. degrees as his own Th.D. majors. In addition, a number of his students took Christian ethics seminars but for some reason were unable to finish the doctoral program.

An especially significant group of graduate students are those persons who minored in ethics, made it a related field of their doctoral program, or enrolled in one or two of the graduate seminars. For instance, two of the six presidents of Southern Baptist seminaries are Maston doctoral graduates. Two others studied with him in their graduate programs.

Cal Guy, a former Maston student and now professor of missions at Southwestern Seminary, says, "Tom Maston was clearly known as a friend to students. Professor Maston didn't run from the lecture platform and say 'hang you' to students. He always had time for them." Maston's academic grandchildren and great-grandchildren number into the tens of thousands. The impact of those whose lives have been touched by Maston's students continues to grow exponentially.

T. B. Maston's impact is seen in more than the vast numbers of students he influenced and in more than his model of personal interest in students. His entire approach to teaching Christian ethics as an academic discipline was peculiarly suited to Southern Baptists. His pioneering grasp of Christian ethics shaped his distinctive influence on his graduate students. He did not accept unquestioningly the traditional approaches to the study of ethics. It was not for him simply moral philosophy or practical theology or Christian sociology or any of the other routine understandings of the field of study. Rather, he fashioned a practical, philosophical, political, biblical, theological approach to the study of Christian ethics. He often reminded his graduates to speak to Baptists "where they are."

In addition to his organization of the subject, the content of his ethics courses defies neat categories. He often bemoaned "libel by label." His ethic is not liberal though his passion for justice often plunges him into league with liberal Christian ethicists. He cannot be considered "fundamentalist" as they are usually perceived, but he takes the Bible seriously. His teaching cannot be honestly labeled neoorthodox even though many of the insights of neoorthodoxy inform his perspective.

In addition to these reasons for the disproportionate impact of his forty-nine doctoral graduates, certain other factors must be considered: (1) The Social Gospel, so closely linked with theological liberalism, had largely by-passed Southern Baptists. The Southern Baptist Convention was virgin territory for Christian social ethics in the forty years that Maston taught. (2) Maston taught ethics to men who became denominational leaders at the front edge of Southern Baptists' most rapid growth. The time was right for maximum impact. (3) The nature of Maston's Niebuhrian teaching on the stewardship of political power has been a distinctive motivating force for his graduates in their approach to the denominational power structures.

Who are these forty-nine graduates of T. B. Maston? An analysis of his doctoral students' professional accomplishments is most revealing. They have been pastors, professors, denominational executives, and foreign missionaries.

It may be significant that an eclecticism marks the vocational profile of these forty-eight men and one woman. Almost all have been in the three professional roles: pastor, denominational worker, and a professor or administrator in higher education. Among the graduates have been forty-seven pastors, twenty-one denominational executives, fifteen seminary professors, fifteen college professors, thirteen missionaries, four government officials, and two military chaplains. It would be interesting to see if other Baptist seminaries' doctoral graduates have filled as many diverse roles. Further, Maston's graduates include two seminary presidents, two college presidents, four presidents of their respective state Baptist conventions, two vice-presidents and one president of the Southern Baptist Convention.

The Christian Life Commission (SBC), has been disproportionately dependent upon persons trained by T. B. Maston. In the thirty years of Christian Life Commission (SBC) history, the commission and the various state commissions have had thirty professional staff persons as full-time employees. Of these thirty professional Baptist ethicists, seventeen have been Maston people. Twelve studied with him and another five with his students C. W. Scudder and William Pinson.

It is immodest for me to quote from a letter of Henlee H. Barnette regarding the influence of the Christian Life Commission on Southern Baptists, but his letter is one of tribute to T. B. Maston. Barnette, for twenty-five years professor of Christian ethics at Southern Seminary, says: "You have trained and taught the real prophetic leadership of Southern Baptists: Allen, Pinson, Valentine, Dunn and a host of others."[1] One reason for this impact has been the high degree of involvement in denominational life by the Maston graduates. All but two of the forty-nine persons have remained active Southern Baptists. It may be that the highest tribute that could be paid by his graduate students to T. B. Maston has already been offered in their seeing themselves as teachers. This has been true whatever the particular vocation of the moment.

The personal commitments of Maston have colored the work of his disciples. His sense of urgency and his emphasis upon the primacy of God's will are echoed through many of his students' lives. He concluded every semester of his philosophical ethics course with some candid observations about his personal philosophy. He always said, "Years ago I determined that what you're going to do for others and for the Lord you've got to do in a hurry." His life has demonstrated that sense of holy hurry. In those same classes he would also say, "Life is too short to do anything other than the will of God. The place of duty is the place of safety . . . the will of God is always best."

He also pled with doctoral students to be good stewards of their educational opportunity by writing. He has always set the pace, encouraged, urged, and challenged his graduates to write. In this area the graduates as a whole have not measured up to the challenge. Foy Valentine, William Pinson, C. W. Brister, and C. W. Scudder are prolific writers. Browning Ware and Jimmy Allen have had exceptionally successful newspaper columns. Beyond these, most of the rest of us have written some but have not quite measured up to the professor's expectations.

T. B. Maston has been the clearinghouse, the catalyst, the resource, the point of reference, the center of a strange and wonderful fellowship of those who did doctoral work with him. I have felt a sense of kinship with those who studied with Maston years before. I seem to know persons I have never met and to appreciate and trust men with whom I have had no contact because of the person and the common beliefs that bind us together.

Some people criticize this sense of loyalty to one another, this primary group orientation or family bond. Like any group so closely bound together in a minority intellectual perspective and fueled by religious zeal, this one has generated misunderstanding by its apparent exclusiveness. We have not been without fault in flaunting this relationship. We have not been without pride that is born of defensiveness. Commitments to racial justice, unpopular economic theories, sex education, church-state separation, and other views held by a minority of Baptists tended to lead us at times to see ourselves as an embattled band of prophets.

There has been, however, a basis in fact for the sense of fellowship among ethics graduates, and there is some evidence to indicate that these persons have contributed to the formulation of a Baptist biblical social ethic. The nature of that ethic is described in the last half of this book.

Bill Moyers, nationally known commentator who studied with Maston, says:

> When I'm asked to define Christian ethics, my best answer is Tom Maston. What the Old Testament prophets taught, he lived. He showed us that the theater of Christian ethics is not the pulpit, the classroom or the counselor's corner but all of life. Christian ethics encompasses all of the arrangements of men. Dr. Maston's message has gone far beyond the notes that we all took.

T. B. Maston often begins his public prayers with, "Accept the gratitude of our hearts, Dear Father." Those of us whose lives have been profoundly touched by his life may pray, "Accept the gratitude of our hearts, Dear Father, for T. B. Maston."

Those who completed Th.D. work with T. B. Maston are:

1. Jimmy R. Allen, First Baptist Church, pastor, San Antonio, Texas
2. Eldon W. Bailey, retired, professor of Sociology, Bishop College, Dallas, Texas
3. Wayne Barnes, First Baptist Church, pastor, Zachary, Louisiana
4. Harold G. Basden (deceased), Personnel Division, Foreign Mission Board, Richmond, Virginia
5. Lt. Col. D. Yates Bingham, United States Air Force chaplain, San Antonio, Texas
6. Tal Bonham, director, Department of Evangelism, General Convention of Oklahoma, Oklahoma City, Oklahoma
7. Julian C. Bridges, head of the Department of Sociology and Social Work, Hardin-Simmons University, Abilene, Texas
8. C. W. Brister, professor of Pastoral Ministry, Southwestern Seminary, Fort Worth, Texas
9. Thurmon E. Bryant, secretary for Eastern South America, Foreign Mission Board, Richmond, Virginia
10. James D. Cates, *Arizona Republic*, Phoenix, Arizona

11. James M. Dunn, director of the Christian Life Commission, Baptist General Convention of Texas, Dallas, Texas
12. Gary Farley, professor of Sociology, Oklahoma Baptist University, Shawnee, Oklahoma
13. Joel Ferguson, community development specialist, Community Services Administration, Dallas, Texas
14. James E. Giles, theological professor, Cali, Colombia, Foreign Mission Board
15. Guy F. Greenfield, White Rock Baptist Church, pastor, Los Alamos, New Mexico
16. Felix M. Gresham, dean of student affairs, Southwestern Seminary, Fort Worth, Texas
17. Cleve R. Horne, Jr., executive director, Christian Civic Foundation, St. Charles, Missouri
18. John C. Howell, dean and professor of Christian ethics, Midwestern Seminary, Kansas City, Missouri
19. Earl Humble, director of the Division of Social Science and Religion, Southern Baptist College, Walnut Ridge, Arkansas
20. Charles P. Johnson (deceased), director of libraries, Southwestern Seminary, Fort Worth, Texas
21. A. Jason Jones, area director, Department of Interfaith Witness, Home Mission Board, Marble Falls, Texas
22. Thomas J. Logue, director of student work, Arkansas Baptist State Convention, Little Rock, Arkansas
23. W. Randall Lolley, president, Southeastern Seminary, Wake Forest, North Carolina
24. Charles E. Myers, Alta Woods Baptist Church, pastor, Jackson, Mississippi
25. Ralph A. Phelps, Virginia Hill Baptist Church, pastor, Athens, Texas, and president emeritus, Ouachita Baptist University, Arkadelphia, Arkansas
26. W. W. Phelps (deceased), dean of students, Belmont College, Nashville, Tennessee
27. William M. Pinson, Jr., president, Golden Gate Seminary, Mill Valley, California
28. Lee Porter, senior adult consultant, Sunday School Department, Baptist Sunday School Board, Nashville, Tennessee
29. Robert E. Presnall, First Presbyterian Church, pastor, Borger, Texas
30. Edward Rickenbaker, Jr., First Baptist Church, pastor, Belton, South Carolina
31. James M. Robinson, Country Estates Baptist Church, pastor, Midwest City, Oklahoma
32. Olan H. Runnels, vice-president, Southwest Baptist College, Bolivar, Missouri
33. C. W. Scudder, administrator of internal affairs, Midwestern Seminary, Kansas City, Missouri
34. Billy Don Sherman, Woodmont Baptist Church, pastor, Nashville, Tennessee
35. Paulo W. da Silva, professor of ethics, North Brazil Seminary, Recife, Pernambuco, Brazil

36. Ebbie C. Smith, associate professor of Christian ethics, Southwestern Seminary, Fort Worth, Texas
37. Rogers M. Smith, administrative associate to the executive secretary, Foreign Mission Board, Richmond, Virginia
38. Cecil L. Thompson, Baptist Spanish Publishing House, El Paso, Texas
39. Lt. Col. Kenneth R. Thompson, United States Air Force chaplain, Wichita, Kansas
40. Joe E. Trull, Calvary Baptist Church, pastor, Garland, Texas
41. Foy D. Valentine, executive secretary-treasurer, Christian Life Commission (SBC), Nashville, Tennessee
42. Browning Ware, First Baptist Church, pastor, Austin, Texas
43. Weston W. Ware, program operations officer, ACTION, Dallas, Texas
44. Stanley O. White, director of missions, Los Angeles Association, Southern Baptist General Convention of California, Los Angeles, California
45. Keith C. Wills, director of libraries, Southwestern Seminary, Fort Worth, Texas
46. Rodney Wolfard, General Evangelism, Brazil, Foreign Mission Board
47. Marguerite Woodruff, professor of sociology, Mercer University, Macon, Georgia
48. G. Ray Worley, senior consultant, National Scientific Corporation, Arlington, Virginia
49. Kenneth W. Wright, First Presbyterian Church, pastor, Golden, Colorado

Note

1. Henlee H. Barnette to T. B. Maston, August 5, 1977.

III
THE THOUGHT OF T. B. MASTON

Biblical Ethics

James Giles

T. B. Maston is widely known for beginning with the ethical teachings of the Bible as he deals with any ethical issue or moral problem. While others might look to some other source of authority to give direction and form the ethical underpinnings, Maston is unapologetic in insisting that the basic ethical principles should be derived from the Bible. That biblical basis should be correctly interpreted and applied to daily life.

How is the Bible to be interpreted and applied when dealing with moral conduct? Is every commandment equally applicable to all mankind for every generation? Certainly not, Maston insists. A thorough understanding of the historical-critical method of interpretation would lead one to conclude that the statements which have to do with ethical principles and moral conduct must be interpreted in the light of the age, social customs, and sense of values of the day in which they were written or spoken. Our task is to discover the meaning of those statements for our generation and apply them in a creative way which moves mankind closer to God and to his ideals for living. To do this is to make the message of the Bible relevant to our day.

The Bible teaches that ethical living finds its beginning in a dynamic religious experience and that man's moral conduct is the fruit of a warm, personal relationship with God. Maston believes that when man drifts from this religious basis, the effects become evident in his lack of concern for his own personal testimony and his indifference to the needs of others. Moral drifting leads man into overt sin. A deepening relationship with God keeps man clean morally and alert to the opportunities to serve God through service to others. A constant study of the Bible and a facility in recognizing the ethical and moral emphases will contribute to right living. Thus one of Maston's major contributions is his detailed study of the ethical material in the Scriptures, *Biblical Ethics: A Biblical Survey*.

The Law

Maston, while being aware of the divergent positions regarding the authorship of the Pentateuch, held to, taught, and wrote from the perspective that Moses was the author of these books.[1] Although one must recognize the purpose and value in the ceremonial and civil sections of the Law, the concern of Maston, the ethicist, is focused principally on the moral law.

The book of Genesis gives one a perspective concerning God which includes his sovereign power in creation and in the affairs of man in history. God is concerned about man and his attitude toward his fellowman (Gen. 3:9,13; 4:9). God's righteousness is declared and forms the basis for the expectation of this same behavior in man (Gen. 18:23; Ex. 9:27).

Genesis emphasizes the unity of the human race and the spiritual dimension in man's nature. This truth is seen in the Genesis accounts of the creation of man in the image of God (Gen. 1:26-27; 2:7-25) and means that man is different from the animal creation. He is created with the need for and an ability to have communion with God.

Sin separates from God. Man's disregard for God's ideals and his own egotism cause him to fall short of God's expectations and to bring evil consequences in divine-human relations (Gen. 3:1-24). Though sin affects God's image in man, this image is not destroyed through sin. Each person is capable of responding to God's revelation and of becoming a channel through which harmony can be promoted in interpersonal relations.

Maston, along with many scholars, discusses the "moral difficulties of the Old Testament." These difficulties grow out of the apparent contradiction between what is presented as God's nature and his commandments. While there are passages which depict God as cruel and vindictive and commanding acts of savagery toward one's enemies, the moral difficulties of the Old Testament can best be explained by recognizing that "God reveals himself in different ways in different periods of human history, and makes different claims on the obedience of his people in accordance with the general spiritual situation, without at the same time qualifying the reality of his fellowship."[2] The principle of progressive revelation would indicate to us that more is expected of man in our day than in the days of the early stages of man's spiritual and moral development.

A study of the Ten Commandments reveals the prominence of the ethical element in man's duties. Four of the Ten Commandments have to do with God's nature and how man should respond to him (Ex. 20:1-11). God's unity and uniqueness and his spiritual nature are affirmed in the first two Commandments. Worship involves an experience in which God's spirituality is underlined. Reverence for God and his name is commanded in the Third Commandment, and due worship of God is assured through the separation of one day each week for rest and spiritual and physical renewal.

The second table of the Ten Commandments emphasizes man's need to be rightly related to his fellowman (Ex. 20:12-17). The Fifth Commandment emphasizes honor toward one's parents, who are representatives of God. One's attitude toward his parents forms the basis of his attitude toward all constituted authority. Since this Commandment is in the center of the Decalogue, it may be seen as the one which makes possible the transition from one's duties to God to his relationship with his fellowman. The other Commandments involve a regard for life, marital fidelity, property, truth, and justice. The Tenth Commandment, prohibiting covetousness, is an internalization of the other Commandments and moves the demands of the Decalogue from the letter to the spirit. The Ten Commandments present the basic principles which, if followed, will guide man toward a right relationship to God and his fellowman.

Exodus also contains many other instructions given by Moses to the Israelites. They formed a mixture of civil, moral, and religious practices for the nation Israel in its early development. We can see that these laws had the purposes of increasing the worth of human life, elevating the sense of dignity of every person, whether he be a slave (Ex. 21:2-11), a criminal (Ex. 21:12-27), a widow, an orphan, or a regular citizen of the community (Ex. 22:1-28). These laws brought a "deepened moral sensibility" which became one of the distinctives of the nation Israel in this epoch of her history.

The book of Leviticus contains the Holiness Code (chs. 17—26), and makes indelible in the mind of the reader the challenge: "Ye shall be holy: for I . . . am holy." Scholars have struggled to determine if the word *holiness* included the ethical aspect this early in the Old Testament history. At stake here is the authorship and date of the various books of the Pentateuch. Those who adhere to the developmental approach consider that the word *holy* at first carried a ceremonial connotation of separation as to relationship and that the ethical element in the meaning of the word came later in history. Maston follows Eichrodt and other scholars in insisting that the holiness mentioned in Leviticus 19:2 and other passages implies moral purity and blamelessness as well as a separation unto God. This is clearly illustrated in the five pentads which appear in Leviticus 19:2-18. These verses deal with provision for the poor, widows, and orphans at harvest time (vv. 9-10), the protection of personal property (vv. 11-12), relationships with one's neighbor (vv. 13-14), justice in judicial matters (vv. 15-16), and a prohibition of hatred and vengeance (vv. 17-18).

The book of Deuteronomy may be called a summary of the other books of the Pentateuch. It is rich in its presentation of the nature of God and emphasizes his love for his people. The book synthesizes the moral requirements for man in his relationship to God and to others. Deuteronomy reminds the people of the commitments which they had already acquired through the nature of their covenant relationship. The Ten Commandments are repeated in chapter 5. An emphasis is placed upon the importance of teaching the laws of God to one's children in chapter 6. Reverence for God would be manifest in obedience. The Shema, "Hear, O Israel: The Lord our God is one Lord: and thou shalt love the Lord thy God with all thine heart, and with all thy soul, and with all thy might" (6:4-5), is a declaration that has served as a basis for both Jewish and Christian belief and behavior through many generations. To love God as this commandment states is to obey all his other commandments. Deuteronomy gives practical instructions to man in the varied circumstances of life.

Maston sees the Law as containing the foundational principles for all other biblical revelation. When one understands God's purpose for mankind as revealed early in the biblical material, he acquires the basis for ethical and moral living.

The Prophets

The prophetic material of the Bible claims much of Maston's attention. A prophet is one who speaks forth the message from God to the people, especially in times of crisis. The prophets saw the cause of irreligious and immoral behavior as an abandonment of God's laws or an indifference to what God expected of man. Thus social reform began for the prophet in the return to God and a renewal of the vertical relationship which man has with him. "They perceived what God was like and, hence, what men must become to be acceptable to God."[3]

Ethical monotheism, the view that there is only one true God and homage to him involves moral conduct, was a central theme in the prophetic message. Most of the prophets lived in times when the worship of other gods was common and the practice of syncretism seemed to be acceptable. Repeatedly they called to their people to repent and be faithful to Jehovah, the only true God (Isa. 44:22; Jer. 25:5; Ezek. 33:11; Hos. 12:6).

The prophets also preached in a day in which ceremonial worship was hollow and meaningless. Therefore, they emphasized righteousness as more important than ritual, obedience above oblations, and justice instead of ceremonies. Man's moral conduct is to be the fruit of a vital, personal relationship with God.

The eighth century B.C. produced four prophets—Amos, Hosea, Isaiah, and Micah—whose ethical teachings thundered forth to bring a decisive dimension to the destiny of Israel. They emphasized that to be religious was to be moral and that the evidences of a vital religion were justice and honesty in business affairs and righteousness and humility in one's personal and religious life (Amos 5:24; Mic. 6:8; Hos. 6:6; Isa. 1:16-18).

These prophets announced that judgment would result from the people's unfaithfulness to God (Amos 5:2; Hos. 4:12; 5:7; 9:1; Isa. 1:21), and injustice toward their fellowman (Amos 2:6-7; 5:11-12; 8:4,6; Isa. 1:23; 3:14-15; 10: 2-3). *The day of the Lord,* a popular phrase to refer to this judgment, would be a day of punishment, of discipline, and of sadness. God would use the pagan kings of Assyria, Egypt, and Babylon and their armies to bring Israel to her knees. But these same nations would also suffer the consequences of their infidelity (Isa. 10:12; 45:1-7; 47:1-11).

The prophets offer hope for those who repent. Even Amos, whose messages are full of angry denunciations of injustice, oppression, and corruption, offered hope to those who repent and seek the Lord (5:4,6,14; 9:8-9,11,14-15). Hosea offered hope if Israel would turn from her spiritual harlotry to her loving and forgiving God. Isaiah gave hope in his emphasis upon the remnant that would exist after the destruction had taken place. Micah offered eschatological hope beyond temporal existence when the ideal age would be ushered in and God would reign supreme, doing away with war and conflict (4:1-5).

Individual prophets tended to emphasize one special theme. Amos cried out for justice (5:24). Hosea sobbed forth the message of God's forgiving love (11:1-9). Isaiah proclaimed the message of the holy and transcendent God who draws man to himself like a magnet and evokes from man righteousness (5:16) and peace (9:6-7). Micah spoke repeatedly of the sins of oppression (3:1-4,9-11), idleness and greed (2:1-2; 6:12), and gave the most comprehensive statement of the ethical teaching of the prophets in his call for justice, mercy, and humility (6:8).[4]

Limitation of space does not permit a presentation of each of the other prophets, but a word must be said about the ethical emphases of Jeremiah and Ezekiel. They were contemporaries, although their prophetic ministries were exercised in different geographic areas and under different circumstances. Jeremiah prophesied in Jerusalem until he was taken to Egypt in captivity (Jer. 43:6-7). Ezekiel was taken captive from Jerusalem to Babylon in 597 B.C. and prophesied while in Exile against the foreign nations (chs. 25—32). He brought messages of comfort and hope to the expatriates (chs. 33—48). Both prophets struggled to bring God's expectations before the people and to warn them of the consequences of their indifference and disobedience to God (Jer. 4:22; 5:1; 16:5; Ezek. 22:25-28).

Both prophets brought emphases in their teachings which were especially relevent for their day and whose concepts became even more significant in succeeding generations. They were: the new covenant (Jer. 31:31-34; Ezek. 16:60,62), and individual responsibility of each person before God (Ezek. 18:5-20; Jer. 31:30). These are basic principles which form a part of the gospel and have been taught by Jews and Christians through the centuries. God still calls his prophets to speak his message of judgment and hope and to hold before man God's ideals for human behavior.

The Writings

The Jews divided their Scriptures into three divisions: the Law, the Prophets, and the Writings. The Writings cover a broad span of history and a variety of classes of literature. While the ethical emphasis is not as obvious as in the other sections, the central themes which we have already mentioned are present and reiterated through many specific statements and developments in history. God is ethical in nature and expects behavior on the part of man that is consistent with his nature and purpose. While men and nations drifted away repeatedly from this norm, these ideals are held up and man is brought back to them through diverse historical events, divine intervention, and men and their divinely inspired messages.

Hebrew poetry, found in the Psalms, was used by God to transmit laws to man. The book of Proverbs is a book of practical wisdom which pictures the moral life as the way to happiness and success. The emphasis is upon the practical rather than the theoretical and personal rather than social or institutional. The book of Job deals with suffering, one of the most significant questions and one of the most difficult problems that men face. Job 31 sets forth some of the highest moral concepts to be found in the Old Testament. The other five books of the Writings, the Five Rolls, contain important ethical truths. For example, Ecclesiastes presents the pursuit of wealth, pleasure, power, and fame as unsatisfying. The summum bonum for man is to fear God and keep his commandments (12:13-14).

The Synoptic Gospels

When asked which was the greatest commandment (Matt. 22:36), Jesus quoted two from the Old Testament (Deut. 6:5; Lev. 19:18). He saw love for God as encompassing all that man should do in relation to God and love for one's fellowman as the practicing of all that is demanded of man in horizontal relations. Maston stressed that here we have the union of religion and ethics; we have the deepest challenge and the most dynamic basis for dedication and service. Can anyone define or describe what love looks like apart from individual acts which man performs toward God and his neighbor and which spring from his own inner sense of value and dedication? The Golden Rule is the highest expression of this love, stated in positive form, and moves man from actions based on duty to grace.[5]

Maston saw that instead of being bound by the legalism of the Pharisees, Jesus freed himself from their stifling rigidity. With reference to the observance of the sabbath he gave three fundamental principles: (1) The Son of man is lord even of the sabbath. (2) It is lawful to do good on the sabbath. (3) The sabbath was made for man and not man for the sabbath. Jesus' teachings conflicted with those of the scribes and Pharisees basically because they were interested in externals; Jesus was interested in motivation.

The kingdom of God is a prominent idea in the teachings of Jesus. He taught that entrance into the kingdom should be sought before material wealth or other physical pursuits (Matt. 6:25-34). The words in Matthew 6:33: "Seek first his kingdom and his righteousness, and all these things will be given to you as well" (NIV) are an ever present challenge. Conditions for entrance into the kingdom include repentance (Mark 1:15; Matt. 4:17), childlikeness (Mark 10:15; Luke 18:17), obedience (Matt. 7:21), righteousness (Matt. 5:20), and single-minded devotion to the things of God (Luke 18:24; Matt. 19:23; Mark 10:23). Jesus stated that greatness in the kingdom is to be based upon humility (Matt. 18:1-4), and unselfish service (Mark 10:43-44; Matt. 20:26-27).

Jesus gave some basic teachings which have to do with ethical living. The paradoxes of the gospel, an important study to Maston, continue to challenge the believer: (1) We find life through death to self. (2) Freedom comes through accepting our role as slaves of Jesus. (3) Greatness comes through unselfish service in the kingdom. (4) Exaltation comes through humbling ourselves in service.[6] The fulfillment of practical duties illustrates that one is a follower of Jesus. Jesus speaks of the meaning of humility and its significance (Luke 14:11), the requirement to be forgiving toward others if we are to experience forgiveness (Matt. 6:14-15; Mark 11:25), the importance of service to others as the basis of our reward in heaven (Matt. 25:31-46), the need to bear spiritual fruit as an evidence of our belonging to Christ (Matt. 7:16,20; Luke 6:44), and the acceptance of the principle that we as Christians are to follow Christ's example and bear the cross (Luke 9:23). This involves having love toward that which does not elicit love, denying ourselves personal preferences in order to render the highest service to God (John 15:13; 20:21; Eph. 5:25), and being willing to follow in the footsteps of Jesus and lead a life of selfless service to others (Mark 10:28; Matt. 19:27; Luke 18:28).

Jesus emphasized that real goodness begins in one's inner being and then expresses itself in outward behavior. The scribes and Pharisees were concerned about defilement from without; Jesus taught that one's own evil desires already contaminate him (Mark 7:15; Matt. 15:17-20; 23:25-26). Jesus emphasized the importance of following principles instead of laws and rules. Laws and rules lead to legalism and rigidity; principles free one up to apply them to the best of one's ability in each individual circumstance. Jesus illustrated these principles with specific examples. He told the rich young ruler to go and sell all that he had and give it to the poor (Luke 18:18-27). This is not to be taken as a commandment for all rich people to obey; rather Jesus wanted to show that riches kept this young man from entering into the kingdom.

Jesus held up the ideal of perfection (Matt. 5:43-48). Our inability to reach this goal creates a tension which motivates us constantly. Love is limitless in its application. Forgiveness and service cannot be measured quantitatively. Thus the ethical demands of Jesus become "impossible possibilities."[7] The perfect ideals of his teachings are constantly relevant for every Christian.

Jesus' life exemplified what he taught. Many experiences illustrate this fact (John 6:38; Phil. 2:8; Luke 23:34; 22:27; 1 Pet. 2:23). Jesus responded to human need in compassion and in a willingness to expend his own energies to meet those needs. His life and death illustrate how he saw purpose in his own teaching: "I am come that they might have life, and that they might have it more abundantly" (John 10:10).

The Pauline Epistles

While Jesus spoke frequently of the kingdom of God, Maston taught that Paul emphasized the same truth with the phrase *in Christ*. To be in Christ is to have the living Christ dwelling within the believer and guiding in the decisions that determine the present and the future in one's life.

Since Paul preached to many who had formerly been a part of a pagan culture, his message of necessity contained more appeals to leave the immoral practices of heathenism (Col. 3:1-9) and adopt a pattern of morality that exemplified one who has become a follower of Christ (Col. 3:10-17). Paul emphasized this same truth within the framework of the fruits of the flesh (Gal. 5:16-21) and the fruits of the Spirit (Gal. 5:22-26).

Paul's ethical teachings emphasize the need for Christians to apply high ethical and moral standards in daily living and thereby be a leavening influence in the community. Paul sought to help Christians who faced persecution from unbelievers in governmental positions and in the business community to be firm in their faith and moral practices while facing opposition (Gal. 6:10; 2 Cor. 6:17).

Most of the epistles of Paul reflect his firm conviction that a deep and genuine religious experience forms the basis for moral living. Paul insisted that good behavior is an outgrowth of correct theology. For this reason he emphasized the basic theological and ethical truths first in his epistles (Rom. 1—11; 1 Cor. 1-15; Gal. 1 to 5:15; Eph. 1-4; Col. 1-2) and then usually put a practical section toward the end (Rom. 12-16; 1 Cor. 16; Gal. 6; Eph. 5-6; Col. 3-4). While this practice is not completely consistent in all of Paul's epistles, it does occur with sufficient frequency to illustrate his conviction that religious experience should be basic to living the good life. Maston calls these two concepts Paul's basic and applied ethic.[8] Some of the basic theological and ethical truths which formed the underpinnings for Paul's emphasis on morality are: In Christ the Christian is no longer required to obey the law; he has been set free. This freedom is expressed as a freedom in the Spirit. The Christian is free from the stifling effects of the law, he is free from the crippling effects of the world, and he is free to surrender this freedom and in love submit to others when people of the world might push toward complete domination (Rom. 14; 1 Cor. 8).

Paul insisted that one's behavior should blossom forth from healthy motivation. His basis of appeal for the Christian life includes the fact that Christ redeemed us from our sins. Therefore we should glorify God with our bodies (1 Cor. 6:20; 10:31; Eph. 1:12; Phil. 1:11). Paul called on believers to imitate Jesus (Phil. 2:5-8; Col. 3:13; 1 Cor. 11:1). Fear and reward were also motives to which Paul appealed (Rom. 2:5; 8:13; 1 Cor. 5:5; 10:8; Gal. 5:21; Eph. 5:5-6; 1 Thess. 2:12; 2 Thess. 1:5).

Since Paul dealt with Christians who were struggling as they became converted from paganism, he spoke frequently about the need to separate oneself from the vices which were detrimental to the Christian's testimony. Paul dwelt on sins connected with the misdirection of the sexual drive, drunkenness, and excesses which prove harmful to the body. He also emphasized the virtues of faith, hope, and love (Rom. 5:1-5; Col. 1:4-5). In 1 Corinthians 13 Paul gives the great tribute to the power of *agape* love. Love is called the supreme, all embracing, transcendent virtue which binds everything else together in harmony. (Col. 3:14, RSV). Paul admonished the practicing of this Christian virtue in every relationship as a solution to conflicts which come in one's life (Eph. 5:25,28,33; Rom. 13:8; Gal. 5:14). He knew that when people love, their behavior will be such as to promote the good life for others.

Other New Testament Writings

The Johannine literature contains an emphasis upon the importance of love. In John 13:34 Jesus adds the dimension "as I have loved you" to the commandment to love one another. To lavish love unselfishly is to bear much fruit in fulfillment of the challenge in John 15:1-7. Maston sees this commandment as new in its source, its motive, its nature, and its dimensions.[9] The same theme is repeated in 1 John, where the author offers tests or proof based upon love that one is a child of God (1 John 2:9-17; 3:15; 4:7-21; 2 John 4-6). He also talks of following the way of light (1 John 1:5; 2:10) and righteousness (1 John 2:29; 3:6,9).

In the Revelation to John, there is an emphasis upon faithfulness to God in the face of persecution and the need to trust in the triumph of God and his righteousness over the forces of evil, whether they be personal or political. Some have criticized the vindictiveness that comes out in Revelation against the hostile state (Rev. 6:10; 16:6; 18:6-8), but one must recognize that the writer and the people to whom he wrote had been victims of cruel persecutions. The longing for a day of justice and victory when the forces that had usurped God's authority would be destroyed came forth in the form of rejoicing over the future victory of God's forces.[10]

The book of Acts has limited ethical content, but it does offer much concerning the work of the Holy Spirit. This involves bringing conviction for sin (Acts 5:1-5), working upon racially prejudiced Jews (Acts 10:1-44), and helping Christians to reach compromises which are mutually beneficial (Acts 15:28-29). The presence of the Holy Spirit enriched the fellowship of Christians and created within them a willingness to share (Acts 2:42; 4:32).

The epistle to the Hebrews presents the thesis that the revelation of God in Jesus Christ is superior to all other revelation. It also enjoins the Christian to remain faithful to Christ and not be tempted to drift back into Judaism or some other false teaching. The epistle ends with a series of exhortations which have ethical and moral significance. They are to be free of immorality (12:16), continue in brotherly love (13:1), show hospitality to strangers (13:2), fulfill conjugal responsibilities in marriage (13:4), be free from covetousness (13:5-6), and submit to spiritual leaders (13:7).

The epistle of James is "the most exclusively practical and ethical book of the New Testament."[11] James emphasized the careful use of the tongue and how one should be a doer of the Word as well as a hearer (1:22-26). He insisted that the Christian should not show partiality based upon one's social standing or riches (2:1-13; 5:1-6). He showed that faith and works are inseparable, and strikes at those who would say that faith is sufficient without the need for good works (2:14-26). One of the most graphic teachings in the epistle deals with one's speech (3:1-12). He illustrated the power of the tongue by showing that it must be dominated as one uses the bit in the mouth of the horse to control the animal. A ship may be huge, but it is governed by a small rudder. The tongue is as a small fire that can set ablaze a great forest.

First Peter speaks of the need to be sober and self-controlled (1:13), to live in brotherly love, and to be generous in hospitality (1:22). It appeals to Christians to submit as a basic strategy. They are to submit to constituted authorities, slaves are to submit to masters and wives are to submit to their husbands (2:12 to 3:9).

Conclusion

The Bible gives an abundance of specific instructions about moral behavior that is pleasing to God and self-enhancing and contains numerous prohibitions about those things which are to be avoided. Maston taught that while the Bible is not a rule book that we can consult for every imaginable problem or situation, obvious principles which have proven valid through the centuries should not be discarded simply because they are either commandments or prohibitions. We should be able to recognize their worth, apply them to our age and culture, and obey them accordingly.

The Christian life is characterized by freedom, openness, and an inner enthusiasm for goodness in contrast to the negative legalism which has sometimes been all too evident in some persons and groups. If the ethical implications of a religious experience are activated, a person will find peace, happiness, purpose, and meaning in life. To survey the ethical teachings of the Bible is to hold before one the ideals that lead to perfect (healthy and complete) living. To follow these teachings is to experience life at its best, Maston believes.

Notes

1. T. B. Maston, *Biblical Ethics: A Biblical Survey* (New York: World Publishing Company, 1967), pp. 1-2. It is significant that this footnote gives a complete survey of the different points of view regarding the critical problems related to the Pentateuch.

2. Ibid., p. 6, quoting Walter Eichrodt, *Theology of the Old Testament*, trans. J. A. Baker (Philadelphia: Westminster Press, 1961), I, p. 284. Maston seems to lean heavily on Eichrodt's ideas in his presentation in *Biblical Ethics.*

3. Ibid., p. 37.

4. Ibid., p. 58, quoting Albert Knudson.

5. Ibid., p. 150, quoting from A. B. Bruce in the *Expositor's Greek Testament.*

6. Ibid., p. 158. "The paradoxes of the Christian life" formed a strong theme in the teachings of Maston in his classes.

7. The idea of the "impossible possibility" comes from Reinhold Niebuhr, *An Interpretation of Christian Ethics* (New York: Harper), p. 113.

8. Maston, *Biblical Ethics*, pp. 187-188.

9. Ibid., p. 222.

10. Ibid., p. 239.

11. Ibid., p. 258.

Theology and Ethics

C. W. Scudder

T. B. Maston is a man with a purpose. That purpose has not changed in the thirty years this writer has known him. His purpose always has been to get people to do the Christian thing. He has spent his professional life seeking to achieve that purpose through his ethical teaching and writing.

T. B. Maston is a prophet out to change the world—in some way to bring the world more and more under the lordship of Christ. He is not a violent reformer, yet he is a prophet with a passion for getting the will of God done.

W. T. Conner, a colleague of Maston for many years, is quoted as having said that the Christian minister is a great reformer until he starts out to be a reformer. Maston fits Conner's idea of a great reformer. He is a gentle man who has been content to do the Christian thing and then wait for God to give the victory. God has given him many victories as he has seen many changes take place as a result of his prophetic influence.

T. B. Maston is not a systematic theologian nor is he a systematic ethicist, yet his ethic is thoroughly theological. He starts with God. He believes that he must build a theological foundation before he builds his ethic. He would explain that ethics without theology would be like a house without a foundation; theology without ethics would be like a foundation without a house. Theology without ethics would lack relevance; ethics without theology would lack power. Ethics and theology go together and need each other.

Maston starts with the Bible in his search for the will of God; he then turns to history. He believes you will find God at work in history as well as in the present. He sets his ethical teachings in both biblical and historical perspective. He believes that every current issue has its roots in the past, that there is a biblical principle that will fit every issue, and that the living presence of God will help in discovering and doing the circumstantial will of God.

Maston's later books focus on his major concern—the Christian life or Christian living. His theological ethic is presented clearly in *Why Live the Christian Life?*[1] That book is used to support this brief interpretation of Maston's ethic and is recommended reading. Another small book throws further light on his theological ethic by showing how it works out in actual living. He titled the book *Real Life in Christ.* It is characterized on the title page as being "Bible guidance for walking the Christian way."

Two of Maston's most characteristic statements are that the Bible is not concerned primarily with theology or ethics but with life and that he has no place for a doctrine that is not livable. Thousands of students have heard him give such strong emphasis to the Christian life. It has been no surprise, then, to find him communicating his most mature Christian insights under that subject in these later years of his professional life.

T. B. Maston always has been pragmatic in his ethical teachings, always looking for ways to get people actually to do the will of God. Mere theory without action never has been acceptable to him. In an effort to interpret the full sweep of his theological ethic, brief emphasis now is focused on his purpose, his authority, his power, and his strategy.

The Christian Life—His Purpose

We have noted that T. B. Maston is a man with a purpose. We now consider his purpose a bit more precisely. According to Maston, "Christian ethics is basically an attempt to study and interpret the Christian life."[2] However, Christian ethics doesn't provide a blueprint for the Christian life, for a constant reformulation always is in process because the experiences and problems are changing.

The present situation, to some extent a product of the past, requires a fresh interpretation of moral concepts and principles of the Christian faith. But Maston is careful to insist that "while every decision may be situationally conditioned, it is not situationally determined."[3]

Before a person can live the Christian life, a basic change in perspective and direction of life is necessary. "Man needs help from outside himself to overcome sin in his life. He receives that help when he comes into union with the resurrected Christ."[4] It is significant that Maston and the thousands of students he has taught have believed that the work of evangelism must be done first in order that man may receive from the outside the help that he needs to become a Christian and to live the Christian life. Evangelism and ethics go together, and none have believed that more than those who have majored in Christian ethics with T. B. Maston.

Two things are necessary to experience union with Christ. "The first is grace; the second is faith."[5] God's outreach to man must be matched by man's upreach to God. God takes the initiative, but man must respond with a leap of faith.

Union with Christ is a continuing experience as well as an initial experience.

The Christian's faith commitment to Christ must include commitment to Christ's way of life. "An outgoing life of service for God and to our fellowman was the basic purpose of the initial experience when we became new creations through union with Christ."[6]

Maston refers to John 15:16 in the vine and branch passage to indicate that the Christian life is to be characterized by bearing Christian fruit. Maston believes that union with Christ creates a desire to bear fruit for him. However, "the ultimate measure of our maturity in and for Christ is how much we are like him."[7]

Maston's purpose, then, is that men may be united with Christ by faith and may grow in Christ's likeness. That is God's intentional will—God's redemptive purpose—and that is Maston's purpose too.

The Will of God—His Authority

"The will of God is the source of authority for the child of God in all of the decisions of life."[8] With that statement Maston clearly characterizes his ethic as a will-of-God ethic. God's will always is right and best for every person in every situation.

Maston acknowledges that not all Christians are agreed in regard to the way a person can know God's will or the sources for an authoritative word concerning the content of that will, but he believes that those who hold different theological and ethical positions usually agree that God's will is the ultimate or final authority for a child of God. He quotes Bonhoeffer as saying that "the only appropriate conduct of men before God is the doing of His will."[9] This affirms the action dimension of Maston's ethic—the will of God is to be done or put in action once it is known.

Maston states that every person has native equipment such as common sense and conscience to use in seeking to know God's will. He also lists judgment as native equipment and defines conscience as being a sense of oughtness. He states that other human resources are available, but that "there are two major divine resources for a knowledge of the will of God: the Bible (objective) and the Holy Spirit (subjective)."[10] He also states that the church is an important interpreter of both of those divine resources but is never superior nor even equal to the Bible or the Spirit.

God's will is authoritative because it is tied to the very nature of God; God's will expresses his nature. Maston concludes that "this means that the ultimate source of authority for the Christian is God himself."[11] And since God is sovereign over the totality of our lives, he has a will for every decision. The will of God is as broad as human experience.

Maston is careful to state that God has an ultimate, ideal, or perfect will, and he insists that the Christian should seek to know that will in every time of decision. He is equally careful to note what Leslie Weatherhead has called the circumstantial will of God. Maston states that both intentional and circumstantial will of God are important in a study of the Christian life.

The conclusion to which Maston comes is that the intentional or perfect will of God will be found to be impossible on many occasions. Each decision must be related to a set of circumstances. "This means that in most times of decision we seek God's circumstantial will."[12] Maston affirms Paul Tournier's statement that "at every moment, no matter what the accumulated ruins may be, there is a plan of God to be found."[13] He also quotes Bonhoeffer as saying, "Through every event, however untoward, there is always a way through to God," and adds, "and hence a way through to his will."[14]

Maston holds that the idea of the circumstantial will of God is similar to the lesser-of-two-evils theory. He believes that no damage is done with that theory if the individual is careful to remember that the decision involves the lesser of two evils. In fact, he believes that there will be a tug toward greater good or the intentional will of God. "This means that the circumstantial will of God, when properly understood, will tend to move us toward his intentional will."[15]

The Bible is important, according to Maston, whether we are seeking the intentional or circumstantial will of God. "The Bible is the main tangible, objective source for a knowledge of God and his will."[16] The Bible is not the exclusive or only source for a knowledge of God's will, but it is a unique source. Maston is careful to insist, however, that as sacred as the Bible is, it cannot take the place of Christ. "Back of the Bible is the divine Person who gave birth to the Bible. His authority is prior to the Bible, but it is also expressed through the Bible."[17]

Man needs both the Scriptures and the Holy Spirit's guidance in his search for an authoritative word from God. Both speak the same word as they speak of and for "*the Word* made flesh." "In general, the Scriptures speak *of* Christ, the Spirit speaks *for* Christ. The unity of their authority rests in Christ."[18]

The Holy Spirit inspired the writers of the Scriptures and illuminates the words of the Scriptures for the reader. Therefore, he is the best interpreter of Scriptures, making them come alive. When no direct word is found in the Bible for a particular situation, Maston states that the Christian "then can seek the guidance of the Spirit."[19] However, he insists that both the Scriptures and the Holy Spirit are needed, and quotes Brunner's conclusion that "as the Scriptures without the Spirit produces legalism, . . . so the

Spirit without the Scriptures produces false antinomianism, and fanaticism."[20]

The Holy Spirit not only guides the Christian in finding the will of God but he also empowers for the doing of that will. Maston says that the Christian desperately needs both the guidance and the empowering if he is to find and do the will of God.

Maston rejects the idea that the Bible is authoritative only as interpreted by the church. He rejects the idea of a mediatorial church. There is no room for such a church with Christ as the Mediator between God and man. "He through the Spirit speaks the final and authoritative word to the child of God."[21] However, Maston acknowledges that the Spirit does speak through the Christian fellowship, and he says that "any Christian should consider very seriously the judgment of his church."[22]

Not only does man have the right to seek the will of God for himself but he must accept full responsibility for his decisions also. He must finally determine God's will for his life. "He is the ultimate interpreter of the Bible and of the leadership of the Divine Spirit."[23] Maston wants no misunderstanding at this point. He says, "Let us again emphasize that the individual Christian is to read and interpret the Bible for himself and to apply it to his own life." He insists that when he can find no direct guidance in the Bible, "he is to decide for himself under the guidance of the Holy Spirit what is the will of God."[24]

It is Maston's deep conviction that God will give a Christian the light he needs to know the will of God in each situation, but he believes that God gives only the light needed for each step in the will of God. He states that "the best assurance of being within God's will tomorrow is to be in his will today."[25]

The Demonstration of the Cross—His Power

T. B. Maston considers the cross to be the symbol of the fundamental law of the universe. He also believes that only the redemptive love symbolized by the cross possesses the power needed to advance the purposes of God in the world.

"If we had eyes to see," Maston says, "we would see a cross written at the center of that universe. The first or basic law of life is not self-preservation; it is self-denial and self-sacrifice, it is 'the way of the cross.' "[26]

Maston also views the cross as "the unifying symbol of a distinctly Christian life and the more distinctly Christian the more prominent will be the cross."[27] The cross will be a reality in the lives of those who seriously desire to be a real Christian rather than a nominal one.

Considering the cross as the unifying symbol of the Christian life is not intended to detract from the historical event of the cross of Christ. However, Maston desires that we understand the cross in relation to the life of Christ as well as to his death. "His death on the cross was in a very real sense a continuation of the type and quality of life he had lived. His incarnation really involved the cross."[28]

Maston believes that "we can properly speak of the atoning life of Christ as well as of his atoning death. He is the atoning person."[29] Christ's death cannot really be separated from his life; his death was the natural culmination of the life he lived. Christ demonstrated the redemptive love of God both in his living and in his dying.

The cross, according to Maston, is neither exclusively a thing of the past nor exclusively for Christ. "It is made visible, at least to a limited degree, through the lives of those who have come to the Christ of the cross and who, in turn, have taken up their cross and are following him."[30] Maston quotes Bonhoeffer's statement that "when Christ calls a man, He bids him come and die."[31]

The cross has an important place and meaning in the life of a Christian. "It involves for the Christian the crucifixion of self with selfish ambition and purpose."[32] Jesus made clear that the cross involves self-denial in the life of the Christian. Maston compares accounts of the conversation at Caesarea Philippi in Matthew 16, Mark 8, and Luke 9 and indicates that "(1) Taking up the cross is voluntary: '*if any man would* come after me.'. . . (2) It is necessary: 'If any man would *come after* me.'. . . (3) Taking up the cross is personal: 'if *any* man.'. . . (4) It is universal: Mark 8:34 says that 'he called to him the multitude with his disciples and said to them. . . .' Luke 9:23 says, 'and he said to all.'. . . It applies to all God's children. (5) . . . According to Luke, Jesus said, 'If any man would come after me, let him deny himself and take up his cross daily and follow me' (Luke 9:23). It is a daily or continuing experience."[33]

As Christ demonstrated the redemptive love of God in his living and his atoning death, we Christians are to demonstrate redemptive love in our living. It is not necessary for us to die on a cross for the sins of men; Christ died once for all. However, redemptive love must be shared with others, and Maston says that "men around us will come to know that kind of love to the degree that we, in response to his love for us, take up our cross and follow him."[34] Maston believes that the Christian, by his cross bearing, becomes a source of life to others. He says, "We cannot redeem men but we can be a redeeming influence among men."[35]

Maston's own summary could hardly be improved. He says: "Since none of us is perfect we are forced to say that to the degree that we deny self, to the degree that we take up our cross, to that degree and that degree only we will reveal God and his power, will discover life abundant, and will be a source of life and blessing to others."[36]

One term cannot adequately describe the ethic of the Christian life, but Maston believes "that the cross is the one symbol or general principle that most nearly unifies, ties into one bundle, and illuminates the various aspects or approaches to the Christian life and its ethic."[37] The cross is dominant in the theological ethic of T. B. Maston, and it is demonstrated clearly in his own life.

The Perfect Ideals—His Strategy

T. B. Maston believes that we need to recognize that tension is part of life and that constructive tension is necessary to healthy growth. "Tension," he believes, "is natural and inevitable for the serious Christian."[38] In fact, he believes that "every phase of the Christian life, when understood properly and considered seriously, is a creator of tension for the seeking, searching Christian."[39]

When we consider the condition of the world and the purposes of God for the world, we always are conscious of falling short of doing what we should do and being what we should be. When we study the Scriptures carefully and consider the quality of life lived by Jesus, the sense of falling short increases.

Maston believes that the perfect ideals are the most relevant part of the Bible. They will never be achieved and are always out before us. They always are there to challenge us and to judge us. We need the tension produced by the perfect ideals, for, according to Maston, "there is no progress without tension."[40] Tension produced by the perfect ideals contributes to our growth in the Christian life.

Maston believes that there is no cure for the tension in the Christian life, but that release and relaxation are possible. He suggests four things that provide release for the Christian (1) "recognition that tension is a natural and necessary part of creative living," (2) "make an honest effort to apply fully the Christian spirit and ideal to his life and to the world," (3) "when we realize that we have failed, that we have fallen short of the purposes of God in our lives, we can cry unto him for forgiveness," and (4) "an abiding faith in God is still another means for release of tension."[41] Maston believes that the serious Christian can enjoy the "peace that passeth understanding" while at the same time experiencing constructive tension in his life.

Maston believes that it is by creating tension between the ideal and the real that progress is produced in advancing God's purposes. The church is in the business of creating such tension and in producing such progress. "The more the church itself becomes a prophetic community the greater will be the tension between it and the world."[42] Maston believes that it is the prophetic members in the church who become the creative force. Prophetic Christians take the Christian message seriously and seek to apply it in their own lives, to the life of the church, and to the world.

Maston notes that "some churches have so completely made their peace with the world that there seems to be no tension between the church and the world," and he concludes that "such a church has lost its power to lift the world toward God's purposes for it."[43] Tension between the church and the world is most constructive when it is produced both by what the church preaches and what it practices.

Maston challenges preachers to be prophetic, but his students have heard his warning not to become too prophetic. The context for the preaching must be considered carefully. Being too prophetic may break the tension in a certain situation and may result in the preacher losing his opportunity to minister.

Many prophetic Christians are too impatient to settle for Maston's strategy of producing tension and letting God work out his will in the lives and affairs of people. Yet God still is producing Christian growth in the lives of the thousands of people who have come under the prophetic influence of T. B. Maston. They go on living with the constructive tension he first produced by his teaching and his writing. And they go on finding the peace that passes understanding which their teacher always encouraged them to claim.

Many lives have been blessed and the world is a better place because of the quiet yet prophetic influence of T. B. Maston. It is the prayer of this former student that God will give us many more such prophets.

Notes

1. T. B. Maston, *Why Live the Christian Life?* (Thomas Nelson Inc., Nashville, 1974).
2. Ibid., p. 11.   3. Ibid., p. 106.
4. Ibid., p. 61.   5. Ibid., p. 63.
6. Ibid., p. 65.   7. Ibid., p. 69.
8. Ibid., p. 106.   9. Ibid., p. 93.
10. Ibid., p. 106.   11. Ibid., p. 94.

12. Ibid.   13. Ibid., p. 95.
14. Ibid.   15. Ibid.
16. Ibid., p. 96.   17. Ibid., p. 98.
18. Ibid., p. 99.   19. Ibid.
20. Ibid.   21. Ibid., p. 101.
22. Ibid., p. 100.   23. Ibid., p. 102.
24. Ibid., pp. 102-103.   25. Ibid., p. 104.
26. Ibid., p. 172.   27. Ibid., p. 156.
28. Ibid., p. 158.   29. Ibid.
30. Ibid., p. 161.   31. Ibid., p. 162.
32. Ibid.   33. Ibid., p. 164.
34. Ibid., p. 165.   35. Ibid.
36. Ibid., p. 166.   37. Ibid.
38. Ibid., p. 174.   39. Ibid., p. 177.
40. Ibid., p. 178.   41. Ibid., pp. 182-183.
42. Ibid., p. 181.   43. Ibid., p. 185.

Marriage and Family

John C. Howell

It may be possible for interpreters of Maston's life and teachings to select several major emphases in his work, but it is certain that the family will have to be included as one of his most important areas of writing and lecturing. On a typed personal letter to me, Maston penned the additional note, "I have done more writing and speaking about the family than anything else." The home has had a definite priority in his life's ministry.

This emphasis on family was grounded in his own personal family experiences. His relationship to his father contributed a dimension of appreciation for authentic Christian faith practiced in the home that colored all of his interpretations of man's place in the home. In his taped lecture on the Bible and family relations, Maston said, "My daddy had a tremendous influence on my life. He was a great Christian, the most sincere, genuine man that I have ever known." Dying virtually penniless after a life of limited education, he might have been considered to be a failure. "But you can't tell me he was a failure. He taught me more Bible and more about the Christian life than any teacher I ever had."[1]

In his recurring emphasis on care for the aging in the family, Maston again wrote against the backdrop of his own experience. His mother lived as a widow for seventeen years after his father's death and had to be provided for by the family. Mrs. Maston's mother, who lived to be ninety-five years old, was a widow for nineteen years and lived with the Mastons each winter for as much as six to eight months for seventeen years. These experiences shine through his teachings on the meaning of personal care for elderly family members.

But the family experience with Tom Mc, their older son who suffered brain damage at birth, may have contributed more than anything else to the sensitivity which he communicated to students about family love and family care. He and "Mommie" have shared day and night duties of total care for Tom Mc throughout his lifetime. Her strength as well as his have been a blessing to students who gathered in their home for fellowship during graduate student days. Many of these same students have had the opportunity to have the Mastons, including Tom Mc, on their church fields or other places of ministry and have been inspired by their presence.

In *God Speaks Through Suffering*, Maston wrote: "As you would know, Tom Mc's presence in our home has influenced in many ways the other members of the family."[2] That influence, in many tangible and intangible ways, has also reached out to touch the lives of countless others who felt the compassion as well as the strength of the Maston home. The priority of the home in his teaching and writing is based firmly on the priority of the home in his own life and ministry.

The Fundamental Significance of the Family for Human Development

It is clearly evident in Maston's writings that he considered marriage and family relationships fundamental to human nature and human development. As a religious educator he demonstrated a basic commitment to the development principle of human growth and focused much of this development in the home. In 1957 he wrote

One of the distinct advantages of the home as a developer of human personality is the fact that in the home there is carried on a continuous educational process. It is continuous not only in the sense that it goes on hour after hour and day after day, but it also continues through life—from birth to the grave![3]

The family is God's first institution for human fulfillment. Maston maintained that the four basic institutions through which God makes provision for man's well-being are home, school, church, and state. Each has its own importance but "the home is the most basic of these four institutions."[4] The home is first not only in time of creation but also in importance. In fact, Maston concludes that "there is a sense in which every other institution of society has evolved from the home."[5]

The home is therefore basic to human development socially, spiritually, and morally. Socially, the child is equipped to live responsibly in society since "through the influence of home he is led to conform, in the main, to the mores and traditions of society." This conformity is never absolute, however, because the "home has a responsibility to help the maturing individual to know when and how to disagree and protest." Children will be influenced toward this type of social maturity when they have been reared in homes where "the adult members had made a satisfactory adjustment to one another and had maintained a wholesome tension with and yet a healthy attitude toward the world and life in general."[6]

Spiritual nurture is also home centered since Maston affirms the home as "a more basically important religious institution than the church." Because the home is the setting within which Christian experience must be lived on a daily basis, neither adults nor children can grow spiritually unless the home encourages such spiritual growth. "Really," says Maston, "about all the churches can do is try to supplement what the home has done or to make up for what it has not done. And the Church cannot completely make up for the failure of the home."[7]

One specific challenge for the Christian home is to encourage children to accept Christ as Savior and to make him the "integrating center" of their lives. Their moral decisions will then be related to their developing Christian faith. Thus the child's moral development in the sense of "his systems of values, his conception of success, and the driving motives and purposes of his life" will find basic grounding in the spiritually sensitive home.[8]

Does this imply that only homes in which God is worshiped have validity as authentic families? No, since marriage and the family are "written into the nature of men, women, and children," marriage belongs to the natural order.[9] Even if God is not recognized in the home, basic natural laws govern the relationship. Acceptance or rejection of these natural mandates for life will affect the success or failure of family life, but a valid marriage exists even where God is not known. The words of Jesus, "What therefore God has joined together, let no man put asunder" (Matt. 19:6), do not refer "to some hazy concept of a spiritual union."[10] Jesus refers instead to God's purpose for all marriages consummated by sexual union into a one-flesh relationship. Maston emphatically declares, "God does not have one set of basic laws for the Christian couple and another set for the non-Christian."[11] Therefore, "Christian marriage is not a particular kind of marriage, although it should have a unique quality."[12]

Healthy family life is essential for social well-being in any society. Since the family is a natural element of all societies, the condition of family life often mirrors the health of a given society. Based on this belief in the strategic importance of the family to all human societies, Maston affirms that the development of healthy families is an essential task of the church. The home is God's most important institution, thus "we are on the mainline when we do anything that will strengthen and stabilize our homes."[13] Maston was an early advocate of the marriage and family enrichment emphasis which is now gaining impetus in churches of all denominations. The fundamental significance of the family can be reinforced by such enrichment emphases in the churches.

Trends and Issues in Maston's Teachings on the Home

The Bible is foundational to Maston's understanding of marriage and family living. Even though his emphasis on the Bible is discussed in another section of this book, it is essential that attention be given to it briefly in this context. In relationship to his interpretation of family life, the recurring emphasis is on God's revelation being in accord with the basic nature of mankind and therefore relevant for all men. For example, referring to the Sermon on the Mount, Maston declares, "The teachings of the New Testament in general and of Jesus in particular express and conform to the basic laws as God has written them into our nature and into the nature of our world."[14]

This focus on the Bible as the source of one's basic family ethic is an emphasis greatly needed in contemporary family-life education if there are to be authentic Christian standards to guide educators. There are times, however, when the unquestioned acceptance of some biblical passages as authoritative truth does not adequately deal with the complexities these statements create for persons living in families. Maston is inclined to affirm the explicit statements of the Bible because they are in the canon of the Scriptures while giving too little attention to the critical and textual problems involved in interpretation. A case in point is the treatment of Proverbs 22:6 in his tape on parents and children. Three possible interpretations of this passage are cited but his conclusion does not deal with the many questions parents raise about the passage as a general revelation of truth. This failure at times to grapple with problem passages is in accord with Maston's desire in Bible study to emphasize "the positive rather than the negative." However, the result of this approach often communicates a certain naiveté concerning the Bible's relevance to life in the family where conflict and anger are realities of experience.

There is emphasis upon the democratic style of Christian family life. In his 1957 survey of the family and its future, Maston related the growing interest in a democratic style of family life to respect for human personality and to individual rights in relationships. He declared that "the tendency toward a democratic type of family living seems to be a natural and necessary trend in the contemporary period" even though this same emphasis might contribute to family instability during the transitional period of moving from traditional to democratic marriage styles.[15]

Respect for human personality is centered in his conviction that all human life is created in the image of God. "One who has been created in the image of God should never be treated as a mere means to some other end," therefore "in the family the husband, the wife, or the child should never be used as a mere instrument, as a means of personal gratification."[16] In his strong plea for mutual respect and for equality in personhood, Maston anticipated the present struggle in contemporary literature over appropriate marriage styles for the Christian family. He identified himself at the companionship or partnership end of the spectrum rather than at the chain-of-command end, but he argued for a strong sense of male responsibility in the home. Equal personhood and functional inequality can coexist in the home just as they do in the state.

Maston declares that God "has ordained that man shall be head of the house and that the wife should recognize that headship and fulfill her own distinctive functions in the home." This functional subordination is not based upon inequality in Christian personhood but is "to be the subordination of an equal to an equal for the sake of order." He is concerned that popular cultural images of equality destroy the authority of the father thus leaving a vacuum in responsibility which the wife and mother must often fill. Such an abdication of male headship is contrary to God's purpose for the wife as well as the children since children "need the loving but authoritative symbol of the father in the home." His conclusion is that "the modern American home must be basically democratic, but unless there is to be chaos and anarchy, there must be some final source of authority in the home," and man should exercise that authority.[17]

Maston, however, is no supporter of the type of individualism which encourages personal fulfillment regardless of its effect on the communities within which Christians live. He declares emphatically that "the individual is so dependent, however, on the community that unbridled individualism is destructive of the best interest of the individual and the community . . . . This is true of all the communities to which the individual may belong: the play or work group, the family, the church, the neighborhood, the nation, and the world."[18] The unity of the family must never be sacrificed on the altar of selfish individualism (male or female) which seeks personal gratification regardless of the consequences for others in the family.

A case-study method for teaching family life was used in his courses. In contemporary theological education, the case study has become an important type of teaching methodology for applying academic principles to human life situations. Through the influence of the Case Study Institute (and the Harvard Business School), a basic technique has evolved for writing and teaching cases. Maston, of course, has not been involved in this development since he retired prior to the inception of the Case Study Institute. However, in the 1948 syllabus for his family problems course, Maston included sixty-nine brief cases to be used by students as catalysts for discussion and response to specific issues. Thus his students were always forced to consider the application of ethical principles to life rather than study principles in isolation from reality.

In all of his writing and lecturing, Maston also made excellent use of questions to stimulate thought and application. By this means he encouraged personal development of one's own position through reflection on the issues. This technique is also prominent in the case-study methodology as well as in the more recent concern for theological reflection as a tool for teaching. Probably it was his excellence as a stimulator of thought that influenced his students to grapple with the issues of family living in our contemporary world even more than the specific content of his courses.

Adequate care for aging family members was a central concern in his teaching. In his family life conferences as well as in his classes, Maston always expressed deep concern for the family's relationship to its aging members. Once again, his attitude toward the family's responsibility for older members of the family is grounded in biblical principles. In 1968, he said, "It is my judgment that the shifting to such a large degree of the responsibility for needy parents from the children to any institution or agency, public or private, violates the plan and purpose of God and is not best for the parents or for the children."[19] This position is based upon Jesus' words recorded in Mark 7:9-13 and Paul's instructions in 1 Timothy 5:3-8,16. He summarizes his position by saying, "My viewpoint is that the order of responsibility for those in need is first, the natural family or relatives; second, the spiritual family or the church; and third, the human family or society in general."[20]

Need must be interpreted as more than physical care. The basic needs of the elderly include somewhere to live, something to do, and someone to care. Living accommodations should always be planned to maintain the independence of the aging person as long as possible. The "something to do" should contribute to their sense of being needed and of having something to give to other people from their own skills and resources. Each of these is important for the emotional and spiritual health of the aging. But the third is absolutely vital—having someone to care for them in a way that expresses appreciation and love to them in their declining years. This is "one real test of the character of a son or daughter, or even of a society . . . and also reveals how much the spirit of Christ has permeated our lives."[21]

Responsibility for parents in their senior years may include caring for one or the other of them in the home of a child or children, but this is not always the wisest move as long as parents can remain independent.

The exercise of caring love requires the maintenance of the dignity of the aged even when the ultimate decisions for custodial care must be made by the children. Many alternatives for places to live are discussed in his writings which seek to present a positive attitude toward care rather than a defeatist attitude. "There can be real blessings to all concerned in the associations of the old and the young," and Christian families can experience such fulfillment when they carry out God's plan for the elderly.[22]

The home is an extension of the kingdom of God for Christians. As has been noted in other sections of this book, the kingdom of God concept is basic to Maston's theological perspective. He usually identifies the kingdom with God's rule in human life and maintains that one of the purposes of the home is to celebrate the rule or kingdom of God in the family. Since the church and the Christian home are both called-out ones, "they both exist for the same big overall purpose: the promotion of the kingdom of God among men."[23] He is convinced that if couples being married realized that their home existed for this purpose among others, "such a perspective would eliminate or solve most of the potential problems they might have."[24]

Family life is lived in the tension between the ideal and the actual. Maston's emphasis on tension created by living between God's kingdom or rule and the world is well known to his readers. He suggests that the tension between the ideal and the real is "one basic conflict" that summarizes all of the conflicts which confront human life in the world. Such tension is also existent in the biblical teachings about family relations, especially in the teachings of Paul. Maston believes that Paul expressed the ideal for family relationships in Galatians 3:28, but demonstrated the necessary adaptation or compromise of that ideal in confronting the actual living experiences of his converts. "Paul started with the people to whom he wrote and ministered where they were. He had to do that if he was to succeed in moving them in the direction in which he wanted them to go." To recognize and live with such tension is to understand the pull of the gospel toward the kingdom-type of life even though conflict and pain must be faced in the actual experiences of life. So Maston concludes that "the presence and validity of such tension is one of the abiding contributions of Paul's epistles."[25]

Some Specific Teachings on Marriage and Family Relations

Marriage is in God's purpose. In all of his writings, Maston consistently describes marriage as a monogamous and exclusive relationship between a man and a woman which is to last throughout their lifetimes. Four essential purposes for marriage are to propagate the race, to provide intimate fellowship and mutual love, to provide a positive expression of sexual passion, and to promote the kingdom of God among men. The propagation of the race is usually placed first in this order of purposes even though there is great emphasis on sex in marriage as a source of emotional and spiritual intimacy when the possibility of procreation is prevented by contraception. Husband and wife relationships are based upon mutual equality, as expressed in Galatians 3:28 and 1 Corinthians 7:3-5, but functional subordination based upon fulfillment of purpose in the marriage is assumed to be God's ultimate will for marriage. Maston's most recent word is contained in a taped lecture on husband and wife relationships in which he says that the New Testament writings stress mutuality in the relationship as primary.

The Bible speaks about the relationship of parents and children. The general perspective which Maston discovers in the Bible is that propagation is a natural purpose of marriage and that children are one aspect of parental stewardship before God. He is emphatic in declaring that "any husband and wife who can and should have children and who deliberately and permanently thwart this basic purpose of marriage are violating a fundamental law of marriage and will have to pay a penalty for their violation."[26] But merely bearing children is not sufficient. Parents must also give adequate love, guidance, and discipline to enable their children to live successfully in the world. The right kind of discipline will be beneficial to the child and also will be beneficial to the home in which the child lives.

The child's responsibility to the parents is to honor, obey, and care for them as needed. This caring responsibility of child to parent has already been treated in some detail earlier in the chapter.

Christian attitudes toward sex and sexual relations are important. Maston clearly teaches that sex which expresses itself in sexual relations is a good gift from God to human life. It is by sexual union that the couple become one flesh and establish the marital relationship. Since sexual union symbolizes the uniting of personalities as well as bodies, any sexual intercourse apart from that of marriage is contrary to God's purpose for human sexual relationships.

Since sex is such a powerful symbol of human emotion, it also expresses sin in vivid ways. This does not mean that sex is bad; it means instead that sex is affected by human sinfulness and is often used to exploit and hurt other people.

Attitudes toward divorce and remarriage need to be examined. In all of his writings and lectures on divorce, Maston considers divorce to be a violation of God's purpose for marriage and therefore sinful. There is also, however, a clear understanding that the sin involved in divorce is not an unpardonable sin. Instead, "the sin that leads to divorce and that may be directly involved in divorce itself can be forgiven as is true of any other sin."[27] He defends the position that divorce may be the lesser of two evils in a marriage which has died to all meaning and purpose of love between two people.

During the course of his own teaching career he moved from a position which encouraged pastors to marry no one who had been divorced to a position encouraging pastors to decide about remarriage for a given couple on an individual basis after sufficient counseling with the couple to determine whether there was a reasonably valid basis for the establishment of a sound, stable marriage.[28]

Notes

1. T. B. Maston, "The Bible and Family Relations," *Family Life Tapes* (Fort Worth: Latimer House, 1976).

2. T. B. Maston, *God Speaks Through Suffering* (Waco: Word Books, 1977), p. 18.

3. T. B. Maston, *Christianity and World Issues* (New York: The Macmillan Company, 1957), p. 62.

4. T. B. Maston, *The Christian in the Modern World* (Nashville: Broadman Press, 1952), p. 33.

5. T. B. Maston, *The Christian, the Church, and Contemporary Problems* (Waco: Word Books, 1968), p. 67.

6. Maston, *World Issues*, pp. 62-63.

7. Maston, "The Bible and Family Relations."

8. Maston, *Christianity and World Issues*, p. 62.

9. Ibid., pp. 68-69.

10. T. B. Maston, "Sex and Sex Relations," *Family Life Tapes* (Fort Worth: Latimer House, 1976).

11. T. B. Maston, "Divorce," *Family Life Tapes* (Fort Worth: Latimer House, 1976).

12. Maston, *Christianity and World Issues*, p. 69.

13. T. B. Maston, "Husbands and Wives," *Family Life Tapes* (Fort Worth: Latimer House, 1976).

14. Maston, *God Speaks Through Suffering*, p. 37.

15. Maston, *Christianity and World Issues*, p. 81.

16. Maston, "Husbands and Wives."

17. Maston, *Contemporary Problems*, pp. 78-79, 121.

18. T. B. Maston, *Why Live the Christian Life?* (Nashville: Thomas Nelson, Inc., 1974), p. 42.

19. Maston, *Contemporary Problems*, p. 118.

20. T. B. Maston, "Parents and Children," *Family Life Tapes* (Fort Worth: Latimer House, 1976).

21. Maston, *Contemporary Problems*, p. 91.
22. Ibid., p. 96.
23. Ibid., p. 84.
24. Maston, *Why Live*, p. 121.
25. Maston, "Husbands and Wives."
26. Maston, *Modern World*, p. 70.
27. Maston, *Contemporary Problems*, p. 102.
28. Maston, "Divorce."

Women in Church and Society

Marguerite Woodruff

After Maston had encouraged me to write my doctoral dissertation on Paul's teachings concerning women, I went to my first teaching position in a Baptist women's college. When I meekly requested the president to consider permitting me to teach in the Bible department, he reared back in his chair and said, condescendingly, "Now, Dr. Woodruff, I'd rather have a broken down preacher who is tired of battling a board of deacons teach Bible here than to have a *woman* do it." For the first time, I experienced discrimination against women. The apostle Paul has been given credit many times for such attitudes since he said for women to keep silence in the churches and not to teach or have authority over men. Should Paul be cited in these few instances without considering all of his writings and his behavior toward women and without looking at the context and the cultural influences on his life?

Christian churches have often lagged behind the society on social issues when the original impetus for humane treatment of all people came from the New Testament and should have been exemplified by the churches first.

The Old Testament and Women

In traditional Judaism, women's place was in the home, married, and with children. This does not mean that she was not self-assertive, however. Sarah illustrates the fact that she felt secure enough to raise her voice to Abraham and demand in the Piel (a very emphatic Hebrew verb form) that he get rid of Hagar and Ishmael (Gen. 21:10). If the Hebrew woman had felt that she was only a notch above a slave, she would probably have been much more demure. And God approved of this type of self-assertiveness (v. 12). Whether the woman described in Proverbs 31 is ideal or real, she does not lack self-confidence. In addition to ruling her own house, she trades with the merchants and even deals in real estate. This exemplifies a great deal more freedom than was experienced by women in Greece at the time of Paul. In Athens, married women stayed behind the walls surrounding their homes and never went out on the streets unless they were accompanied by a slave.

130

Women usually were not mentioned in a census, as exemplified by the statement in Numbers 26:62 concerning the number of Levites there were counting "all males from a month old and upward." However, in that same chapter the daughters of Zelophehad and the daughter of Asher were mentioned by name. In Numbers 27, the daughters of Zelophehad came to Moses and requested their father's share of the Promised Land. Moses went to the Lord about it and again God came through for women's rights, even extending their case to a general law (Num. 27:8).

Several women were classifed as prophetesses by the Old Testament writers, and it seems to be accepted without any question. It is interesting that the word *prophet* means "one who speaks forth." God told Moses in Exodus 7:1 Aaron would be his "prophet," that he would say what Moses told him to say and Moses would be acting as God to him. So God used women as well as men to speak forth or proclaim for him. Miriam, Huldah, and Noadiah are called prophetesses (Ex. 15:20; 2 Kings 22:14 ff.; Neh. 6:14). Deborah is probably the most outstanding prophetess and was also a political leader. She held court and "the children of Israel came up to her for judgment" (Judg. 4:5). She summoned Barak to her and *he came*. When she told him God wanted him to go into battle against Sisera, he agreed to go only if she would go with him. She assented but warned him that the honor of conquering Sisera would go to a woman instead of to him. Deborah gave the orders from God; Barak obeyed; and the woman Jael took the general!

Even though the Jewish man thanked God every day that he had not made him a woman, still Jewish women were honored coequally with the men as parents and no doubt Jewish women were regarded more highly and had more freedom than their counterparts in the cultures surrounding them.

Jesus and Women

Jesus was born into a Jewish home and studied in a Jewish synagogue. Thus he understood from earliest childhood that his mother was to be honored along with his father. After his experience of confounding the teachers of the law at age twelve, he came back to Nazareth with his parents and was obedient to *both* of them. He dared to violate the taboos of the day regarding male-female relations by talking to women in public, touching them, and allowing them to touch him. Indeed, his violation of the social customs of the day probably did as much as anything else to antagonize the Jewish leaders and lead subsequently to his death. He fraternized with publicans and sinners, even eating with them. He touched lepers. He talked with a woman in Samaria who had a notorious reputation and thus violated three taboos. He permitted a woman who suffered from continual bleeding to touch him and instead of rebuking her for contaminating him, he healed her and sent her away in peace. He graciously accepted the touch of a sinful woman who bathed his feet with her tears, wiped them with her hair, and poured perfume over them. Then he forgave her sins and sent her away in peace under the disapproving gaze of a Pharisee host who had neglected the social amenities but who could not see the worth of a human soul, certainly not a female one (Luke 7:37 ff.).

Although the writers of the Gospels often failed to mention the fact that there were women in the crowds following Jesus, hearing his teachings, and accepting them, they did on occasion mention this. All four Gospels recount the feeding of the five thousand men; only Matthew mentions "besides women and children" (Matt. 14:21; compare Mark 6:44; Luke 9:14; John 6:10).

There is no indication that there were women among the seventy whom Jesus sent out, but Luke uses *heteros* for "others" which means different kinds of people so this heterogeneity may have included some women (Luke 10:1). At any rate, Luke does mention women accompanying Jesus and the twelve on one of their preaching missions. Mary of Magdala, Joanna, Susanna, and many other women ministered to these men from their own personal resources (Luke 8:3). It is from Luke's account that we get many of our insights into Jesus' relation to women. When Luke recounts the healing of a slave upon the request of his master, he immediately follows this with the raising of the son of a widow (7:2-18). When he concludes the story of the good Samaritan, he goes in the following verse to Jesus' visit to the home of Martha and Mary (10:30-42). Martha was fulfilling the traditional female role of serving her guests while Mary broke with tradition and sat listening to Jesus' teaching, expanding her mind and spirit. Jesus commended Mary for choosing the better part. Martha evidently got the message, for when Lazarus died, it was she who went to meet him and expressed her confidence that he could handle the situation. It was to Martha that Jesus made his declaration, "I am the resurrection, and the life" (John 11:25).

When Jesus healed on the sabbath, he did not discriminate. He healed a woman who was bent double; he healed a man who had dropsy (Luke 13:10-13; 14:2-4). When he was seeking to help his audience understand what the kingdom of God was like, he used an illustration of a man sowing a mustard seed; then he added one of a woman putting yeast in her bread (Luke 13:18-21). He told a parable about a man who lost a sheep, and then to help his female audience identify with the story, he told about a woman who lost a coin (Luke 15:3-10). When he was explaining the suddenness of his return, he talked about two men asleep in the same room: one taken, the other left; and two women working together at household tasks: one taken, the other left (Luke 17:34-35).

Letha Scanzoni and Nancy Hardesty observe, "In a day when most rabbis refused to teach women because their minds were supposedly incapable of grasping God's truth, Jesus taught women openly."[1] When Jesus engaged the Samaritan woman in conversation and she tried to keep him talking on theology rather than getting personal, he did not insult her intelligence by saying, "A woman shouldn't be concerned about theology," but he answered her question straightforwardly and then zeroed in on her personal life.

Rosemary Ruether thinks that even more significant than all of his consideration of women and his violating of the taboos of Jewish tradition is the fact that he modeled the Christian ministry on the role of service. "The waiting on tables, the lowly role of women and servants, is to be the model for the ministry."[2]

It is obvious from their devotion to him how much women appreciated Jesus' treating them as persons worthy of divine grace. They were the last at the cross and the first at the tomb. To Mary of Magdala he revealed himself first and entrusted the message to be delivered to his disciples. Whether or not women were present to receive the Great Commission, they have unstintingly devoted themselves to it for two thousand years.

Paul and Women

Peter, in writing to encourage Christians of the dispersion, said that Paul had written some things that were "hard to be understood" (2 Pet. 3:16) and certainly on the subject of women, this is true. While Paul respected women and complimented them for serving right alongside the men, he seemed in other places to contradict his own behavior by his words. Explanations for these hard sayings have run the gamut from taking them literally and seeking to apply them to the twentieth century, to saying flatly that Paul did not write them. Perhaps there are some satisfactory in-between explanations. Paul's most rigid teachings concerning women are found in 1 Corinthians and 1 Timothy. Paul was in Ephesus when he wrote to Corinth, and Timothy was in Ephesus when Paul wrote to him (1 Cor. 16:8; 1 Tim. 1:3). Ephesus was the center of the worship of Artemis or Diana and, as was true in Corinth at the temple of Aphrodite, priestesses came as virgins to the temple and were dedicated to prostitution in the temple service. At the temple of Aphrodite in Corinth there were at one time a thousand temple prostitutes. The message of Jesus Christ was a message of freedom, and Paul was anxious that the women who became Christians not go overboard with their freedom so that their dress or conduct associate them with these prostitutes rather than with the modesty becoming a Christian.

It must also be kept in mind that at least 1 Corinthians was written to answer specific questions which had been addressed to Paul by the church at Corinth. And as Maston says in the cassette tape, "The Role of Women in the Church" (*Broadman Ministers' Tape* series) "Wouldn't it be wonderful if someone discovered the letter from the Corinthians!"[3]

Constance Parvey introduces the idea of gnosticism as an influence Paul was combatting in Corinth, in addition to Aphrodite.

Paul's concern with the Corinthians is not so much with women as such as with a whole cluster of difficulties in the congregation, all of which show signs that agnosticized, pneumatic believers had penetrated its midst, disregarded established customs, and among other problems they had created, had also influenced some of the women. The Gnostics in the Corinthian congregation, both men and women, give evidence of acting like spiritual libertines. They considered themselves carried away by a higher loyalty and were preoccupied with their own private ecstasies. Because they believed they were acting on the instructions directed by the divine spirit-possession within them, they considered themselves superior to others, and thus considered their action independent of any human judgments, criticisms or control. The disorderly conduct of the women fits into a general picture of turmoil and breakdown in the congregation.[4]

With reference to marriage or celibacy in 1 Corinthians 7, Paul suggested two reasons for his position. One is his eschatology: He expected the imminent return of Christ and since this was true, "why cumber yourself with the problems of marriage for such a short time?" Probably related to this is his second reason: It is easier to devote all of one's time to spreading the gospel if one does not have a marriage partner to think about.

In considering whether God would desire some of these practices applied in twentieth-century churches, it should be noted that in some of these instances Paul definitely stated that it was his own will or opinion, not necessarily a voice from heaven. See for example 1 Corinthians 7:12 in the Revised Standard Version (RSV), "I say, not the Lord"; 7:17 (RSV), "my rule"; 7:25 (RSV), "I have no command of the Lord"; 7:39 (RSV), "And I *think* that I have the Spirit of God" (author's italics); 1 Timothy 2:8 (RSV), "*I* desire" (author's italics); 2:12 (RSV), "*I* permit no woman" (RSV). Of course, in 1 Corinthians 14:37, he did say that what he was writing was a command of the Lord, and two verses before, he had told the women that if they wanted to know anything to ask their husbands at home. This was assuming their husbands would know the answers and many dedicated, church-attending ladies know that is not necessarily so. It is likely that Paul was thinking in terms of his Jewish heritage when he said this, for a Jewish man would have been thoroughly educated in the synagogue where the Jewish woman would not have been. He also drew upon Jewish tradition for his reasoning that Adam was not deceived but Eve was (1 Tim. 2:14). The literature of the Targums, Josephus, Philo, and the Apocryphal literature were all very emphatic in reminding men that women were responsible for their problems. However, as Scanzoni and Hardesty point out:

Nowhere does Jesus refer to the Fall. He does not suggest that the woman is weak and easily deceived. He does not forbid her to study theology or teach his word. He does not blame her for the first sin or remind her that men will rule over her because of it. Rather he treats all daughters of Eve as persons created and recreatable in his image and likeness.[5]

Despite these hard-to-understand things which Paul said, he commended many women for their work in the churches. Before his conversion, when he was seeking letters to the synagogues at Damascus, he specifically included women as among the followers of the Way that he wanted permission to drag out and throw in jail. Even then, he was aware of their activity in the new faith. After his conversion and leadership in the church, he utilized their homes and services. Lydia, the businesswoman of Thyatira, took Paul and Silas into her home both before *and* after their prison experience in Philippi (Acts 16:15,40). At Thessalonica and at Beroea "not a few" leading women believed (Acts 17:4,12, RSV). He sent greetings to ladies and the churches meeting in their houses (Col. 4:15; Philem. 2; Rom. 16:5; 1 Cor. 16:19). He urged Euodia and Syntyche to be of one mind (Phil. 4:2) and commended Lois and Eunice (2 Tim. 1:5) and nine other faithful women (Rom. 16).

One of the most outstanding of these women was Priscilla who, with her husband, hosted the church and also instructed Apollos when he was not fully informed regarding the Way (Acts 18:26). Out of six instances in which the names of Aquila and Priscilla appear, Priscilla assumes preeminence four times and the instance of their expounding to Apollos was one of those times.

Paul said for women to be submissive to their husbands immediately after he had said that all the members of the congregation ought to submit themselves to one another: male and female (Eph. 5:21). And he said husbands should love their wives as Christ loved and gave himself for the church (5:25). If love is self-giving, is it not also submitting? In Galatians 5:13, Paul said to all Christians, not just women, "by love serve one another."

So, even though he made the husband the head of his wife, he made all Christians submissive to each other. To quote Maston,

It possibly should be added that Ephesians 5 implies that the relation of the Christian husband and wife should be on such a high and holy plane that it would be an appropriate symbol of the relation of Christ and his church, with Christ as the head and the church as his body. In 1 Corinthians Paul said, 'The head of every man is Christ, the head of woman is her husband, and the head of Christ is God' (11:3). Everyone, even Christ, has a head or someone over him. This implies that there must be some order, even where two who basically are equal before God, are living together as husband and wife. There at least must be some distribution of responsibility and certain distinctive functions for each to perform.[6]

Women as Deacons

Depending upon the translation given for *diakonos* describing Phoebe in Romans 6:1, she was a deacon or a servant. It is interesting to observe how different translators deal with that word which occurs so frequently in the New Testament. In twenty instances of Paul's usage of *diakonos*, *The Bible in Today's English Version* (TEV) translates it consistently as "servant" except in 1 Timothy 3:8,12 where the word is translated "helper." The translation *deacon* does not occur. *The New English Bible* (NEB) is not consistent. Where Phoebe becomes a "fellow-Christian," Paul becomes a "minister" (Eph. 3:7; Col. 1:23), and the officers in 1 Timothy 3:8,12 become "deacons." Other translations are used in other places. The Revised Standard Version makes Phoebe a "deaconess," Paul a "minister," and the officers in 1 Timothy 3 "deacons." In Philippians 1:1, the bishops and deacons of the church are saluted without specifying male and/or female. The *Amplified Bible* (Amp.) makes Phoebe a "deaconess" and *The Living Bible, Paraphrased* (TLB) makes her a "dear Christian woman." Helen Barrett Montgomery, the only female translator, most frequently uses the word *minister*, even for Phoebe *(The New Testament in Modern English)*. In Philippians 1:1 and 1 Timothy 3:8,12, she uses "deacon" and in 1 Thessalonians 3:2, she calls Timothy "God's fellow worker." With reference to deacons in 1 Timothy 3, she gives a footnote, "The office of deaconess is later than the New Testament. Deacons were both male and female in the apostolic church."[7] The King James Version prefers to think of Phoebe as a "servant" while Paul and Tychicus and Timothy are all "ministers" (Eph. 3:7; 6:21; 1 Thess. 3:2).

It is possible that the translators since the 1600s have helped to perpetuate the idea that Phoebe could not possibly have been a deacon, even though the masculine form of the word is used to describe her. It is also possible that the translators have simply reflected their culture rather than be fair and consistent in their translation of the word *diakonos*. Another point needs to be made regarding 1 Timothy 3 where the qualifications of deacons are spelled out. Verse 11 interrupts the requirements of deacons to say, "Likewise *gunaikos.*" Most translators have chosen to call them "wives," but the insertion would be more sensible if they were women deacons. J. B. Moody, writing in 1910, cites a commentary which says:

"there is no reason that special rules should be laid down as to the wives of deacons, and not also to those of bishops. Moreover, if the wives of deacons were meant, there seems no reason for the omission of 'their,' which is not in the Greek. Also the Greek for 'even so' or 'like manner' denotes a transition to another class of persons."[8]

One further observation needs to be made regarding Phoebe. Not only did Paul call her a *diakonos* but he also called her a *prostatis*. This is the only time the noun is used in the New Testament. In the Greek translation of the Old Testament, the word occurs as "rulers" (1 Chron. 27:31; 29:6), "officers" (2 Chron. 8:10; 24:11). The verb form appears in the New Testament as rule (Rom. 12:8; 1 Tim. 3:4,5,12; 5:17) and "are over you" (1 Thess. 5:12). In all these instances the descriptions are ruler or manager or officer or overseer and yet Phoebe (Rom. 16:1-2) is only a "helper" (RSV, Amp.) or a "good friend" (TEV, NEB) or a "succourer" (KJV).

The Present Day

Even though Paul said in Galatians 3:28 that there is no difference between male and female for we are all one in Christ Jesus, still women have suffered discrimination in our churches. As Maston points out,

Some men as well as an increasing number of women have become conscious of the inequities suffered by women in most if not all of our churches. In churches where women frequently considerably outnumber the men, they have little voice in determining the church's programs and policies. They seldom hold a place of significant leadership responsibility in the work of the church. Even if they are represented on committees they are usually on a committee of minor importance, such as the Flower Committee, or as a minority member of a major committee. As teachers they are restricted to the teaching of children and women. There are comparable limitations for women in the work of the denomination.[9]

Women have fared slightly better in denominations other than Southern Baptist from the standpoint of ordination as pointed out by William and Priscilla Proctor.

At this writing (1976) there are an estimated 5,000 ordained women in the country. Among the top ten Christian churches in the United States, the United Methodist Church boasts the largest number of ordained women—about 500. Second is the United Presbyterian Church with 189. Since they opened up ordination to women in 1970, the Lutheran Church of America has ordained 24 women and the American Lutheran Church 5. The twelve-million-member Southern Baptist Convention, which is the largest Protestant denomination in the country, has only about 15 ordained women. By contrast, two relatively small denominations, the United Church of Christ and the American Baptist Convention, have a high proportion of women clergy: the United Church of Christ has more than 350 ordained women and the American Baptists about 150. But many of these women who have full pastoral powers on paper are finding they cannot get satisfactory preaching jobs.[10]

In a resource paper which Maston prepared for the Christian Life Commission (SBC), he made the following suggestions:

1. Southern Baptists need to be more concerned and informed about ERA and the women's liberation movement in general.
2. Churches and church leaders ought to realize that "equal pay for equal work" applies to women employees of local churches and denominational agencies and institutions.
3. Christian men and women are equal before God (Gal. 3:28). They should recognize, however, that generally speaking their abilities differ and hence they have some distinctive functions to perform without feeling superior or inferior to the other.
4. Southern Baptists should study the Scriptures concerning women, giving careful attention not only to the teachings of Jesus and Paul concerning women but also their relations to women.
5. The ordination of women as deacons (deaconesses) or ministers is a local church decision. A church considering such action should study, among other things, ordination in the Scriptures.
6. Qualified women should be elected to serve on church and denominational staffs without discrimination.
7. More qualified women should be selected to serve on the boards of state and Southern Baptist Convention agencies and institutions.[11]

Southern Baptists have been encouraged through the years to maintain awareness of human rights by the Christian Life Commission and by outstanding committed Christians such as Maston. At the meeting of the Southern Baptist Convention in Atlanta in 1978, resolutions were passed which urged the constituency to fight for human rights for blacks, the poor, women, the elderly, and others. More women were elected to Convention boards than in the past, although female representation still only totals about 19 out of 216 positions filled at the Atlanta meeting. May we in the future become leaders rather than lagging followers on behalf of the rights of all people whom God created and for whom Christ died.[12]

Notes

1. Letha Scanzoni and Nancy Hardesty, *All We're Meant To Be* (Waco: Word Books, 1974), pp. 56 f.

2. Rosemary R. Ruether, *New Woman New Earth* (New York: Seabury Press, 1975), p. 65.

3. T. B. Maston, 20 September 1973, Broadman Ministers' Tape, Baptist Sunday School Board, Nashville, Tennessee.

4. Constance F. Parvey, "The Theology and Leadership of Women in the New Testament," in Rosemary R. Ruether, ed., *Religion and Sexism* (New York: Simon and Schuster, 1974), p. 124.

5. Scanzoni and Hardesty, *All We're Meant To Be*, p. 37.

6. Maston, Broadman Ministers' Tape.

7. Helen Barrett Montgomery, trans., *The New Testament in Modern English* (Philadelphia: Judson Press, 1924), p. 566.

8. J. B. Moody, *Women in the Churches* (Martin, Tenn.: Hall-Moody Institute, 1910), p. 103.

9. Maston, Broadman Ministers' Tape.

10. Priscilla and William Proctor, *Women in the Pulpit* (Garden City: Doubleday and Co., Inc., 1976), p. 21.

11. T. B. Maston, "Ethical Issues: 1978 and Beyond" (Nashville: The Christian Life Commission of the Southern Baptist Convention), p. 3.

12. Maston has not discussed the subject of women in the systematic way. However, in several of his books he does lay down principles regarding Christian relationships that would be relevant to this subject.

Citizenship

Julian Bridges

It is often said that there are no two areas which are more controversial than religion and politics. When the two are discussed together, there is often an emotional explosion. Not so in the writing and thinking of T. B. Maston.

Maston's writings reveal an uncanny ability on his part to deal with delicate issues in an unusually thought-provoking but tactful manner. In the judgment of the present writer, Maston's masterful tact is a result of maturity, experience, and insight into various issues related to the two topics discussed in this chapter. His evaluations of religion and politics avoid extreme positions, often assumed by writers with less wisdom.

A Balance Between Dyads

One distinctive of T. B. Maston's writing is his dyadic-type thinking. Examples of this emphasis are his frequent discussions of such topics as personal and social ethics, positive and negative morality, evangelism and social concern, worship and service, and decisions regarding right and wrong.

In the areas of Christian citizenship and political participation, Maston's readers soon become aware of a desire on his part to strike a balance between opposites or counterparts of a common theme. Conservatism and liberalism, civil obedience and disobedience, order and justice, local and state responsibilities, national and international commitments, and the relationship between church and state—all of these and other topics are dealt with effectively by suggesting that both parts of the dyad should always be kept under consideration. Neither should be neglected completely, and, where necessary, conciliation rather than conflict should be the dominant, overriding theme.

Without compromising what ought to be accomplished under certain sociopolitical conditions, Maston is able to stimulate thinking on both sides of an issue and yet demonstrate a "love for all the brethen." Perhaps this is a primary reason that he has been able to speak prophetically yet patiently and often successfully to Southern Baptists and others for over a half century. Often employing the Socratic, interrogative form of writing, he has been able both as a peacemaker (Matt. 5:9) and one who exhibits "zeal" (John 2:17) to challenge his readers to act on vitally important political issues through the years.

Recently the Christian Life Commission (SBC) asked Maston to prepare a resource paper which would serve as an overview of contemporary ethical issues.[1] Before he discusses particular issues in the paper, Maston entitles the first section of the paper "Need for Balance." Typical of the tenor of his writing and the spirit of his speaking on political and religious issues is his view on the subject of compromise.

Compromise does not do any serious damage to the integrity of an individual or a group so long as the end attained is greater or more significant than the sacrifice that was made. This is particularly true when the end could not have been attained without the compromise.[2]

Characteristics of Christian Citizenship

Any consideration of T. B. Maston's political ethic should include at least a brief synopsis of his concept of what a Christian citizen should be.

First, Christian citizenship is a *comprehensive* task. The citizenship is both secular and sacred, both temporal and eternal. "The Christian is a citizen of two worlds—this world and the next world; of two kingdoms—the kingdom of Caesar, and the kingdom of Christ."[3]

Christian citizenship is a comprehensive task also in that it is worldwide and all-inclusive in scope. In commenting on Christ's Great Commission (Matt. 28:19-20 and other texts), Maston states incisively, *"All* of the children of God are to go to *all* the world with *all* of the Gospel."[4] By the last phrase he means that Christians are to evangelize and are to obey all that Jesus has commanded us, including his teachings on being a citizen *in* the world, though not *of* the world (John 17:15).

Christian citizenship encompasses political life at all levels. "As a citizen of this world, he (the Christian) is a citizen of his local community, county, state, nation, and the broader human community."[5] The Christian faith is to be applied to the totality of life. Biblical teaching is as broad as life itself. "The God we worship is the sovereign God of the universe, the God of the street as well as of the sanctuary."[6]

Secondly, Christian citizenship is a *challenging* task. It demands that the believer be an informed, intelligent citizen. One is reminded of the statement of Karl Barth to his theological students that the Christian today must face the modern world with the Bible in one hand and a newspaper in the other. The Christian must know what is happening in his world. An effective Christian citizen must have at least a measure of understanding of social, economic, political, moral, and religious trends and issues. He should be alert to facts such as the emergence of phenomena like the Third World, human rights, world hunger, war and peace, the energy crisis, and other issues of international scope. Examples of national and local problems are poverty and welfare, crime and punishment, family life, the status of women, older adults, sex and sex relations, pornography, the mass media, alcohol and alcoholism, racial and ethnic relations, church and state, economic systems, biomedical ethics, and the Christian life-style.[7] Although no one can be an authority in more than two or three of these complex areas, the Christian should try to maintain an interest in all areas of ethical concern where the teachings of Christ can be applied. The intelligent Christian citizen needs also to understand the nature of three contemporary movements: Communism, effective materialism, and secularism.

Christian citizenship is challenging because it requires a proper historical perspective, and this obviously necessitates considerable study. Maston states: "In a very real sense we can never understand anything fully unless we understand it historically . . . . We cannot sense the direction in which the world is now moving unless we have some insight into the route it has traveled."[8]

Thirdly, Christian citizenship is a *constructive* task. It is basically positive and optimistic because it is based upon the sovereignty and supremacy of God. God will have the last word. He will win the ultimate victory in the affairs—all affairs—of this world. The Christian citizen will try to maintain a transcendent perspective concerning all that occurs in his world, seeking always to catch step with Christ as he moves among his creation and extends his rule and reign in the hearts of men and in all human societies of the world.

The Christian citizen will work constructively for a synthesis of conservative theology and social concern and action in society. He will seek to apply the spirit and teachings of Jesus to all social institutions of society—to the political, economic, educational, and domestic (to the family), as well as to the religious and moral areas of life. The Christian citizen will emphasize ethics as well as evangelism, works as well as faith, social service as well as individual ministry.[9]

Finally, Christian citizenship is to be just that—*Christian*. The believer in Christ is to be a *Christian* employer or employee, a *Christian* family member, a *Christian* student, a *Christian* voter or politician. Maston says that "in all the other relations of his life, the word 'Christian' is to precede and to be underscored in front of every role he plays in life."[10]

Some Specific Aspects of Citizenship

Government as such is crdained of God (Rom. 13:1) and obtains from him its authority (John 19:11) and its purpose to maintain order and accomplish good in the world (Rom. 13:2-4). Christians should respect political office holders (1 Pet. 2:13-17) and pray for them (1 Tim. 2:1-3). They should also pay their taxes (Rom. 13:6-7).

Maston believes the New Testament teaches that the Christian who opposes a government's position on a matter should ordinarily do so with a passive or "suffering" resistance, rather than one of hostile rebellion. "The way of victory for the Christian and the Church is 'the way of the Cross.' "[11] The church's role, in those countries where it can be exercised, is to warn the state against its legitimate limits, particularly if it seeks to persecute those who seek to proclaim the gospel (Acts 5:29; Rev. 13:1-2).[12]

Concerning the issue of *human rights* today, a number of suggestions are made by Maston:[13] (1) The United States should seek to be impartial in stressing human rights in countries which are its political friends as well as its political foes; (2) Christians should support political leaders in this country and elsewhere who champion the cause of human rights nationally and internationally; (3) nations should be strongly urged to adhere to the Declaration on Human Rights of the United Nations or to similar statements located in many of their own national constitutions; (4) states and political bodies should be reminded that they do not create or grant human rights; they merely recognize and proclaim them; (5) Christians should insist on equal treatment of all persons, without preference to color, culture, or life condition.

(6) Human rights of citizens include the right to vote, to be treated with respect and dignity, to be able to disagree with those in authority without repression, and to have a job and opportunities for education without discrimination; (7) such rights entail accompanying responsibilities and are limited by the rights of others; (8) Christians should try to help all people understand that basic human rights are rooted in biblical concepts such as the intrinsic worth and dignity of all individuals, which is based upon the belief that persons are created in the image of God; and (9) we cannot be Christian and remain aloof from the needs for granting greater equality of opportunity in our nation and in other nations of the world.

With respect to *the Third World* (the relatively neutral nations, largely still in economic development), the following statements are paraphrased from Maston's views:

(1) We, in the West, should recognize that there is considerable shift of power from the more highly industrialized nations to the nations with abundant natural resources.

(2) Most of the nations of the Third World stand, in political philosophy, somewhere between communism and the [developed] nations of the West.

(3) Christians should encourage our political leaders to shift our nation's foreign policy to a more favorable position in relation to the developing nations.

(4) It must be remembered that the vast majority of Southern Baptist missionaries serve in countries of the Third World. The revolutionary movement of the masses that led to self-government was the product, to some degree, of the message of the Christian missionaries. Some of the basic concepts of the Christian faith are very revolutionary. These include the fact that people of all races and cultures are created in the image of God, that Christ died for all, that God is no respector of persons.

(5) Christians in general but missionaries in particular need to make a distinction between the legitimate grievances of the masses and the methods they may at times use in seeking the alleviation of these grievances.[14]

Regarding *world hunger* and *the energy crisis,* it is impossible to separate the political aspects from the economic and social aspects of these complex problems. An estimated one-half billion to a billion people are currently hungry in our world. Senator Mark Hatfield has said that this fact "is the greatest threat to this nation and the stability of the whole world."[15] Freedom from hunger is certainly one of the fundamental freedoms of man. Government leaders should be urged to formulate programs that will reduce and ultimately eliminate hunger in the world. Included in these programs should be the sharing of means of population planning, industrial development, and agricultural advancement. Since one third of the world's people have an annual per capita income of $100 or less, while that of our citizens is approximately $5,600, means should be found to more equally distribute the wealth of our world. This will undoubtedly mean some sacrifice on the part of American Christians and others in this country.[16]

The president of the United States has said that the shortage of energy in the world is "the most crucial issue of our day . . . the moral equivalent of war."[17] It is calculated that air conditioners alone in the United States expend each year as much energy as the 800 million people of China. World peace may be at stake as balances of power shift toward those countries which still contain relatively large reserves of energy-producing, natural resources. Political leaders should be encouraged to develop energy conservation programs but see to it that the poor are not penalized further by being made to pay unfair amounts of their income for energy needs. Christian citizens, churches, and denominational organizations and agencies should lead the way in energy conservation, setting the example of a simpler life-style.[18]

Law and order on one hand and individual and social justice on the other must be kept in proper balance. At times law and order can break down but possibly because justice has been neglected or denied for certain citizens. The past and continued struggle in this country for civil rights and equality of opportunity is a case in point. Maston states:

> Extremists at both ends of the struggle have contributed to the breakdown of respect for law . . . . Some of those who now cry loudest for "law and order" are the very ones who sought in every possible way a few years ago to evade compliance with the courts' decisions regarding desegregation. They were and some still are particularly harsh in their criticisms of the United States Supreme Court. Some have even accused the Court of following the Communist line. Such contributes to a breakdown not only of respect for the Court but also of law in general.[19]

On the other hand, some who seek to secure justice for themselves and others use methods which reduce respect for law and order as such. To do so is to ultimately hurt rather than help the cause of justice. There should never be a complete loss of respect for those who seek to enforce the law and maintain order.

However, some persons would want to maintain laws because they give them an unfair advantage over other disadvantaged citizens. In this case such laws will not be respected by those to whom justice is denied, and order ultimately tends to be undermined. May the majority who have the power be just as concerned about justice as they are about enforcing law and order. If not, such law and order will at best be unstable.[20] Maston concludes his thoughts on this topic with a significant statement:

> The relative importance of order and justice are determined by the situation. In a time of rapid change and revolution, such as the contemporary period, justice should be given primacy. This can be done without a reckless abandonment of law and order.[21]

Contemporary *civil disobedience* is a difficult and delicate subject with which to deal. Some have tried to convert Christ himself into a political and religious revolutionary. There is no doubt about his teachings being revolutionary in his day and today. If Christians and others applied the principles he taught and practiced, our world would experience unbelievable and unprecedented revolution. However, Jesus was not revolutionary in the sense that he sought to overthrow the political system of his day. Even his opposition to the religious leaders was directed against false interpretations of religion rather than against the faith itself.[22]

On several occasions the followers of Christ found it necessary to "obey God rather than men" (Acts 5:29). The specific instances were related to the preaching of the gospel, but the biblical statement does contain a general principle. However, any civil disobedience should be carried out regretfully, in such a way as not to undermine respect for authority and with the recognition that the state has the right to punish those who disobey its laws, though the latter may be unjust in the mind of the Christian. Maston's conclusions on this important matter are as follows:

> First, we cannot deny the right of nonviolent civil disobedience. On the other hand, we must conclude that much contemporary civil disobedience would have to be disapproved. This disapproval would be based primarily on the motive and particularly the spirit of the disobedience.
> Each civil disobedience incident or movement would have to be judged on its own merits.[23]

An international application of the above ideas on civil disobedience can be made to the restless masses of the world who are struggling for their freedoms—politically, economically, socially, and religiously. As Christians and Americans we should be sympathetic and supportive of most of their goals, although we may have to disapprove and even oppose some of the methods which may be used by some to try to attain the goals. Let us not forget that, as Americans, we once fought for our own political and economic independence. Nevertheless, as Christians we are always to do everything possible to live in peace with everyone (Rom. 12:18 ff.). This would include working with and through international organizations, such as the United Nations, as imperfect as they may be.

Voting is a highly significant part of the political process in democracies such as that of the United States. The Christian citizen will seek to be as informed as possible about all of the candidates for office in order that he may exercise his franchise intelligently. Not to vote is to surrender one's choice to those who do. It is to approve what others decide for you. It often means maintaining the status quo when there is a need for change or permitting relative chaos when stability could have been achieved.

Maston feels that Christians should vote primarily for the candidate rather than for the party he may represent. Some Christians may serve so actively in a political party that it will be almost impossible for them to disassociate themselves from it and cast their vote for nonparty candidates, but most Christians can and should do so at certain times. Loyalty to Christ and the good of the country should come above allegiance to a party under just any conditions. By being independent, voters have the opportunity to contribute to challenging both major parties to provide clean administrations, rather than allowing corruption to creep in. Also issues, more than labels or personalities, will influence the independent, conscientious Christian voter. The child of God should seek truth and honesty first of all in politics, although these may never be found to perfection. Finally, differences in political views should never be a test of fellowship between believers in Christ.[24]

One-issue voting is a common mistake of many misguided Christians. If they discover that a candidate belongs to a particular denomination or believes a certain way on one issue, they are persuaded to vote for him. There are usually many issues at stake in an election, whether it be at the local, state, or national level. The Christian should not rest until he has informed himself on as many of these as possible and learned the various candidates' views on each major issue. The Christian can consult those whom he holds in high esteem as to their political opinions. Then, before God in prayer he should make his own decision.

We should also be careful that we are not mislead by political propaganda or rhetoric into thinking that because a candidate employs certain moral or religious phrases in a very general manner that he is expressing deep conviction. Such speech may more honestly reflect political convenience. The ability, training, experience, maturity, and integrity of the candidate concerning the issues relevant to the office he is seeking are the major reasons for earning our vote and support.[25]

Issues Related to Religious Liberty

There are three basic theories regarding the relationship which may exist between church and state. Maston refers to these as identification, domination, and separation.[26] Baptists and the majority of Americans have historically chosen the latter theory as one which permits the greatest freedoms for the church, the state, and the individual. It is not by accident that the United States provides for its citizens as great or greater freedom than any other country in the world. One of the primary reasons is because of this nation's doctrine of separation between church and state.

Maston reasons that the separation theory preserves religious liberty, and, in turn, religious liberty or freedom is foundational for all of man's freedoms. If a society does not respect religious freedom, there is no assurance that other freedoms will be respected.[27] The fullest expression of religious freedom includes other freedoms: assembly and association, propaganda or press, civil participation and speech, conscience or belief, and independence from control by the state and protection of the state from control by the church.[28] Maston cautions: "The defense of religious liberty is not optional for those who love the democratic way of life. It means that as goes religious freedom, so will go all the other basic freedoms of life."[29]

A number of specific issues related to religious liberty could be discussed. Examples of these are: Should public schools be used for any sectarian purposes (serving as meeting places for religious worship, baccalaureate sermons, Bible reading, praying)? Should the government provide services to parochial schools (such as free transportation and textbooks)? Should America have a civil religion (one that identifies God with American patriotism, Southern subculture with biblical teaching)? Can churches work together with local, state, or the federal government in areas of social, health, and welfare ministry without violating the principle of separation of church and state?

Although space here does not permit a treatment of the issues mentioned above, two related issues should be dealt with at least briefly. The first of these is *government aid to church-related institutions.*[30] Guidelines urgently need to be developed to aid Baptist and other denominational agencies in knowing just how far they can go in accepting government aid in any form (loans, grants) and retain their distinctly Christian character. Should such aid probably only be accepted in cases where "service has clearly been rendered" the government and rejected under all other circumstances? What is the precise meaning of the preceding phrase in quotation marks?

The second issue of urgent concern where Baptists should seize the initiative to act is the area of *taxation of churches.*[31] Should church or denominationally-owned properties, which are not used strictly for worship or educational purposes, be free from real estate taxes? "Tax-free holdings of churches, hospitals, universities, and other benevolent institutions have contributed to fiscal disasters . . . like that in New York City, where 41 percent of the real property is exempt."[32] Should publishing houses, assembly grounds, church parsonages, parking lots that are leased during the week, unused land, and other revenue-producing property not be taxed? "Sale and lease-back" transactions should certainly be taxed. This is where an individual or company gives a business to a church or denominational agency to avoid paying these taxes, and then leases it back to the original operators.[33] Maston says:

Any time an institution, through apartments or housing, becomes competitive with legitimate business interests in the community, it should pay the same taxes as its competitors. Certainly any property held for investment purposes should be taxed.[34]

Local churches should even pay something voluntarily to local and country governments for the police and fire protection they are now receiving and which must be paid for by all citizens, some of whom are not Christians or members of their churches. Thus, Southern Baptists should study in depth and act on these and other matters related to religious liberty before they are perhaps compelled to do so by the government.[35]

Finally, Christian citizenship calls for actively participating in the political process, from the local precinct level to encouraging the most talented and dedicated young people to enter politics as a divine calling.

Notes

1. T. B. Maston, "Ethical Issues: 1978 and Beyond" (Nashville: Christian Life Commission of the Southern Baptist Convention, 1978).

2. T. B. Maston, *The Conscience of a Christian* (Waco: Word Books, 1971), p. 143.

3. T. B. Maston, *The Christian, the Church, and Contemporary Problems* (Waco: Word Books, 1968), p. 39.

4. Ibid., p. 59.   5. Ibid., p. 39.

6. Ibid., p. 47.

7. Maston deals briefly with each of these issues in "Ethical Issues: 1978 and Beyond," pp. 1-18.

8. Maston, *Contemporary Problems*, pp. 42-43.

9. Ibid., pp. 39-50 passim.   10. Ibid., p. 52.

11. T. B. Maston, *Biblical Ethics: A Biblical Survey* (New York: World Publishing Co., 1967), p. 239.

12. Ibid., p. 240.   13. Maston, "Ethical Issues," p. 15.

14. Ibid., pp. 14-15.   15. Ibid., p. 10.

16. Ibid.   17. Ibid., p. 11.

18. Ibid., pp. 11-12, 17-18.

19. Maston, *The Conscience of a Christian*, p. 129.

20. Ibid., pp. 129-130.   21. Ibid.

22. Ibid., p. 131.   23. Ibid., p. 132.

24. Ibid., pp. 133-134.   25. Ibid., pp. 135-136.

26. T. B. Maston, *Christianity and World Issues* (New York: The Macmillan Company, 1957), pp. 215-224.

27. Discussed by Maston in "Religious Liberty," an unpublished paper presented to The Christian Life Workshop, Southwestern Baptist Theological Seminary, 1972, pp. 5-7.

28. Maston, *Christianity and World Issues*, pp. 233-234.

29. Ibid., p. 236.

30. Maston discusses this topic in an unpublished paper, "Issues Today," 1969, pp. 8-12.

31. Ibid., pp. 12-21.

32. T. B. Maston, "Church-State Tax Study Proposed," *Baptist Standard*, July 21, 1978, p. 4.

33. Maston, *The Conscience of a Christian*, p. 96.

34. Ibid.

35. Maston, "Church-State Tax Study Proposed," p. 4.

War and Peace

Browning Ware

To do creditable research one must go to original sources. The basic source for the thought of T. B. Maston is the man himself. His life is also the most penetrating commentary on his speaking, teaching, and writing. Few persons have focused life and work so keenly as he. Who he is and what he thinks may be interchanged without damage to either.

While researching Maston's written material on war and peace, I reflected on the man. Comprehension of his thought is enriched by exposure to Maston's character and personality. He is simple without being simplistic, reserved without being passive, disciplined without being rigid, confident without being presumptuous; and he is fiercely loyal to Jesus Christ. I have never encountered a person who is more distinctly an individual and less individualistic. His investment of life and work has been for effectiveness rather than effect.

Maston lives, thinks, teaches, and writes as a sympathetic dialectician. He is almost painfully careful in his efforts to understand and to provide a platform for contending points of view. His own conclusions are presented humbly but with conviction. However, a student should be hungry when he comes to Maston's table because this polite professor does not force feed his beliefs.

As a Christian dialectician, Maston maintains tension between differing expressions of thought in order to expose both their error and truth. All positions, including his own, stand under the greater tension of the sovereignty of God and its expression as the will of God. The dynamic tension between God's ideal and the human situation is the key to understanding all of Maston's thought. The lives of Christians are lived in this climate of positive tension. Their decision making is informed by circumstances of the immediate situation but should be directed by conscientious effort to know and do God's will.

War

War continues to be a critical problem in the world. The questions surrounding war and peace assumed new ethical dimensions with the spreading of Christian faith in the Roman empire. Despite the establishment of Christianity as an official religion by Constantine and participation of Christians in holy wars during the centuries, there has been a growing uneasiness about the Christian's involvement in war. T. B. Maston believes an intensifying crisis resides in the possibility of contemporary war. In "Ethical Issues: 1978 and Beyond," he suggests three reasons for this crisis: First, a sectional war, particularly in the Middle East, would be difficult to restrict to the nations of the area. Our nation's painful engagement in Vietnam is a reminder of the need of wisdom in this problem. Also, the emergence of a world energy crisis aggravates tensions which involve the Middle East. Second, the armaments race is being accelerated. An increasing number of nations are engaged in the production and purchase of weapons. Third, "the proliferation of nuclear weapons poses a threat to the whole world . . . . One prediction is that by 1985, forty nations will have nuclear capability; a decade later this number is expected to increase to 100."[1]

Since a brief period in the service of his country during World War I, Maston has demonstrated growing discernment in the complexity of a Christian's relationship to war. He refers to himself as "a limited conscientious objector" in World War II. At no time has he advocated an absolutist position. He contends equally for the rights of the "conscientious participant" and the "conscientious objector."

Maston explains the evil of war in a good creation as an accommodation of God's intentional will. Wrestling with the Old Testament's relationship with war, he sees a twofold picture. "One is a dark, rather foreboding picture which is interpreted by many as being out of harmony with the nature and character of the God revealed by Jesus Christ. On the other hand, we get at least a glimpse into the ultimate if not original purpose of God, which is strikingly similar to the revelation of God in the life and teachings of Jesus."[2]

"An objective reading of the New Testament," according to Maston, "will lead one to conclude that there are no specific teachings in it concerning war and the Christian's relationship to it. War is not explicitly justified or forbidden."[3] After examining the New Testament teachings used in support of both pacifism and war, Maston concedes, "What one finds . . . depends largely on what one wants to find."[4]

Maston finds that both Testaments acknowledge war as part of the human situation; however, they do not accept war as God's ultimate intention. At best, war is God's adjustment to man's sin; at worst, war is man's gross sin against God's best.

Contemporary war continues to be an accommodation between God's ideal and immediate situations. Speaking of Third World countries, Maston points out that "the revolutionary movement of the masses that led to self-government was the product, to some degree, of the messages of the Christian missionaries."[5] What a candid illustration of the irony of the Christian's predicament. Nevertheless, Maston insists that "distinction should be made between legitimate grievances of the masses and the methods they may use at times in seeking alleviation of these grievances."[6] Maston resists an easy accommodation which seizes upon war as the only answer to injustice.

Emerging in the Old Testament are hints of God's original intention: King David, who had "waged great wars," was forbidden to build the Temple (1 Chron. 22:8, RSV). The prayer of the psalmist was that God would "scatter the peoples who delight in war." (Ps. 68:30, RSV). Finally, Isaiah prophecied, "For to us a child is born, to us a son is given; and the government will be upon his shoulder, and his name will be called Wonderful Counselor, Mighty God, Everlasting Father, Prince of Peace" (Isa. 9:5-6, RSV).

Both God's accommodation to sin and the victory of his original intention are demonstrated in the life, crucifixion, and resurrection of Jesus. Any Christian perspective on war and peace must view these issues through the cross of Jesus; any posture of pacifism or nonpacifism must attempt seriously to conform to the spirit of Christ.

Peace

Few persons have exposed the essential relationship of Christian faith and its application to all life as has T. B. Maston in over fifty years of speaking, teaching, and writing. Neither theology without ethical application nor ethics without theological foundation can embrace the Christian life. Faith without works is childless; faith needs application and expression. And works without faith is orphaned; works need source and direction. For Maston the two must be inseparably linked if they are to represent the revelation of God in Jesus Christ.

Peace is a big word for Maston. Peace reflects God's nature and will; it also represents the application of God's will in human life. Maston uses the concept of peace in an elastic sense in order to indicate varying degrees of harmony with God's intention.

Furthermore, he employs the term as does the Bible. Peace may be the image of individual communion with God, harmonious human relationships, absence of violence among nations, and the ultimate fulfillment of God's will. Therefore, peace may be experienced immediately and in process by individuals and groups but never perfectly within history. As long as sin exists in persons, the hope for peace will race ahead of its appropriation. "Nevertheless, the fact that peace is hard to attain does not mean that the hope for it should be surrendered as the idle dream of visionaries. Such a surrender certainly should not characterize Christians."[7]

In the Old Testament Maston sees war as God's accommodation to man's sin and peace as God's intention. Even the dark picture of Old Testament wars is framed by the coming golden age of peace (Isa. 2:4; Mic. 4:3). Furthermore, God's nature and character is increasingly portrayed as that of the peacemaker.

Peace, in the New Testament, is internalized and fulfilled beyond its expressions in Old Testament life. What God had promised is fulfilled in Jesus Christ. However, until Christ is enthroned in the lives of all persons, peace will be experienced more individually than corporately. Even within stress and violence, the Christian may be at peace. Although this peace is satisfying, the Christian cannot be satisfied. His life is stretched by the tension of God's desire of peace for all persons. Although personally at peace in an unpeaceful world, the Christian must work to create peace in corporate structures of life.

Complete peace will always be elusive. Individuals and nations may experience peace in varying degrees, but "wars and rumors of wars" will continue. Maston observes nothing in history, the Bible, or the contemporary scene to modify his certainty about the probability of war. He insists, however, that the apparent impossibility of complete peace is not the major concern of the Christian. Doing God's will is his highest calling and also the greatest contribution the Christian can make to peace. "There may be many defeats; but if we take the long look—and the Christian should always include eternity in his perspective—we can and should believe in the victory of love over hate, of good over evil."[8]

Strategy

How can the Christian do the will of God in a world of war? Maston's strategy emerges from the tension of two contending realities: God's ideal and the actual situation. These extremes create a "Procrustean bed" in which the Christian's decision making is stretched. At the head of the bed is the magnetism of God's intention and at its foot is the pull of concrete circumstances and mixed motivations.

Maston desires no simple standoff between these extremes; he does not call for easy compromise. Rather, the Christian is to do the will of God as well as he can apply it within the situation. The process suggests a type of situation ethics, although this is a term which Maston does not prefer. He differs radically with popular situation ethics in many ways, principally by his view of the sovereignty of God, by his acceptance of absolutes, and by his emphasis on God's ideal rather than the situation as the primary consideration in decision making.

Some theological basis stands behind every strategy in dealing with war and peace. This is true for pacifism and nonpacifism. Maston observes that it is difficult to discover whether pacifists and nonpacifists begin with theology or work out their theology to support their position.[9]

Interpretations of love, justice, and the cross of Jesus are usually significant in determining position as a pacifist or nonpacifist. "For the pacifist, love is primary, justice a derivative of love. Justice may be able to check and punish evil; love alone can overcome and redeem evil."[10] There is no doubt that love is superior to justice in the strategy of Christian pacifism; however, the two must not be divorced.

The position of the nonpacifists does not rest on the superiority of justice but upon its attainability. Maston agrees with Reinhold Niebuhr, William Temple, and Emil Brunner that love is ethically purer than justice; with them he questions whether a Christian love ethic can be applied effectively in human society. For the nonpacifist, justice may be the nearest approximation to love's pure ideal. Maston accepts the tension between love's ideal and its partial realization in justice, and he reluctantly agrees that the Christian may choose war as a means of attempting to attain justice.

Concepts of love and justice tend toward abstraction when they are left without application. Over against these categories stands the cross as God's concrete response to man's sin. In the cross God exercised both justice against sin and love for the sinner. Pacifists and nonpacifists appeal to the cross for support of their strategy about war; however, they emerge with radically different interpretations. "To the nonpacifist the cross reveals primarily the justice of God and God's condemnation of sin. To the pacifist the cross reveals primarily the love of God for man and God's method of overcoming sin."[11]

Therefore, the nonpacifist sees in the cross God's continuing controversy with the nations. War may be a legitimate reflection of God's judgment and justice. In contrast, the pacifist finds in the cross God's nonviolent response to man's sin. War is not in character with the cross.

Maston is empathetic with the agony of each position and its subsequent strategy. He refuses to take an absolutist position on either horn of the apparent dilemma. He is absolute, however, in his conviction that both justice and love are fully realized in the cross. He warns pacifists and nonpacifists to be more concerned about the will of God which they experience in the cross than about the strategics which they derive from their interpretations of the cross. Neither can fully understand God's strategy or his ultimate triumph. "We may not be able to see the victory of the cross in our individual lives; but if our lives are tied in with the purposes of God, then the price we pay today may be part of God's triumph tomorrow."[12]

Application

T. B. Maston's emphasis on the Christian conscience and its relationship to war is a significant feature of his applied Christian ethic. According to Maston, conscience is neither a special human faculty, such as sight or hearing, nor is it the voice of God within the individual. Conscience makes it possible for a person to hear God's voice, but it is not that voice. Rather, conscience is the "God-given sense of oughtness, a conviction that there is such a thing as right and wrong."[13]

The "sense of oughtness" is the moral constant in man's moral nature. The content of that oughtness is the changing factor, a moral variant. Because of many conditioning influences and contributors, conscience cannot be considered an inerrant guide. A restless conscience is an opportunity for moral advance but not a guarantee of it. In the non-Christian, this uneasiness expresses the anguish of both estrangement from God and a deep longing for him. The disturbed conscience of the Christian generally reflects tension created by increasing sensitivity to God's will.

Although Maston agrees that inerrancy of conscience cannot be maintained, he insists that the authority of the conscience must be protected. "What other sense of guidance is available to a man if he will not do what he considers right?"[14] This sense of oughtness, the inner capacity to do right and ability to respond to God's Spirit, must be authoritative for the individual. When the promptings of conscience are dulled from within or the intentions of conscience are abridged from without, the will of God for the individual is being resisted.

The call to war and the claims of conscience may create an agonizing tension within the individual. Maston organizes the responses to this tension under three main groups, while suggesting there are variations within each response.

The first response of the Christian conscience to war is participation as a matter of citizenship. The Christian's responsibility is to obey; conscience corresponds to the nation's call to arms. While conceding that the state may not be able to conform to the Christian ethic, Maston is critical of this posture: "Blind obedience by all citizens would eliminate all hope for moral and social progress."[15]

The second response accepts participation in war as the lesser of two evils. Those who hold this position recognize that many, if not most, of life's choices are not between pure good and obvious evil. Choices must be made in the gray area, with the intention to select a position of more good and less evil. To participate in war may be the decision.

Maston does not agree that war is a part of the natural order. Wars occur because of the violation by individuals and nations of God's laws. Therefore, he does not go easily into that gray night of easy concession to war. In a statement which reveals a more autobiographical tone than most of his writing, Maston states:

> Many Christians fail to see that one can hold to the lesser-of-two-evils theory, at least in one sense of the word, and still refuse to participate actively in war. He may recognize that he cannot escape some involvement in the sin of the world. He may not claim that his position is totally free from evil and sin. But, on the other hand, he may consistently argue that refusal to participate in war, for him involves less evil than participation.[16]

The third response refuses participation in war. This is the position of pacifism or conscientious objection. Maston correctly observes that there are many variations and subtleties in the posture of nonparticipation in war. These range all the way from absolute and unconditional refusal to degrees of limited service which stops short of taking human life. Another kind of conscientious objectors emerged during the war in Vietnam. These were *selective objectors* to the Vietnamese conflict. Some of them had little philosophical or theological basis for refusal; they simply did not want to interrupt their lives. Others rejected this particular war as being unnecessary, illegal, immoral, or on the more traditional grounds of conscientious objection. When refusal to participate in any war represents sincere objection of conscience, Maston believes the right of the conscientious objector should be supported and defended.

Maston believes that the first and third response to war, previously suggested, tend toward unrealism for the Christian. On one hand, unquestioned participation in war is irresponsible to the claims of Christ. On the other hand, the person who fails to be concerned about every aspect of national life, including war, is unresponsive to the claims of citizenship. And withdrawal from the demands of citizenship is almost impossible in this complex world.

T. B. Maston is a fervent advocate of the right of individual conscience. If Christians are consistent, they will respect and defend the right of the conscientious objector just as strongly as they insist on their own right to worship. For many years Maston has contended that the right of one sincere conscientious objector in a denomination of 10,000,000 members should be defended by the other 9,999,999. "To do less is to violate something basic in our Protestant way of life."[17]

Conclusion

During the writing of this chapter on T. B. Maston's thought, Carlyle Marney, another friend and mentor, died. My wife and I talked about these very different Christian giants. She asked what Marney's counsel to the Christian conscience might have been. I replied that Marney probably would have bellowed, "Rock the boat!"

She then inquired what Maston might say. I suggested that Maston would encourage each person to make his own thoughtful and prayerful decision. Then, quietly and firmly, Maston might say, "As for myself, I intend to bail and row."

Notes

1. T. B. Maston, "Ethical Issues: 1978 and Beyond," (Nashville. Christian Life Commission of the Southern Baptist Convention, 1978), p. 13.
2. T. B. Maston, *Christianity and World Issues* (New York: The Macmillan Company, 1957), p. 239.
3. Ibid., p. 241.   4. Ibid., p. 240.
5. Maston, "Ethical Issues," p. 15.   6. Ibid., p. 16.
7. Maston, *Christianity and World Issues*, p. 267.
8. Ibid., p. 287.   9. Ibid., p. 282.
10. Ibid.   11. Ibid., p. 285
12. Ibid., p. 287.   13. Ibid., p. 269.
14. Ibid., p. 271.   15. Ibid., p. 274.
16. Ibid., p. 279.
17. T. B. Maston, *The Conscience of a Christian* (Waco: Word Books, 1971), p. 140.

Economics and Daily Work

Ebbie Smith

"Most of the problems of the modern period are economic, to some degree, and some of the most perplexing of them are primarily economic."[1] These words reveal T. B. Maston's recognition of the overall importance of economic life and daily work. He also sees the necessity for Christian economic involvement if Christianity is to influence the lives of people. Maston says "the great moral principles of the Christian faith are germane to economic life and are of profound economic significance when properly understood and applied."[2]

He clearly perceives the vital role of economics in life and Christian principles in economics. As with all good biblical scholars, he is aware of and in touch with contemporary problems. He projects a statement of ethics that speaks biblically and consistently to contemporary needs with unfailing relevancy.

Basic Christian Principles Related to Economics

T. B. Maston's viewpoints on economic concerns grow out of and are controlled by certain basic concepts. Maston's economic ethic is based on his conviction that God is sovereign over all and concerned about every aspect of the individual's life as well as society's welfare. God's sovereignty and concern lend both responsibility and hope to efforts to influence economic life. Right relations to man and society are the inevitable and necessary derivative of man's relation to God.[3]

This conviction leads to Maston's statement that the church's message, which is germane to economic life, finds its central core in its doctrine of God and his relation to the world. Both man and economics must be studied in the light of God's nature and will. Maston is convinced that the economic order will function effectively only when people seek and do God's will in relation to economic practice and daily work.[4]

The important factor in any economic practice, program, or system relates to what it does to people.[5] Christian approaches to economics must follow Jesus' example of respect for personality.[6] Maston concludes that machines, profits, motives, property, and wealth must be evaluated on the basis of their effects on human life and personal dignity. "The test of the economic institution or system is not the quantity of goods but the quality of life it produces."[7]

The priority of persons relates directly to Maston's evaluation of Communism. He recognizes Communism's rapid progress in the world and the improved economic status it has brought to some. He clearly sees, however, that Communism has been and remains unable to fulfill its promises of equality and freedom. In reality Communism, a form of atheistic materialism, ultimately degrades people because it separates them from God. Communism exalts man but enslaves the individual. Based on the principle of the importance of persons, Maston rejects Communism because it cannot satisfy man's deepest needs and hungers or solve his fundamental economic problems. He rejects Communism less on economic grounds than because of its adverse affect on men, women, and children.[8]

Maston is convinced that God's people must be fully involved in applying the Christian message and spirit to economic problems. "If the Christian forces are interested in influencing the lives of people, they must be concerned with the economic relations and evaluations of these people and with the application of Christian moral ideals to the economic environment in which those people live."[9] In fact, he sees the only hope for lasting economic improvement to be recruiting an increasing number of committed Christians who will honestly apply biblical ideals to economic life and practice.[10]

Maston suggests a method whereby organized Christianity can influence economic thinking and practice. The church's most basic and distinctive task is that of bringing individuals into a vital, life-changing union with God. This new life in Christ must be translated into everyday Christian living. This translation to everyday living in the economic realm is best achieved by restricting Christian activities to general patterns and major goals. "The primary social task of the Christian forces is to set out clearly the general goals or ends of society but leave the technical methods to be used to attain those goals to the practical politician and the socially minded scientist and technician."[11]

Maston is equally convinced that the churches must maintain their independence, refusing to become identified with any particular economic class, system, or program.[12] He advises churches to avoid entangling alliances with economic and social movements.[13] Only a free church can effectively challenge the world in the direction of the Christian economic ideal.[14]

The church, thus, should be an independent critic and guide of the social and economic sector. In this way it maintans tension between biblical teaching and current practices.[15] By creating this holy discontent with things as they are, as compared to God's revealed will, the church can foster a burning desire to make the purposes of God a reality in the world and can provide direction to programs.[16]

Maston's economic ethic rests on the foundations of responsibility and love. "Power involves responsibility."[17] The goal and motive of individual and business economic activity should be service rather than profit. He is convinced that a permanent cure for economic ills will spring only from the practice of self-denial, the sacrifice of personal interests, and cross bearing. Private gain no longer should be the dominant motive in business. Service rather than dividends should be the supreme test of success. Businessmen should be socially motivated and accept responsibility for the power given them.[18]

Love and the cross principle of life constitute basic assumptions of Maston's economic ethic. The cross kind of life is the key to proper economic living. The "cross rather than the club" is to be the Christian method of serving in and the changing of economic structures.[19] Love entails doing good to and respecting the rights and value of all. It involves self-sacrifice for the benefit of others and is, therefore, a crowning virtue in economic life.[20]

The teachings of T. B. Maston on specific economic issues grow out of these basic convictions. These teachings can be divided into those which relate primarily to the individual and economic life and those which relate primarily to society and economic issues.

The Individual and Economic Life

Maston is convinced that economic factors such as property, money, work, and vocation have spiritual significance. "No one is a fully developed Christian until he has applied Christian principles to every area of his life."[21] Hence, a person's relationship to material goods and to the methods whereby such goods are acquired and used is a spiritual matter which affects and is affected by that person's relationship to God.

Maston recognizes the biblical principles of the right to private property. He also realizes that human ownership is not absolute. Christians must be aware of their stewardship responsibilities both to God and fellowman.[22] While the tithe is an integral part of this overall stewardship, tithing alone is not an adequate expression of one's dedication to God. Christians must view possessions as a trust.[23]

Property and wealth should always be subservient to human needs and welfare. Wealth achieves its greatest meaning when used for the welfare of the community. "Whatever property the Christian may have, little or much, should be used for God's glory and the common good."[24]

Maston believes that material things are of secondary consequence and never to be sought as ends. When one seeks first the kingdom of God—then the material will find its rightful place. While never depreciating wealth or property, Maston emphasizes the danger of riches. Riches are to be considered in relation to their value to the kingdom of God, for one cannot serve both God and money.[25]

God intends work for mankind. Work is not a result of man's temptation and the Fall. Maston considers work both a right and a duty. Since work is a right, he believes that unemployment is always an evil. Moreover, since work is a duty, people should labor rather than seeking to live on the work of others. Christians should consider work a way of cooperating with God in his creative activity.[26]

Maston places some restrictions on work. Making money is never to be the Christian's primary emphasis. Moreover, the teacher feels that Christians should engage in beneficial, honorable work and perform it honestly. Christians should avoid work that either compromises their influence or embarrasses the cause of Christ. They should also guard against any unjust, unfair, or unchristian practices. Christian honesty, according to Maston, includes full and honest work on the part of workers.[27]

Honorable, beneficial, and honest work should be respected among Christians. Maston deplores tendencies to depreciate the value of manual labor. He feels that both churches and society should regain a wholesome respect for the dignity of one who works with his hands and the work this person does.[28]

The concept of vocation is extensively treated in Maston's writing. He believes that God has a plan for every person and that Christians should seek diligently to find and perform that plan. Christians should recognize their partnership with God in their vocation and glorify God therein.[29] He sees that every Christian is called to servanthood within their vocations. In fact, he feels that Christians will be satisfied only with vocations that God can use.[30]

While Maston believes that every child of God has a vocation, or calling, and is involved in God's ministry, he recognizes a unique calling to church-related functions. Such calls are neither more holy nor more honorable than others. The emphasis is on service. Vocational Christian service, according to Maston, receives its importance from its primary task—that of perfecting and equipping the body of Christ. Thus, the church is strengthened.[31]

Along with teachings about producing wealth, Maston also projects principles concerning the use of money. He acknowledges spending for normal necessities. However, he emphasizes that expenditure for necessities are justified only to the extent that such spending fits the Christian for more effective service and contributes both to the welfare of society and the glory of God. Furthermore, Christians should use their wealth for the cause of Christ.[32]

There is a commendable emphasis on Christian sharing in Maston's teaching. He reminds Christians that the church is a family and that family members should help one another in times of need.[33] He reflects on the Jerusalem fellowship and the radical nature of their giving to the extent that none among them had any need (Acts 2:44-45). The Jerusalem pattern of selling possessions to meet the group's need was not Communistic but spiritual. It did not become the accepted pattern for all churches. The Jerusalem model does reveal an eternally valid spirit which indicates that need within the fellowship should be met through Christian sharing.[34] Maston concludes, "One wonders if the Christian movement has not lost considerably in its impact on the world by shifting its emphasis from caring for the members of the fellowship to the promotion of a program."[35]

Maston also speaks about Christian responsibility concerning indebtedness. Unlike some contemporary teachers, he does not prohibit all credit buying or indebtedness. He emphasizes that Christians must maintain a "keen sense of responsibility for a debt of any kind." Bills are to be paid promptly. A good credit rating is an asset to the Christian, the church, and the cause of Christ.[36]

In summary regarding the individual and economic life, Maston emphasizes the right but not the absolute right to private property. Stewardship directed both to God and fellowmen is central to his concept of wealth. He sees work as both a right and a duty but contends work should be honorable, beneficial, and honest. All Christians serve God through vocation. Money is to be spent for necessities, for others, and for the cause of Christ. Christians must maintain absolute integrity and responsibility in all economic endeavors, especially in regard to indebtedness.

Society and Economic Issues

T. B. Maston tackled economic issues that relate to society as well as those related to individuals.

Maston contends, for example, that no economic or political system is either sacred or holy. This is as true of capitalism and democracy as of movements that seek to replace them. There is neither a "Christian economic system" nor is there any system that can claim unconditional divine approval. "Christians and churches should not be concerned primarily with the economic or political system but with what the system or systems do or will do to individuals and to the basic social institutions founded by men."[37]

This principle means that no economic system can consider itself established by God. In fact, Maston says, "Any economic system that cannot solve the human problems it creates, such as unemployment and poverty, without throwing the load on a government that cannot indefinitely carry it, will die ultimately and should die."[38] Whatever economic system exists must be built on biblical principles. Maston concludes, "it is my conviction as deep as my own soul that a permanently sound economic order can be built on the principles that Jesus established for his kingdom and on those principles alone."[39]

Maston also addresses the problem of economic classes. His resistance to prejudice, racism, and discrimination is well known. He allows no divisions of class or race in the Christian community. However, he understands that so long as people are of unequal ability, economic classes are inevitable.[40] He admits the reality of class churches. These class churches actually serve the differing desires and needs of the various groups who express religious life differently. Class churches, according to Maston, are not particularly bad if the spirit of Christian fellowship between congregations is maintained. Denominations must, however, be certain not to neglect the common, working people.[41]

Maston speaks to both sides of the labor-management problem and considers Christianity's relation to it. He calls for the application of Christian ideals of concern for others, self-denial, and love in the business world. Private gain should not be the dominant goal of management. In the economic arena, according to Maston, the only escape from revolution or dictatorship is the voluntary application of Christian principles to economic life by businessmen. "In business life the choice is Christ or chaos."[42]

This conviction naturally forced Maston to consider the profit motive. He gives some credence to the idea that the profit motive and service to mankind go hand-in-hand. He quickly adds, however, that all motives and incentives must be brought under and evaluated in the light of Christian love and infused by love. Love alone allows one to give primacy to the service motive and keep economic incentives under proper control.[43]

Maston recognizes the need for organized labor and the advantages gained for workers through unions. He does not, however, suggest unrestricted support for unions. The labor movement has become powerful, independent, and self-assertive. This fact, says Maston, gives greater independence to the church's approach to economic conflicts. The church is under no compulsion to take either the side of labor or management but is free to see the good and evil in both approaches to an issue.[44]

The church should seek to help all its members, union and nonunion, to understand the labor movement. Maston is certain that Christianity should not identify with labor or any other class or group but should seek to influence both labor and management. "When labor, through its unions, does something that violates the Christian spirit and principles, the church should just as readily, but no more readily, remind it of its error as it would remind management."[45]

Closely related to the issue of labor is that of a just wage. Just wage is not necessarily the same as legal wage or the agreed wage. Just wage is one sufficient to meet the needs of the worker and those for whom he is responsible. It should be adequate to provide health, comfort, and security. Maston believes that this "living wage" should be the first charge on the profits of any industry.[46]

Maston addresses the problem of economic planning and freedom. He understands that every economic system has some mixture of planning and freedom. In fact, in today's world, governments are obligated to do some economic planning.[47] Planning should stabilize employment, assure a more equal distribution of wealth and goods, and allow the greatest personal freedom.[48]

Poverty and its attendant problems make up another area of economic ethics which Maston addresses. He notes that the Bible is consistently on the side of the poor, the disinherited, and the weak. He astutely points out that the Old Testament considers wealth a sign of God's favor and never glorifies the poor although they are seen as special charges of the Lord. Proverbs 30:7-14, according to Maston, presents the ideal as a golden mean between poverty and wealth.[49] The letter of James teaches that God allows no partiality based on wealth.[50] Thus, Maston sees clearly the biblical truth that the poor should be respected and cared for.

Moreover, Maston indicates a basic understanding of and sympathy for the poor. Without relieving the poor of responsibility, he explains the difficulties of those trapped in poverty and indicates his understanding of the frustrations of living in the "ghetto." He speaks to the difficulty of extracting self from the situation.[51]

Maston admits the need for a certain amount of government provision for social security in a highly industrial society. At the same time, however, he raises strong warnings concerning the danger of such government care. He points out that people tend to willingly give up freedoms and easily develop overdependence on government for the sake of security. He questions the possibility that a government can provide extensive social security service without also developing a centralized, paternalistic, bureaucratic government.

The result, he says, will be to limit, to a degree, the liberties of citizens.[52]

The problem of distribution, as discussed by Maston, relates both to poverty and world hunger. Maston is convinced that feeding hungry people at home and abroad is primarily a matter of distribution.[53] He believes that the Christian conscience demands a more equal distribution of wealth, not only as an economic expediency but also on moral and religious grounds. This problem of distribution must be solved in the economic order.[54]

Maston is not seeking equality. Equality can serve as a corrective principle but not an attainable goal. The desire is for more equitable distribution rather than absolute equality. He does feel that equality of opportunity for health, education, and self-realization should be immediate and continuing goals.[55]

These problems of welfare, justice, and distribution that are interrelated with poverty are critical problems in Maston's thinking. He believes that such efforts as minimum wage laws, social security, and other measures can effect a more equitable distribution. He further is convinced that both in the United States and on a world scale, such broadening of distribution would be advantageous as well as more in line with Christian principles.[56]

"The Christian should pay his taxes." Thus, without equivocation, Maston sets forth the Christian duty to fulfill the citizen's tax obligation. He sums up his convictions saying, "the Christian should pay his taxes promptly and cheerfully, never seeking to evade any tax responsibility."[57]

Maston has had much to say about churches and tax exemption. He believes that only the buildings used for worship and educational purposes should be tax exempt. His conclusion is, "Let church-related institutions be more concerned with what is fair and right than they are with what will be most advantageous to them."[58]

Conclusion

Maston joins biblical principles with contemporary issues. There are no idealistic suggestions that indicate a lack of contact with world problems. Maston uses relevant material from the social sciences. He refuses, however, to fall to the temptation to place social science, contemporary issues, or idealistic programs ahead of the Bible.

Maston contributes much to Christian discussion of economics in both basic principle and practical methodology. His family demonstrates the qualities of sharing, responsibility, and simpler life-style. As with Maston's teaching in general, what he says about economics is reinforced by who he is and what he does.

Notes

1. T. B. Maston, *Christianity and World Issues* (New York: The Macmillan Company, 1957), p. 117.

2. Ibid., p. 119.

3. T. B. Maston, *Why Live the Christian Life?* (Nashville: Thomas Nelson, Inc., 1974), pp. 20-23, 58-59.

4. Maston, *Christianity and World Issues*, pp. 119-120.

5. Ibid., p. 120.

6. T. B. Maston, "Christianizing Economic Life," *Graded Bible Lessons for Sixteen Year Pupils*, part 4 (1933), p. 247.

7. Maston, *Christianity and World Issues*, p. 134.

8. T. B. Maston, *The Christian in the Modern World* (Nashville: Broadman Press, 1952), pp. 81-82.

9. Maston, *Christianity and World Issues*, p. 119.

10. Maston, *The Christian in the Modern World*, p. 69.

11. T. B. Maston, "The Relation of Christianity to Modern Social, Economic, and Political Ideologies," (paper delivered to the Southwestern Society of Biblical Research, Texas Christian University, January 31, 1948), p. 1.

12. Maston, *Christianity and World Issues*, p. 146.

13. Maston, *The Christian in the Modern World*, p. 83.

14. Maston, "The Relation of Christianity," p. 2.

15. Ibid.

16. Maston, *Christianity and World Issues*, p. 146.

17. Maston, "Christianizing Economic Life," p. 247.

18. T. B. Maston, "Christian Business Ethics" (Unpublished paper, 1934), pp. 4-5.

19. T. B. Maston, "Organized Christianity and New Economic Order" (Unpublished paper), p. 15.

20. Maston, *Christianity and World Issues*, pp. 127-128.

21. Maston, *The Christian in the Modern World*, p. 69.

22. T. B. Maston, "Making and Using Money," *Graded Bible Lessons for Sixteen Year Pupils*, part 4 (1933), pp. 242-244.

23. Maston, *Christianity and World Issues*, p. 129.

24. T. B. Maston, "Rich and Poor," *Graded Bible Lessons for Sixteen Year Pupils*, part 4 (1933), pp. 236-237.

25. Maston, *Christianity and World Issues*, pp. 122-123, 128-130.

26. Maston, *The Christian in the Modern World*, pp. 74-75.

27. Maston, *Christianity and World Issues*, p. 131.

28. T. B. Maston, "The Dignity of Manual Labor," *Baptist Standard* (October 23, 1968), p. 16.

29. T. B. Maston, *God's Will and Your Life* (Nashville: Broadman Press, 1964), p. 34.

30. T. B. Maston, "Choosing a Life-Work," *Graded Bible Lessons for Sixteen Year Pupils*, part 3 (1933), pp. 182-183.

31. T. B. Maston, *The Conscience of a Christian* (Waco: Word Books, 1971), pp. 29-30.

32. Maston, "Making and Using Money," pp. 244-245.

33. Ibid., p. 244.

34. Maston, *Christianity and World Issues*, pp. 123-124.

35. T. B. Maston, *Biblical Ethics: A Biblical Survey* (Waco: Word Books, 1967), p. 250.

36. Maston, *The Christian in the Modern World*, p. 74.

37. Maston, "The Relation of Christianity," p. 2. See also *Christianity and World Issues*, pp. 142-143.

38. Maston, "Organized Christianity," pp. 1-5.

39. Ibid., p. 8.

40. Maston, *Christianity and World Issues*, pp. 143-145.

41. Ibid., p. 145.

42. Maston, "Christian Business Ethics," pp. 2-6.

43. Maston, *Christianity and World Issues*, p. 134.

44. Ibid., p. 135.   45. Ibid., p. 136.

46. Ibid., p. 132.   47. Ibid., p. 139.

48. Maston, "Christianizing Economic Life," p. 249.

49. Maston, *Biblical Ethics*, p. 95.

50. Ibid., pp. 260-261.

51. Maston, *The Conscience of a Christian*, pp. 120-123.

52. Maston, *Christianity and World Issues*, p. 137.

53. Ibid., pp. 140-141.

54. Maston, "Organized Christianity," p. 6.

55. Maston, *Christianity and World Issues*, pp. 140-141.

56. Ibid., p. 142.

57. Maston, *The Christian in the Modern World*, pp. 89-90.

58. Maston, *The Conscience of a Christian*, pp. 95-96.

Race Relations

Charles Myers

For half a century the term *race relations* has been common to our society. And for the past thirty-five years relations between the races has been the number one problem of our nation and perhaps the world. Through these years the voice and influence of T. B. Maston have contributed immeasurably to the efforts of the Christian community to deal with the problem.

His Thought

To Maston the problem has never been just differences between American whites and blacks. The differences here are representative of differences of people all over the world. In a book written in 1946, he said, "What was formerly considered a backyard domestic situation has become a front porch international issue."[1] The people of the world are on the march and the minority groups in our country have been joining in the march. Though there are political and economic factors involved, to him the problem is primarily moral and spiritual.

There are many things which have contributed to the problem, but Maston points to two attitudes as the major contributors. These are what he calls the we-you psychology and our prejudices. In the first instance, the we group usually belongs to the majority and considers itself superior to other groups. The you group is composed of some minority group and is excluded from most of the privileges enjoyed by the majority. These could be Jews in any part of the world, being discriminated against, being feared and ridiculed. They could be the Japanese or Chinese who were denied citizenship in the United States in the early part of this century because they were not white. They could be those same Japanese who were moved away from their homes on the West Coast and many of them confined to prisons, immediately following Pearl Harbor. They could be the Mexicans who have always been considered foreigners and treated as second-rate citizens. Or they could be the blacks who have been forced to live "across the tracks" in the sorriest neighborhood, having the worst streets and the poorest sanitary conditions. Because of their color they were discriminated against economically, politically, and spiritually. These groups were not like the majority, so they were excluded from the way of life of the majority.

The second factor, prejudice, is the common lot of every person, according to Maston. Everyone has blind spots and has this in common with all his ancestors. There are many things that have contributed to this condition. One major factor is social heritage. We are born into a community where certain discriminations are practiced. We assume these to be a part of life, so we take these as our standard. Prejudice is not innate; it is caught like one catches the measles. Later it is probably intensified by economic and social competition. Regardless of how prejudice comes, it casts a dark shadow across the life of every person it touches. It is like a cancer eating away at one's soul and the soul of society. Prejudice is at once the cause and effect of racial tensions.

These are the factors which Maston feels have resulted in discrimination and segregation. This is an extension of the master-slave tradition in the United States. It is based upon the idea that one group is inferior to another group. There would be no segregation, though there might be some separation, if it were not for prejudices. Neither would there be a feeling of superiority and inferiority among the races. This discrimination has not only been a blight on society but also it has had a devastating effect on its victims. It has created in them a sense of inferiority, defeatism, and resentment. It has also created a determination to get even, which has resulted at times in violence.

Maston has never accepted the idea of racial superiority or of one group being more intelligent than others. He has decried discrimination in public services such as medical treatment, travel, restaurants, and other public facilities. In specific instances of discrimination like the seminary student who was denied a burial place for his wife because she was Mexican, the Harvard graduate who was denied the privilege to vote because he was black, and the economic injustice which caused these minority people to be the "last hired and first fired," always moves him with indignation. He cannot accept this kind of discrimination because when he prays "Our Father," he knows he is declaring himself a potential brother to every man.

Basis for His Thought

Like every other conviction Maston has, his position on race relations is based upon his concept of God, the teachings of the Scriptures, and good common sense. To him the nature of God is a point of reference and the source of authority. He believes God to be a moral person. He believes God to be the creator of all things and the ruler of all things. The final authority rests with God. He believes God expects his children to be laborers with him in creating a better society. To say that being a Christian has nothing to do with one's relation to the blacks, or any other group, reveals a limited concept of the Christian life and a very distorted view of the nature of God.

His concept of God includes the conviction that God created man in his image. This means that all people are created in the image of God and are from one family stock. Also included in this is the fact that Christ died for every person. These are the ideas that give a person his worth, his value, and his dignity. God loves every person: the dope addict, the filthy, the immoral, and the clean. No one can be so degraded that God does not love him. No life is more precious than any other. God shows no partiality.

In addition to that, Maston believes that every person who comes into the family of God comes through an experience of faith in Christ. In this experience one is born into the family. We become children of God, brothers in Christ. We are children of the same Father. Therefore we are kin to each other in the creation experience and in the redemption experience. This eliminates any idea of superior and inferior people.

Added to Maston's concept of God is his acceptance of the teachings of the Scriptures. Foremost in these teachings is the example of Christ. Jesus crossed the Jewish-Samaritan line which was the nearest thing to a color line in his day. He dealt with the Samaritan woman at the well which was contrary to good Jewish practice on two counts, her race and her sex. He ate with publicans and chose one of them to be a disciple. He answered a question about which was the greatest commandment by saying it was love for God and the second was love for one's neighbor. When he told a story to answer the question concerning who is a neighbor, he made the central figure in the story a Samaritan. He was saying every man, regardless of race or position, is our neighbor. He further stated that we are to love one another as he loved us. And he loved us enough to die for us.

In this respect, to Maston, the Golden Rule is certainly applicable. If the person in the majority group would remember to treat the minority peoples as he would want to be treated were he in that place, we would solve most of our race problems.

The problems of racial prejudice arose in the early church and were dealt with by the Lord. The message that Peter received in his vision on the housetop was that "God is no respecter of persons" (Acts 10:34). Based on this, Maston is convinced that our goal should be to eliminate all distinctions and discrimination based on color or class. This was the message proclaimed to the early church. Though Onesimus was a slave, he was to be treated as a brother. Paul said there were to be neither bond nor free, but that "ye are all one in Christ Jesus" (Gal. 3:28). This new relationship in Christ destroyed all barriers based on external differences.

Since Pentecost the Holy Spirit has been active in the life of the church seeking to break down barriers that separate people. Maston is convinced that unless the Holy Spirit leads present church people in this area, we will be fragmented, but we can find unity if we follow the Spirit's leadership. He asserts the Scriptures teach that right relations with one's fellowman inevitably result from one's right relation with God and that being right with one's fellowman is a proof that one is right with God. "Paul suggests that the Christian's ethical and spiritual maturity, his likeness to the image of God can be measured by the degree that cultural, national and racial differences have no significance for him."[2]

He also feels that many people are quite mature in most areas and yet are terribly immature in attitudes on race. They frequently are controlled by emotions and prejudice rather than sound judgment based upon Christian principles. This immature attitude frequently handicaps missionaries in their work. Failure in this area is to him like placing handcuffs around the arms and legs of missionaries, for it is well known that what we do here today makes headlines around the world tomorrow.

It is also Maston's conviction that the teachings of Jesus and Paul are quite clear in stating that the Christian should be law-abiding. There should be a respect for those in authority and the Christian should pray for them. The law of our land is quite clear concerning respect for all races. The Christian will want to obey the law.

Application of His Thought

Maston has always insisted that it is not enough just to have a conviction based upon one's belief but that conviction must be expressed in everyday living. Though he recognizes the need for a tremendous change in race relations among us, he advocates caution in the changing process. It is his conviction that the method of change must be just as much in harmony with the spirit and teaching of Jesus as the idea calling for the change. He maintains that good can never be attained by doing evil. There are Christian methods as well as Christian goals and only those methods that can stand the tests of Christian principles should be used to achieve Christian ends.

In keeping with this concern, in his book, *Of One*, published in 1946, he commended the Home Mission Board for the financial help being provided for teachers in black colleges. He conceded that the method was not perfect but, at least for the moment, seemed to be the most constructive approach to a "very difficult and delicate problem." In that same book, in dealing with theological training for blacks, he noted that a few Southern Baptists had suggested that the white seminaries should be opened to young ministers of all races. His observation was that only time would tell what the denomination would do in this regard, but he felt all would agree that in some way black ministers should have available to them training comparable to that provided for white students.

In 1959 Maston wrote in a book entitled *Segregation and Desegregation* that there was a Southland of many Souths. He said that it was not so much a battle between segments in the South as it was a battle within the soul of individual Southerners. He felt that the inner nature of the battle gave hope for a constructive outcome. He said that a man will fight with himself only so long before he would sue for peace and come to terms with himself.

He has little use for people who deliberately fan the flames of prejudice for their own gain, and he does not hesitate to speak out against them. "Unfortunately, some people today are making the arousing of racial prejudice their business. An appeal to prejudice gives to them their greatest opportunity for recognition and leadership. They seek to arouse prejudice in others in order to make themselves popular. They are the political, religious, and social demagogues who have been and are a curse to the South. Some of these men, particularly those whose popularity has depended entirely on the present racial situation, might be shrugged off if it was not for the memory of Adolph Hitler who used some of the same strategies and techniques as the race baiters of the present day."[3] Naturally some of these religious demagogues resented being exposed for what they were, and Maston became the object of their hate mail and the subject of some of their tirades.

But exercising caution is, in his mind, not to be confused with a total lack of action. Maston feels progress in the area has to be made and feels the primary responsibility lays with individuals, particularly individual Christians. It is his conviction that Christians need to start with the world where it is and maintain a steady tension toward where it needs to go. Radicals may break the tension and destroy the effectiveness of the cause. His reminder is that if Christians do not begin to comprehend more fully what it means to be impartial and apply the truth of the gospel, future historians will write that fight promoters and baseball managers did more to emancipate the blacks than did Christians.

The real need, in Maston's thinking, is to quit talking so much about

God as a Father and act like he is. "There is no real solution for the race problem or any other basic human problem apart from the family spirit, which stems from the unity of God, who is our Father and who is redemptive in his purposes."[4] Human problems cannot be solved without the spirit of love and brotherhood. On the other hand, there is no real basis for love and brotherhood apart from a faith in and a vital relation to the living God.

To Maston, one related to God speaks his language, which is the language of love. He will not speak a language of hate. He will not join with those who stir up racial animosity. He will not designate people by undignified and odious names. He will not appeal to prejudice or to baser human emotions. He will not be blind to the problems faced but will approach those problems with intelligence rather than emotions. Love that enables the individual to live thus is stronger than human love; it is a divine quality. It comes from a union with Christ and makes the individual treat others as a "thou" and not an "it."

In a paper entitled "Integration," prepared in 1956 for the Advisory Council of Southern Baptists for work with Negroes, Maston stated some things the individual Christian needs to do in light of existing conditions. He needs to accept court decisions as the law of the land. He needs to help create an atmosphere that would help the public schools. He needs to recognize the serious difficulties faced by many communities. The greater the proportion of the population that is black the more difficult it is for the schools to comply with the court's decision. To push integration too rapidly in some communities in the South might conceivably create more problems than it solves. Integration involves more than the mere presence of children from two races in the same school. It could be cruel to admit a child to a school unless he was really accepted by the children and teachers in that school. We need to be patient with one another. At the same time he insists we must continue to admit that the contemporary problem is basically a moral and Christian problem.

In this same paper Maston observed that it could be that some conscientious Christian would defend segregation for the time being. He said this in itself would not do any particular damage as long as these recognize that the segregation pattern is out of harmony with the spirit and teachings of the Bible, particularly as revealed in the life and ministry of Jesus.

In a pamphlet entitled *Interracial Marriage* published by the Christian Life Commission (SBC), Maston states that such a marriage is unwise but certainly not because one race is superior and the other inferior. He believes that one cannot make a case against interracial marriage on the basis of any specific teachings of the Scriptures. However, such marriages, at least in our culture, are unwise. It is difficult enough to achieve a satisfactory adjustment in marriage within one's own race and culture. These difficulties are multiplied when the marriage crosses the line of race. He further states that such a marriage is not only unwise but also may be positively wrong for the child of God. Consideration must be given to the effect that such a marriage would have on other people and upon the cause of Christ.

As important as the individual is, Maston is convinced that he cannot turn the tide alone. There must be groups of individuals standing together. These groups are the churches. If the race issue is primarily moral, it is Maston's contention that these moral forces should take the lead in solving the problems.

The only way the churches can lift the world toward the Christian ideal is to maintain a constant tension between what the world practices and what the churches preach. Christian groups that defend as Christian the practices of the world that fall below Christian ideals, will never challenge the world. This is just as true in the area of race relations as in any other realm.[5]

In another book he placed the responsibility for right relations squarely on the church.

If the church will not dare to be the church in the fullest possible sense, if it will not take seriously the Christian ethic, applying its principles to race and other areas of life; then it will lose its own soul. Without the Christian ethic the Christian church becomes an empty shell, a corpse that has lost the power to give life because the life principle no longer resides in it.[6]

One of the crying needs of man is to be taught. One of the main purposes of the church is to teach. Just because a person has been saved does not mean that all his attitudes and actions have been changed. He needs to grow, and he grows as he is taught. None of us fully and perfectly practices all Christ has commanded. We constantly fall short. We are as a church to keep on teaching and to keep on being taught. To fail to teach is to fail in the mission of the church.

It may be difficult, and some would say impossible, in some sections to rise now to the high level of the ultimate will of God in race relations. The difficulty, however, of reaching or attaining God's will does not nullify or abrogate that will. Admittedly, we have to start where we are and move toward full achievement of his will.[7]

The church has a heavy responsibility, a responsibility in keeping with her privilege. She can fail to measure up and that would be tragic. But even far more tragic would it be if by precept and example she taught the wrong thing. Perhaps in some instances she has been doing just that. Maston takes note of that in one of his books.

However the actual practice of segregation is not the most damaging phase of the picture. The practice would not be so bad if so many churches and church leaders did not place the stamp of divine approval upon it. When the church identifies the Christian ideal with something less than the ideal, it loses the vision of the ideal and its ability to challenge and lift the world toward the ideal.[8]

Maston has repeatedly said that in a world that is rapidly becoming one neighborhood we must become one brotherhood or resort to enslavement of minority groups and handicapped people in order to maintain our status quo. The choice is not only between brotherhood and slavery but also between brotherhood and chaos. We really have no choice but to accept every person as a potential brother in the Lord.

Some say that this is idealistic. True. Our Christian faith is idealistic, but this does not make it irrelevant. Let those of us who approach the human situation, race or otherwise, from the Christian perspective remember that ours is a distinctive contribution. Let us not become so involved in the political approaches to the problem—approaches that are valid and valuable—that we fail to magnify and to be channels for the love of God. And we need to be sure that we ourselves are so solidly grounded in that love that we can and will continue to love when our love is rebuffed or rejected.[9]

Finally, he warned us often that our refusal to do right could only lead to trouble. In a prophetic statement made in 1959 he said:

There is always a possibility that the members of a "you" group, under the continuing pressure of a dominant "we" group may develop a deepening racial consciousness with an intense pride in the accomplishments of their race. When that happens, they tend to become a competing "we" group. They no longer are willing to accept as permanent and inevitable a secondary status in society. They challenge the majority to treat them as equals, to accept them as full partners in the culture.

When this stage is reached in the relation of two great racial groups, adjustments must be made in previously accepted patterns, or friction and serious trouble usually will result.[10]

Throughout his ministry Maston has faced the problem honestly, has with love stated his convictions which were based on his concept of God as revealed in Christ, and has tried to maintain a constant tension in his own area pulling those about him to a higher level. One could not ask for more from any Christian.

Notes

1. T. B. Maston, *Of One* (Atlanta: Home Mission Board of the Southern Baptist Convention, 1946), p. 8.

2. T. B. Maston, *Segregation and Desegregation* (New York: The Macmillan Company, 1959), p. 93.

3. Ibid., p. 48.

4. T. B. Maston, *The Bible and Race* (Nashville: Broadman Press, 1959), p. 26.

5. Maston, *Of One*, p. 79.

6. T. B. Maston, *Christianity and World Issues* (New York: The Macmillan Company, 1957), pp. 94-95.

7. Maston, *Segregation and Desegregation*, pp. 103-106.

8. Maston, *Christianity and World Issues*, p. 106.

9. T. B. Maston, *The Christian, the Church, and Contemporary Problems* (Waco: Word Books, 1968), p. 147.

10. Maston, *The Bible and Race*, p. 62.

Personal Morality

Joe Trull

"He is the most Christian man I've ever met." These words of a fellow student were my first introduction to T. B. Maston. In the years that followed I knew him as teacher, major professor, counselor, and friend. During the last few years before his retirement, I served as his grader and teaching assistant. After more than twenty years acquaintance, that first one-sentence introduction has not diminished. To know Maston the man is to know a great deal of the spirit of Jesus Christ.

The personal life of husband/father/deacon/neighbor Thomas Maston, reflects like a mirror his deepest convictions about personal morality. In attitude and actions Southern Baptists' best known ethicist has lived the truth he taught and taught well the truth he lived.

The greatest single influence upon Maston's thought concerning personal morality was his father.

I learned more about the Bible and the Christian life from my Daddy than anybody else. He was a man of real integrity; that impressed me the most . . . . But as far as personal morality, I had so much respect for him, that even before I was a Christian, there were certain things I just wouldn't do.[1]

Often he stated that his father taught him more about the Christian life at the end of a corn row while they rested the mules than did all of the theological giants of his student days.[2]

Another important influence was the study of the Bible itself. Converted at the age of sixteen, young Tom read the Bible through at least twice during that first year of his new spiritual life. He read the Bible so much, he humorously recalls, that his mother worried about him. "I think," he relates, "a great many of the ideas and ideals that shaped my life came out of that period of reading the Bible."[3] To study the seminary professor's ideas about personal morality is to be constantly referred to the teachings of the Scriptures.

Basic Theological Concepts

A constant emphasis in Maston's teaching was the impossibility of divorcing theology and ethics. The latter depends on the former. The dedicated scholar

177

taught that without a strong theological base, ethics becomes only a house of humanism built on the shifting sand of culture. His personal ethic is built on a strong theological base. To understand his concepts of personal morality, one must grasp the teacher's basic theological presuppositions.

For Maston, the Christian ethic is founded on the nature of God—a personal, moral, sovereign Creator who is also our heavenly Father revealed in Jesus Christ. To be right with God, one must be right on a personal and moral basis. What a person thinks about God will ultimately determine his attitude toward himself and his neighbor.[4]

Also, we cannot be right with God unless we are right with our fellowman (Isa. 1:10-18). God is holy and he expects his children to be holy (Lev. 19:2). He is light (1 John 1:5) and we are to walk in the light as he is in the light (1 John 1:7). . . . We are challenged to be like him.[5]

Man, created in the image of God, is a moral person with moral responsibility. Though marred by sin, this *imageo dei* has not been totally destroyed. There is enough of the image of God left in man for restoration through union with Christ. The companion fact that Christ died for all mankind gives to each person dignity and worth.

The Christian experience of salvation is the dynamic of the Christian life. Union with Christ brings a person into the family of God. Jehovah expects each of his children "to be like him—like him in character and concern."[6] To the degree this salvation experience is meaningful, the Christian will embody God's perspective towards the world.

A vital, life-changing union with the living Christ is basic to Christian morality.

To be a real Christian means to let that which was a potentiality in the initial experience become a living, dynamic reality in our lives. Another way of expressing the same concept is to say that the real Christian is one who lets the resurrected Christ live in him and through him.[7]

For Maston, the essence of the kind of life Jesus lived is found in Luke's five word biography, "He went about doing good."[8]

Maston's understanding of the Christian life is his key theological concept for his view of personal morality. Every Christian, he feels, is called and challenged to give his best in following Christ. "If Christ is our Lord, and he is if we are his followers, then we are his servants or slaves. Our supreme allegiance belongs to him. This means that every area of our lives must be open to him and to his control."[9]

The source of authority for the Christian life is the will of God. Because he believes this deeply, Maston wrote an entire book on the subject, *God's Will and Your Life.* In this book he noted that the will of God was central in Jesus' life, the North Star of his compass. So it is for the Christian, he affirmed. God's will is as broad as life itself; it includes the totality of the life of the individual as well as society. Through the resources available to him, a Christian can know the will of God. The mature Christian also discovers what the Bible has taught him, that the will of God is always best. To do God's will is the supreme goal of the Christian life.[10]

The ultimate ideal in the Christian life, according to Maston, is perfection. Not the kind of sinlessness often connected with perfection but the biblical idea captured in the Greek term *teleos*—"complete, full-grown, mature."[11] The best test of this ideal is *directionalism,* a coined word which asks, "In what direction are you moving?"

The biblical ideals of perfection, such as, "Therefore you are to be perfect, as your heavenly Father is perfect" (Matt. 5:48, New American Standard Bible), inspire the child of God to be on a perpetual quest. These "impossible possibilities" (Niebuhr's term) make the Christian faith abidingly relevant and create a healthy constructive tension in the Christian life. Maston liked to quote Cromwell's note on the flyleaf of his Bible, "He who stops being better stops being good."[12]

In order to lead people from where they are toward a biblical ideal, tension must be applied to pull them upward. When the ideals of perfection as established by Christ are applied to individual lives (Maston calls this "pew tension"), the child of God is drawn toward God's ideal. One of the paradoxes of the Christian life is that a believer can have the "peace . . . which passeth all understanding" within him, even while standing under this constructive tension.[13]

What is the highest good for the Christian? It is the kingdom of God. This summum bonum alone unifies and integrates the Christian life. To enter the kingdom is to submit to the rule and reign of God. To be a citizen of God's kingdom is to allow the ethic of Jesus to be a present reality.

The Kingdom is a vital inner experience that will undoubtedly express itself outwardly. It is eternal and spiritual, inner and outer, present and future, ethical and apocalyptic. The ethics of Jesus are the ethics of the Kingdom.[14]

Love is the crowning virtue of the Christian life. Jesus made it the chief commandment (Matt. 22:36-39). Christ taught that love for God and man belong together. The love that comes from God is the source of love for our fellowman, and love of our neighbor is proof of our love for God.[15]

Those who know the Maston family know how much they demonstrate this virtue in their personal lives. "We are particularly interested in people who are neglected and lonely . . . . She [Mrs. Maston] does more of that kind of visiting than anyone in our church . . . . One thing I do know— I love folks."[16]

The ultimate symbol and unifying principle of the Christian life is the cross. Perhaps it is the most influential concept in Maston's understanding of the Christian life. He often said, "To the degree that we take up the cross, do we follow Jesus."

Quoting Bonhoeffer's *The Cost of Discipleship,* Maston stressed that cross bearing is crucifying self, an essential part of the Christian life (Gal. 2:20). "When Christ calls us, he calls us to death, but it is a death that brings life."[17] To follow Christ is to say no to selfish concerns, yes to Christ's way of sacrificial service, and to keep on following him day by day (Luke 9:23). Only as the Christian bears the cross voluntarily and personally will he reveal God, reveal life, and give life to others.[18]

Specific Moral Concerns

Upon this sound theological foundation T. B. Maston built a superstructure of personal moral concerns. He often stressed that one is not as Christian as he ought to be unless he maintains in his personal life, both from a negative and positive perspective, thoroughly Christian moral standards.[19]

In a resource paper entitled, "Ethical Issues 1978 and Beyond," Maston expresses concern for a balanced perspective by Southern Baptists. Maston feels there is a contemporary danger of neglecting personal morality, with our present emphasis on social morality. Along with this, he adds, is a tendency to ridicule some of the negative emphases Baptists have traditionally given.[20] "While the positive represents the highest expression of the Christian life, there continues to be a need for a negative emphasis."[21]

This new trend is in contrast to the tendency in years past for Baptists to heavily stress the negatives of the Christian life. Maston addressed that imbalance also, pointing out that those who stress rather exclusively personal morality tend to magnify the negative aspects of the Christian life, judging it solely by what one does not do.

Maston feels this present trend away from personal morality and negative emphases is due to the fact that "Southern Baptists, to use Troeltch's distinction, have become more of a churchly type."[22] Nevertheless, with our sect background, which has not been entirely lost, Baptists have an unusual opportunity to work out and maintain a proper balance between personal and social morality.[23]

When a Christian faces a right or wrong decision in personal morality, what should he do? In his popular book on decision making, *Right or Wrong?*, Maston poses three questions to ask when facing moral questions:

1. How will my participation in this activity affect me personally: my body, my mind, my personality, my spiritual life?
2. How will it affect others and my influence on others?
3. How will it affect the cause of Christ?[24]

These principles, along with light from within, light from without, and light from above will help Christians make responsible moral decisions.[25]

What then are the major personal ethical concerns of this man often called Southern Baptists' greatest ethicist? There are so many issues in the general area of personal morality, that an attempt will be made to refer to the most persistent and significant ones.

First, however, note some principles which Maston feels are applicable, to varying degrees, to most contemporary personal moral issues.[26]

Among these principles are: (1) Life is a creation of God and should be considered sacred. (2) The individual will be held accountable by God for his decisions (Gal. 6:7-8). (3) One's body belongs to the Lord, is the temple of the Holy Spirit, and should be dedicated to the purposes of God (I Cor. 6:13-20; Rom. 12:1). (4) Right for the child of God is determined not only by what he thinks is right but also by what others think and by the effect of what he does on the lives of others (Rom. 14:1-23; I Cor. 8:1-13). (5) Closely akin to the preceding is the fact that the strong should serve the weak (Rom. 15:1-3). (6) Whatever the Christian does should be for the benefit of others, for the good of the church, and for the glory of God (I Cor. 10:24,31-33). (7) We who have been recipients of the comfort of God should be instruments of that comfort, letting our Father reach out through us to those who have sinned and fallen short of the glory of God (II Cor. 1:3-7).[27]

It is on the basis of these and related principles, that T. B. Maston comes to feel that "total abstinence from *alcohol,* other *drugs, gambling,* and *smoking* is the only defendable position for a Christian."[28] Since the body belongs to the Lord (1 Cor. 6:20), it should be used for the purposes of God. This means, among other things, that the body is a part of our Christian stewardship. Many issues concerning right or wrong for the Christian (such as alcohol, illicit drugs, and smoking) should be answered on the basis of their effect on the body.[29] At the same time, Christians should have compassionate concern for the victims of these habits.

Alcohol, Maston affirms, is our number one drug problem and alcoholism is increasing among women, physicians, and juveniles. Maston feels alcoholism should be labeled both a sickness and a sin. Christians should oppose the trend of our culture to portray drinking as normal, natural, and wholesome.[30]

Every Christian should support efforts to limit the publication and distribution of pornographic literature and the flagrant portrayal of sex and violence on television. Personal morality is under attack in this "sexploitation" of our society motivated by greed and godlessness. Christians should personally avoid the very "appearance of evil," which means they should neither purchase materials nor patronize the purveyors of pornography.[31]

Another moral issue is the area of health, including mental health. The Christian ideal is that the best medical service ought to be available to all people. Some of the most pressing and perplexing moral problems today are in the biomedical area. Such issues as abortion, euthanasia, genetic engineering, organ transplants, and experimentation confront the contemporary believer.

Christian doctors, scientists and others should ask, "Is this right?" as well as "Is this legal?" One thing that will help in relation to many issues or cases will be a respect for life in particular. In regard to abortion, euthanasia, and organ transplants, the decision at times may seem to be in the gray area when the choice may be between the lesser-of-two-evils.[32]

Maston feels, for example, that abortion is justified only under very serious conditions such as incest, rape, or threat to the life of the mother. He also approves only negative euthanasia, that is, when it simply means the withholding of artificial means to keep a terminally ill person alive. Positive euthanasia, the intentional ending of a life, is always wrong.[33]

Reflecting his father's strong personal morality, T. B. Maston is deeply disturbed by personal dishonesty. Integrity, and the lack of it in so much business, government and social life is antithetical to Christian morality and should bother the conscience of all Christians.[34]

One of the deadliest vices for the Christian, Maston asserts, is the attitude of self-righteousness, the only sin specifically condemned by Jesus. Calling it a "sin of the sanctuary," Maston points out that pride may take many forms, including the unwillingness to be changed by an experience of genuine worship which gives a vision of service.[35]

That Christians today are expressing more concern for people is encouraging to Maston. The essence of the Christian faith is to be like God in character and concern. The God revealed in the Bible is impartial. However, he shows a special concern for the neglected and underprivileged, the poor, the widows, the orphans, the strangers. Christians should evidence that same concern for the welfare of the disenfranchised of our society.[36]

Sensing one of the great weaknesses of contemporary Christianity, Maston has recently sounded the call for a distinctly Christian life-style. He agonizes over the fact that there is not as much difference as there ought to be in the life-style of most Christians and non-Christians.

Southern Baptists, as well as Christians in general, do not make the impact they should on the world largely because so few of us live a distinctly Christian life. The failure is entirely too evident in personal morality, in relation to neighbors and friends, in concern for people in general and the neglected and needy in particular, in daily work as employer or employee, in relation to those of other colors and cultures, and in our attitudes toward and involvement in the moral and social issues of our society.[37]

What is the standard for the Christian's life-style? Without hesitation Maston answers, "It is the life Jesus lived."[38]

This Christocentric thread runs throughout Maston's convictions concerning personal morality. The real test of the good Christian is not found in what he doesn't do (smoke, drink, gamble) or in his faithfulness to religious requirements (tithes, attendance) or his service in the church (teacher, deacon) or even his active participation in the life of the community.[39]

The real Christian is one who lets the resurrected Christ live in him and express himself through him. In other words, we are real Christians to the degree that we are Christlike.

The preceding means that the supreme test of the Christian life is positive rather than negative; vital rather than formal.[40]

He believes that. He taught that. He lives that. I believe I speak for many when I say he is the most Christlike person I've ever met.

E. S. James, for many years the courageous and oft-quoted editor of the influential *Baptist Standard* (state Baptist paper of Texas), eloquently summarized the lasting contribution of Thomas Buford Maston.

More than any other person in the Southwest Dr. Maston is responsible for Southern Baptists being able to envision new horizons in the ethical realm. Quietly and in humility he has gone about the task of teaching and directing the thoughts of others, and God has let him live to see some of the harvest of the seeds he has sown.[41]

Notes

1. Interview with T. B. Maston, April 10, 1978.
2. T. B. Maston, Christian Ethics 31—Class Notes (Fort Worth: Southwestern Baptist Theological Seminary, 1958), p. 4.

3. Interview.

4. T. B. Maston, Christian Ethics 32—Class Notes (Fort Worth: Southwestern Baptist Theological Seminary, 1960), p. 53.

5. T. B. Maston, "Principles of Christian Social Concern and Action" (Unpublished paper presented to the Christian Life Commission of the Southern Baptist Convention, Nashville, Tennessee, 1977), p. 1.

6. T. B. Maston, *The Conscience of a Christian* (Waco: Word Books, 1971), p. 13.

7. Ibid., p. 32.   8. Ibid., p. 18.

9. T. B. Maston, *God's Will and Your Life* (Nashville: Broadman Press, 1964), p. 11.

10. This paragraph abbreviates a few of the major ideas of the book.

11. T. B. Maston, Christian Ethics 32—Class Notes (Fort Worth: Southwestern Baptist Theological Seminary, 1960), pp. 62-63.

12. Ibid., p. 63

13. Don McGregor, "Maston the Teacher," *Baptist Standard* (May 22, 1963), p. 9.

14. Maston, Christian Ethics 32—Class Notes, pp. 33-34.

15. Maston, *The Conscience of a Christian*, p. 24.

16. Interview.

17. Maston, Christian Ethics 32—Class Notes, p. 69.

18. Ibid.

19. T. B. Maston, "Personal and Social Morality," *Baptist Standard* (March 26, 1969), p. 18.

20. T. B. Maston, "Ethical Issues: 1978 and Beyond" (Nashville: Christian Life Commission of the Southern Baptist Convention, 1978), p. 1.

21. Ibid.

22. Interview.

23. Maston, "Personal and Social," p. 18.

24. T. B. Maston, Right or Wrong? (Nashville: Broadman Press, 1955), pp. 29-34.

25. Ibid., pp. 41-46.

26. Maston, "Principles," p. 20.

27. Ibid.   28. Ibid.

29. T. B. Maston, "The Bible and the Body," *Baptist Standard* (May 8, 1968), p. 16.

30. Maston, "Ethical Issues," p. 6.

31. Ibid., p. 5.

32. Maston, "Principles," p. 22.

33. Ibid.   34. Ibid., p. 21.

35. T. B. Maston, "Sins in the Sanctuary," *Baptist Standard* (July 10, 1968), p. 16.

36. Maston, *The Conscience of a Christian*, p. 13.

37. Maston, "Ethical Issues," p. 17.

38. Ibid.

39. T. B. Maston, "Who Is the Good Christian?" *Baptist Standard* (February 6, 1969), p. 19.

40. Ibid.

41. E. S. James, "T. B. Maston's Unique Contribution," *Baptist Standard* (April 20, 1966), p. 5.

Human Suffering

Cecil Thompson

The theme of human suffering is not very prominent in Maston's major writings, nor was it in his classes. It does, however, contribute substantially to our understanding of the man himself and consequently of his thought. Certainly he would have become outstanding even apart from his long encounter with tragedy. Yet his positive reaction to it has evidently heightened the dimensions of his character and thinking.

Human suffering is the principal subject of two of his small books.[1] He wrote both after his retirement, but his basic position had been "hammered out" many years before and has remained essentially unchanged.[2] On occasion he shared in the classroom his perspective toward human suffering, yet many of his students remained unaware of his personal pain or of its exact nature or cause. He seemed reticent to mention details, probably to avoid any appearance of seeking pity. Fortunately he did respond to the repeated requests to publish it from some of those helped by his rather unique perspective.

Both of his books on suffering are dedicated to his older son, Tom Mc. Although the author has had his share of the pain common to all, the background and the primary basis for his perspective toward human suffering is "one particular problem."[3] Let him describe it in his own precise words:

Our real struggle . . . with the problem of suffering began when our first child was born. I had stood by when he came into the world. When I got home, I sat down at the dining room table and wept. . . . His mother had almost literally given her life that he might live. Why?

The question became louder and more persistent when we noticed that his development along some lines was slower than expected. Why? became a shout when we discovered that Tom Mc had been injured at birth.[4]

None of the many doctors, including two of the only four United States cerebral palsy specialists then known to them, offered any hope. For several years Mrs. Maston and others spent multiple hours seeking to help him to talk and to control his body better, but he has never been able to talk, walk, sit alone unaided, or even to shift himself in bed. Almost every voluntary muscle of his body is affected, and his parents do almost everything for him.

The first monograph on this theme was written primarily in Beirut, Lebanon, while Maston was serving as guest professor in the Arab Baptist Seminary. There he shared with us "the distillate of many years of personal experience."[5] He accepted the invitation to teach in the seminary only after Mrs. Maston had agreed that she and Tom Mc would go also so that he could continue helping, as always, with their son.

His second monograph appeared a decade later and required a reprint within months. It represents a complete rewriting of the earlier book. Although the basic position and much of the content remain the same, it is even more readable. The tone is conversational and the style even more personal. He shares more fully his own family experiences; his wife is affectionately referred to as "Mommie." He identifies by name those whose experiences of suffering he cites. It may well represent his finest writing style, especially as a concerned and compassionate Christian. Only a disciplined mind and heart could have produced such literature more than a decade after his retirement following more than forty years of lecturing and authoring several textbooks!

Both books were family productions. His wife participated not only in the original writing but also many of her ideas became part of the contents. Eugene, the younger son, served as "a severe and a most helpful critic." And, of course, the book would never have been written except for Tom Mc. Apparently a doctor's error caused his injury and thus precluded a normal life. Tom Mc, however, has become a genuine person rather than just a problem. He embodies the human dilemma of what Christian parents should feel and do in the presence of innocent suffering with the exacting, unceasing demands on their physical, emotional, mental, and spiritual strength.

The Mastons joined the multitude of those who have cried out, Why suffering? and have struggled with the sequel question of God's relation to it. Maston reveals the intensity of that struggle: "Several years ago I felt I had to find a reasonably satisfactory answer to the preceding questions or lose my sanity and/or my faith."[6] The Maston's deep struggle forms the background for his approach to the theme of this chapter.

His Basic Approach to Suffering

Maston summarizes concisely his own perspective toward human suffering in three of his briefer works, each time with a three-page résumé at the very end.[7] He does not attempt to treat philosophically the problem of evil nor even the various kinds of suffering. For example, redemptive suffering was included only in a limited way. Distinctively Christian suffering he defines as that which results from obedience to the will of God in a sinful world, such as reflected in 1 Peter. Maston treats it in his ethic of the cross for the Christian follower. But this chapter presents his thought concerning suffering common to non-Christians as well as to Christians, suffering that does not result necessarily from one's having obeyed or disobeyed God's will.

His primary approach is not that of the professor but rather of the fellow sufferer whose Christian experience requires him to integrate human suffering into the whole of his basic faith and ethic. His interpretation of Job illustrates this.[8] Accordingly, suffering, and particularly the suffering of the innocent, is seen as very definitely a moral problem because God is revealed in the Bible as moral and sovereign. The why of Job's sufferings was not explained to him, although the reader is aware that they resulted from Satan's challenge to God (Job 1:9). Job disproves the oversimplified theory that all suffering is the result of one's own sins. There is much unexplained suffering and men cannot wholly understand the mystery in it, a mystery that goes back ultimately to God.

A practical conclusion does emerge from Job in that the sufferer who continues to believe in God and humbly submits to him may enjoy fellowship with him even in the midst of suffering. Suffering need not alienate a believer from God but may in reality, lead to a stronger faith in him. This is basic to Maston's perspective. He echoes the teaching of Job that, even though we have no full theoretical solution to suffering, our doubts can be dispelled when we come face to face with God. Thus his basic approach is that of personal experience as a Christian seeking biblical insights into the nature of unexplained human suffering.

The Laws of Life and Suffering

To contend that suffering comes without "rhyme or reason" does not satisfy Maston from the strictly intellectual viewpoint and even less from the Christian perspective. He considers it to be out of harmony with our kind of world. The first statements of his latest summary set forth his foundational concept of "the basic laws of life":

1. All of life is governed by certain basic laws. This means that a cause-and-effect relationship operates in all of life, including the area of suffering and sorrow.
2. The basic laws of life are written into the nature of men and women by the God who created them and into the world in which they live.
3. Some of those laws are known; others, unknown.
4. The benefits for the observance and the penalties for the violation of these laws are not external to the laws but inherent in them. This means that the results of obedience and disobedience are natural and inevitable.

5. Most, if not all, suffering results from the operation of the basic laws of life.
6. God does not in some miraculous way send suffering. In most cases he would have to work a miracle to keep it from coming.
7. Because the basic laws of life are in harmony with our natures, it is wise for us to seek to discover and to live in harmony with those laws.[9]

He quotes approvingly definitions of law as:

"a sequence of events in nature or in human activity that has been observed to occur with unvarying uniformity under the same conditions." *Law* can also mean "any rule or principle expected to be observed: as, the laws of health" *(Webster's New World Dictionary).*[10]

Such laws cannot be broken; they break the one who breaks them, whether recognized or not. They are "closely related to, if not identifiable with, the fundamental laws or commandments and principles found in the Scriptures" and therefore should not be considered burdensome because God provides them for a person's good.[11]

Sin and Suffering

Because suffering and the goodness of God seem antithetical, the question of sin is raised.

8. Since sin is a violation of any law of God, unwritten as well as written, most, if not all, suffering is the result of sin.
9. Sin that causes suffering may be the sin of the sufferer, but it may also be the sin of someone else or of society and/or the institutions of society.
10. Since God is sovereign of the universe, suffering in some way must be within his will. It seems clear, however, that it is a phase of his permissive or circumstantial will and not his perfect or intentional will.[12]

Whose sin is responsible—that of the sufferer or of someone else? His favorite biblical reference here is John 9:2-3. Jesus taught that the man's blindness had nothing to do with his sin nor that of his parents. This is not to be interpreted as exonerating them from all guilt but simply that God did not send blindness in this case as sin's punishment. However, some suffering does result from the personal sin of the sufferer (see John 5:14). Thus he distinguishes between sin as a breach of God's laws for which one is not morally responsible, although possibly affected, and sin as personal guilt.

If suffering comes largely through the operation of God's basic laws, does he send it on the innocent to punish the guilty? He responds that everything we know about God revealed in Jesus suggests that he would not do that. Then, what about God's relation to the suffering of the apparently innocent?

"God may, and evidently does, frequently use suffering, not sent directly by him, as a means to chasten his children." His main purpose, however, "is to purify and mature rather than to punish."[13]

Leslie Weatherhead's threefold distinction of the will of God as ultimate, intentional, and circumstantial helps avoid a fatalistic or simplistic interpretation of the divine will. God's ultimate purpose of redemption fully expresses his sovereignty and will not be denied. Clearly God's perfect will does not intend for men to suffer (see Rev. 21:4). Evidently most suffering is an expression of God's circumstantial or permissive will. Maston's reverence before God leads him to say "most" rather than "all," because he recognizes our lack of full understanding, especially concerning natural catastrophes. Also he does not believe that "any person has the wisdom or the right to say how God will always operate."[14]

The Miracles of God and Suffering

The searching question is often raised as to whether we should expect God in some miraculous way to shield us from suffering. Maston, consistent with his previous statements, neither forsakes his concept of the basic laws of life nor annuls the full sovereignty of God nor denies the evil of human suffering.

11. God the Creator is more powerful than that which he has created. He sees fit, however, with rare exceptions, not to interfere with the laws of life. This gives us a dependable, predictable world in which to live.

12. It does seem that God, at times, steps in in unusual ways to relieve suffering. He may do this by setting aside some of the basic laws of life, but it seems that more frequently he works in harmony with and through those laws. He energizes them and makes them function more effectively than they would without his presence.[15]

Apparently miracles do occur, and Maston cites experiences of personal friends. However, he feels that these are not as common as his own "miraculous" healing from a severe case of pneumonia before the days of the so-called miracle drugs. He believes that he would not be alive today if God had not responded to prayer on his behalf nor if his wife had not gotten him to the hospital as quickly as she did, where he received the best of medical care. To him "prayer and the physician belong together." He is convinced that the presence of God can energize the laws of healing and make them operate more efficaciously than they would otherwise. The divine presence can heighten medical personnel's skills and make medicines more powerful. He believes that this is the method God most frequently uses.[16]

The basic laws of life are not impersonal forces but God's laws, representing his consistent nature, activity, and purpose. Admittedly Maston generally uses *law* in its secondary sense of what man can observe in nature, but its primary meaning as a directive judgment remains, because the lawmaker is God who has written them into our human nature and our universe. Maston rejects the charge that God is "an absentee landlord." He does not directly "send" the hurricane and other forms of natural evil. Nor is it useless to pray for men in such calamities because God might work a miracle and is always concerned with people; therefore, prayer is altogether fitting. He does believe that the main thrust of such prayer should not be for protection from the physically destructive forces but for inner spiritual needs in the midst of whatever comes with life.[17]

The Christian theist, which Maston is, affirms a personal moral God who in his sovereignty has created and sustains every part of the universe. To unify his thinking, the theist seeks to transcend the dichotomy apparent in such concepts as *natural* and *supernatural*. Thus, to represent God as occasionally intervening to set aside a lower law by a higher one raises the question of why should God not more often, if not constantly, use the higher law to achieve the orderly universe we need. Again the matter of God's purposes appears. Even the helpful distinction between the intentional and the circumstantial aspects of the divine will does not completely remove the mystery of suffering. Here his theodicy is based clearly on the revelation of God's will and purposes in the historical Jesus. Maston seems to be greatly comforted in that we have no record of Jesus' intentionally sending suffering upon anyone but we do have multiple instances of his relieving it both for the guilty and for the innocent.

The Contributions of Suffering

13. Far more important than, Why suffering? is, What will we let God do to us, for us, and through us because of suffering?

14. God wants to use the suffering and sorrow that comes to us for our good, for the good of loved ones and others, and for his glory. What he can do for us and through us will depend on our reactions to our suffering and to him because of our suffering.[18]

Our answer to the difficult question about God and his relation to human suffering largely determines our reaction to suffering and our attitude toward the Lord. A mistaken concept here usually leads to a rebellious forsaking of God or to a fatalistic resignation that usually means a dreary, defeated life. Suffering can be a powerful molder of lives. Such experiences, to use an expression of Mrs. Maston, "will make us better or bitter."

Potential contributions to the sufferer include strengthened character, greater maturity, patience, proper evaluation of the values of life, deepened sense of the need for God and of fellowship with him, and a developing capacity to wait for him. Another contribution can be peaceful submission to the will of God or perhaps a better word would be *cooperation* with the will of God, regardless of the outcome. "Earnest prayer that ends with a 'nevertheless' is the way to a peaceful heart for the sufferer and for those who suffer with him." An additional contribution of suffering is illustrated by the strings of the violin that must be made tighter and tighter before becoming ready to fulfill their purpose in the hand of the master musician.[19]

The sufferer and those who suffer with him are not to succumb to self-pity but are to be stewards of their experience (2 Cor. 1:4). First they must adjust to their own suffering before they can effectively be used by the Lord to lighten the burdens of others. In statement thirteen above, the shift to a more important question neither denies the full reality of the tragedy of suffering nor rebels before the God who permits it but moves positively toward overcoming evil with good by humbly consenting to God and by cooperating with him in his purposes.

The Promises of God and Suffering

Concerning his Christian faith, Maston has never seriously doubted the conversion experience in his youth or the dependability of God. He closes his summary on this note of confidence:

15. Regardless of why suffering comes to us or the nature of our suffering, we can sense the presence of our heavenly Father and can confidently rest on his promises.[20]

Biblical promises have deepened and strengthened the faith of many, including his own.[21] His personal favorites include Deuteronomy 33:27, especially at high altitudes in a jet plane; Psalm 23; and Matthew 11:28-30. He uses repeatedly Romans 8:28, preferring the translation that places "God" as the subject who works in everything for good. The "good" is defined in the following verse as conformity to the image of God. Perhaps the most reassuring of all is 2 Corinthians 12:9. A relatively unknown verse, Micah 7:8, has been to him a great source of strength and encouragement for a number of years, especially the phrases, "when I fall, I shall arise" and even more so, "when I sit in darkness, the Lord shall be a light unto me."

The constant theme of God's being awake and near while we sleep appears in the quotation, the illustration, and the written prayer which form the conclusion of his latest chapter on God's promises.[22] One wonders if his years of sleeping in the same room with Tom Mc to care for him throughout the night have not influenced his own interpretation of his relation to the heavenly Father. Be that as it may, his experience of more than fifty years with Tom Mc has indelibly marked his character, thought, and ministry. Without this experience perhaps his achievements would have been quite different from those which we today associate with him. One cannot help but wonder what other contributions Mrs. Maston would have made had she been able to continue as a seminary professor. Nevertheless, by the grace of God, they have touched many lives in a unique way because of their honest and Christian acceptance of personal suffering. They are God's faithful and loving stewards, especially toward those who suffer and those who suffer with them.

Perhaps Maston's writings can be comprehended quite adequately without knowing of his personal situation. However, such personal knowledge not only heightens one's admiration for the man but also enables one to perceive Maston's ethical teachings from a far greater perspective. Acknowledging his incomplete understanding of God's will and way, Maston has demonstrated a trusting acceptance of whatever circumstances life may hold and has eloquently testified by character, word, and deed that the Lord indeed is good and worthy of complete confidence and continuous praise.

Notes

1. T. B. Maston, *Suffering: A Personal Perspective* (Nashville: Broadman Press, 1967); T. B. Maston, *God Speaks Through Suffering* (Waco: Word Books, 1977).
2. T. B. Maston to C. L. Thompson, June 7, 1978.
3. Maston, *Suffering,* p. 1.
4. Maston, *God Speaks,* pp. 13 f.
5. Milford O. Rouse, "Foreword," *Suffering,* p. iii. (Rouse is the Maston's family doctor and friend.)
6. Maston, *God Speaks,* pp. 9 f.
7. Maston, *Suffering,* pp. 85-87; Maston, *God Speaks,* pp. 93-95; T. B. Maston, *God's Will and Your Life* (Nashville: Broadman Press, 1964), pp. 90-92.
8. T. B. Maston, *Biblical Ethics: A Biblical Survey* (New York: World Publishing Company, 1967), pp. 95-99.
9. Maston, *God Speaks,* pp. 93 f.
10. Ibid., pp. 31 f.   11. Ibid., pp. 32,36.
12. Ibid., p. 94.   13. Ibid., p. 44.
14. Ibid., p. 52.   15. Ibid., pp. 94 f.
16. Maston, *God Speaks,* pp. 56 ff.

17. T. B. Maston, *The Conscience of a Christian* (Waco: Word Books, 1971), pp. 154 f.
18. Maston, *God Speaks*, p. 95.
19. Maston, *Suffering*, pp. 71 ff.
20. Maston, *God Speaks*, p. 95.
21. Ibid., pp. 81-90.   22. Ibid., pp. 90-92.

Church and the World

Ralph Phelps

"The world is the field." This portion of Jesus' explanation of the parable of the tares growing in a grain field would seem to be an ideal introduction to a discussion of T. B. Maston's thought concerning the church and the world. One could have neither sat through every course that he taught nor served five years as a teacher in his department, both of which this writer did, nor read his writings without being constantly impressed with the almost infinite range of his social concerns. No problem of mankind and no remote corner of the globe are beyond the boundary of his attention as he seeks to apply the gospel of Jesus Christ to every area of living.

"Where he is coming from"—to use a contemporary expression—is abundantly clear. Maston is not a philosophical ethicist but is a theological moralist whose reference point for everything is "the God we worship and serve . . . the sovereign God of the universe."[1] Maston adds that this God cannot be restricted to any one segment of life. "As sovereign He is interested in and concerned about the totality of the life of the individual and of the world."

More specifically, Maston's ethical base is in Christian theology. Believing that "we become Christians through union with the resurrected Christ," he teaches that being a member of this family of God places on an individual obligations "as broad and deep as life itself."[2] Nor does he simply proclaim this principle; he is as deeply and personally committed to it as one possibly can be. Remarkable indeed is the fact that a person from the hills of East Tennessee—where as a boy it took his family one full-day's ride in a horse-drawn wagon to get from their side of the mountain to the other where his uncle lived, and one who spent his teaching career in one of the world's most conservative theological seminaries—can have such a breadth of vision and can be so remarkably free from provincialism and narrow-gauged thinking.

Maston's combination of theological conservatism and sociological liberalism—both of which are evident in any study of the topics treated in this book dealing with his thought on major substantive issues of the twentieth century—must confound critics who try to label him with one of their in-stock tags. Unquestionably, his theology is ultraconservative by today's theological norms; and some have wondered if he should not properly be labelled a fundamentalist, what with his great respect for the Bible and its revelation and his frequent use of proof texts. However, it would be a gross error to label him thus, for in one very vital regard he breaks with the fundamentalist mentality. This is in his insistence that the spirit as well as the letter of the biblical message must be respected and implemented. No amount of legalistic juggling of proof texts or arguments is justification for abusing any person or principle, and a Christian's highest responsibility is to be faithful to "Christ in you." In the preface to his book, *The Christian, the Church, and Contemporary Problems,* Maston writes, "The chapters in the present volume seek to apply the Christian message and spirit to contemporary social and moral problems."[3] Note the phrase "and spirit." This is typical of his approach to the world.

Frequently Maston said to this writer, then a young teacher much exercised by a multitude of what he thought to be gross injustices and inequities, "You must stay sweet, my boy. There's no way to do the work of the Lord except in the spirit of the Lord." His advice may not have "taken," but it made a profound impression.

While holding to conservative theological views and yet sounding like the liberals in his emphasis on love, Maston has been even more of a paradox when his social views have been known. He may have urged sweetness on a colleague—and he was certainly remarkably free from bitterness and rancor despite the frequent buffetings he experienced, even in the school in which he taught—but he was as fearless as Jesus cleansing the Temple when he dealt with social problems. In times of war, he taught peace and the ideal of nonretaliation. In an era of exploitive racial segregation, he taught the oneness of all mankind and the moral imperative of ending segregation in all its degrading forms. In an age of supernationalism, he taught internationalism and the ideal of world government. At a time when monopolistic capitalism was upheld by many in his own denomination as God's ideal for mankind and when the seminary in which he taught at times seemed more dominated by a hunger for philanthropic donors than for the world redemption about which it talked so much, he emphatically declared that Christianity was not dependent on any economic system and that no single system was the embodiment of Christ's teachings. He even had the audacity to say that some teachings of socialism might be closer to the biblical ideal than was laissez-faire capitalism. In a day when taller church spires and bigger church programs were the idols of the faithful, he served in the 1940s on the board of the then-suspect Urban League in an effort to help the disinherited minorities. He participated in the Religion and Labor Fellowship in an effort to overcome unionism's view that organized religion was the working man's enemy. He met with tiny groups of concerned churchmen and helped organize what was eventually to become the Texas Baptist Christian Life Commission. If not denounced outright for his views, he was constantly suspect and was labeled a liberal, a radical, a socialist, or a Communist (depending on which epithet sounded best in a given forum).

To attempt to encompass within a few brief pages the thoughts of Maston on the church and the world would not only be an exercise in utter futility but would do a gross injustice to this twentieth-century prophet. One interested in pursuing Maston's views on the church and a wide variety of world issues can read at least four of his books: *Christianity and World Issues; The Christian, the Church, and Contemporary Problems; A World in Travail;* and *The Christian in the Modern World.*

Rather than attempt to capsulize his thoughts on many subjects, this chapter will treat his general positions and his recommended strategies where the Christian church and the world in which it functions are concerned.

The Church

While he by no means conceives of the church and Christianity as interchangeable entities, Maston does place great stress on the church as the earthly, visible, institutionalized form which is responsible, in this present world, for nurturing, teaching, spreading, and embodying the intangible principles which comprise the Christian faith. He may be sharply critical of the church's failure to fulfill her mission, her sometimes sickening gap between creeds and deeds, her foot-dragging when a firm pace is needed, her apathy to human misery, her identification with the socioeconomic or political status quo, and her secularization. But he has always recognized the church as a divine institution and never advocates, as some have, nailing her doors shut so that mankind can progress. Like the original purpose of Martin Luther, his intention appears to be the reform of the church, not a break of fellowship with her.

After examining the various usages of the word *church*—a local congregation, a particular denomination, a universal body of believers, an inclusive grouping of all the forces of organized religion—Maston examines appreciatively Gavin's definition of it as "a divine institution, supernaturally founded, endowed by God and governed by the Holy Spirit, the compass of whose domain extends over the whole of human life from the cradle through the grave to the Hereafter."[4] He does question what Gavin means by "domain," saying that if this means the church's influence should be felt in every area of life there would be no great disagreement but that if he means that the church's word should be the final authority for every man in every realm of life this concept of an "omnicompetent church" would not be acceptable.

Maston believes strongly that the church should have "a sense of divine purpose."[5] However, he warns that when this sense carries to the extreme the idea of a "this-worldly domain" it becomes an authoritarian church "which stands between the individual soul and God, claiming authority over the consciences and lives of men."[6] When that happens, he points out, there is a failure to distinguish between original Christianity and organized Christianity.

Perhaps a reason for Maston's continued belief in the church, an institutionalization of Christian values, in spite of its flawed practices is his realistic recognition of the human elements in the church's earthly programs. He declares simply that "imperfection is inevitable because the church cannot escape its humanity."[7] The church is what he frequently calls a "divine-human institution," and though he never says so in these exact words the gist of what he says about the church is this: Her founder and head is perfect, but local management sometimes leaves something to be desired.

This recognition of human frailty is no cop-out or evasion of the church's responsibility. Maston exercises constant tension on the minister and lay person alike as he urges the will of God, the summum bonum of his whole ethical system, upon them.

The State

Because of the constant interaction between church and state as Christianity functions in the present world, it is imperative for anyone concerned with moral imperatives to have a clear understanding of the state as well as of institutionalized religion. Of all the subjects which Maston has carefully explored in great depth, none is more thoroughly or intelligently treated than is the state. While many, particularly Roman Catholics and others believing in the overlapping of authority of church and state, would not agree with his conclusions, even they would have to admit that he has taken a broad, comprehensive look at the many ways the state may be viewed.

Following Paul, Maston holds that the state, or government as such, is a divine institution and a part of God's eternal plan for mankind. "The state stands for or symbolizes constituted authority, the authority to maintain law and order," he declares.[8] Concurring with Aristotle that the state exists for the promotion of the good life and with Roger Williams that it exists for the development of human society, he raises the question of what specific functions the state should perform and then responds:

The functions of the state on behalf of its citizens might be summarized as follows: it is to provide or to secure for them justice, liberty, and security. In some ways the most comprehensive of these and certainly the one most emphasized by leaders of democratic thought has been and is liberty.[9]

The Relation of Church and State

The greatest area of conflict where church and state are concerned is at the point of authority—how it is derived and how it should be exercised. Maston would agree with certain Roman Catholic theologians that both institutions derive their authority from a divine source, but he quickly differs with them in the exercise of their respective authority. He writes:

There is a source of authority beyond the church and the state, and whatever authority each of these possesses is delegated authority. The limitations of the authority of both church and state is most specific in the area of the individual conscience. The final authority for the individual is neither the state nor the church. As William the Silent put it, "Compulsion cannot touch the soul." Neither the state nor the church has the right to attempt such compulsion.[10]

If God is the source of original authority for both church and state, the question which ultimately must be dealt with, in the establishment of a working relationship between these two institutions, is, How does God choose to mediate that authority? Maston considers several possibilities then concludes that God mediates some authority through the people and retains a portion, including ultimate authority, for himself. This view "would mean that the church and the state are responsible both to God and to the people." He adds that if generally held, this position would "save a nation from an authoritarian, totalitarian church or state on the one hand, and from identifying the voice of the people with the voice of God on the other hand."[11] Then he adds significantly, "The latter is one of the abiding dangers in a democracy."

Maston discussed the possible relation of church and state under three main headings:[12]

Identification. There is no clear distinction between the secular and the sacred, between the political and the religious. Judaism and the Old Testament religion are classical examples of identification in biblical times, and an established or state church is a modern example. In the latter case, the assumption is that the whole nation is Christian—a patently false assumption.

Domination. At times both church and state have tried, with varying degrees of success, to control one another. The totalitarian state in the modern era has been either outright hostile to the church or has been on friendly terms as long as the church would do its bidding. At times the state has tried to dominate the church physically and to destroy it; at other times, it has sought to control it through spiritual domination—"the more insidious effort to control the spirit and soul of the church."

Nor has the state alone of these two major institutions attempted to dominate. The Roman Catholic Church, utilizing the two-swords theory, wherein the spiritual sword is wielded by the priest and the secular sword by kings and knights "but at the will of the priest and as long as he approves." History has recorded many case histories of church attempts to control the state albeit under the guise of being "for the common benefit of humanity," as one Catholic writer puts it.

Quite objectively, Maston points out that all attempts on the part of the church to dominate the state have not been Rome originated. Calvin, whose personal point of view was as undemocratic and authoritarian as possible, made the state subservient to the church. Lutheranism, from its early relationship of a love match on a common Christian basis, soon gave up its liberty to the state, a power which it accepted as a manifestation of the divine will. Some think this subservience provided the background for the rise of totalitarianism in Germany and other European countries.

Separation. Of the three possible relationships, the right one is separation, according to Maston. After examining the views and influence of John Locke and Roger Williams on the colonists and the factors which caused the United States from the beginning to provide for the separation of church and state, Maston quotes Thomas Jefferson's famous phrase, "a wall of separation between church and state," and says that there is no doubt that he and Madison intended for the First Amendment to the Constitution "to erect such a wall."

In a single, simple sentence, Maston defines his understanding of this political principle: "Separation of church and state simply means an organizational and functional separation."[13] His position is not that of religious indifferentism, and he quickly adds to his definition: "It is not a separation of religion and political life. Christian principles should be applied to governmental affairs . . . . But neither the church nor the state should seek to control the other or to use the other to promote its interests."[14]

There is one other danger in the position of separation which needs to be recognized by defenders of this position. This Maston terms "secularism, the danger that all of life will be organized as if God did not exist."[15] He believes that "the best assurance against the secularization of all of life is a vital type of religious movement, so dynamic that it will permeate all of life, so pervasive that the secular will be infused with a sense of the sacred."[16]

This type of religious vitality is more apt to be found in the disestablished, free, and sometimes small religious minority, he firmly believes.

In no area does the thinking of Maston on the church and the world come more sharply into focus than in this area of church and state. Although he is ever an idealist, he is also a realist who recognizes that man is going to organize his world along institutional lines and that those institutions will greatly shape his destiny. It is his responsibility to work within the "destiny shapers" to help them fulfill God's ultimate intents of redemption and freedom for all mankind.

The Church's Strategies in Relation to the World

What possible strategies can the church follow in relation to and in the midst of a sinful world? Maston identifies four which the church has historically followed.[17]

The rejection or withdrawal strategy. Throughout Christian history there have been many Christians who have looked upon the world as a kingdom of darkness controlled by Satan. They have, therefore, contended that the best thing a Christian can do is withdraw from the world as far as possible. Those who hold to this position reject culture as far as possible and try to separate themselves from the world and activities within it. Recognizing that there is a valid place in the Christian's life for a limited type of withdrawal and that all Christians should withdraw from the sin of the world, Maston rejects this strategy as a comprehensive approach and declares, "While those heroic groups and individuals who have consistently separated themselves from the world should be respected, nevertheless, their attitude is not compatible with the spirit of original Christianity."

The identification strategy. The exact opposite has been the strategy of other Christians who have sought to reconcile the gospel with the science, philosophy, and general cultural environment of the day, making Jesus "The Christ of culture." Theological liberalism, or what Barth calls "Culture-Protestantism," is within this tradition. Maston rejects this strategy also, making it clear that the Christian movement should not be identified with any particular economic order, political system, or any other form of the status quo or program of reconstruction or change.

Accommodation strategies. Accommodation, a median strategy between the two extremes cited above, has several forms within itself. The first is the practice of closely relating the this-worldly with the other-worldly, the building of a supernatural superstructure on a natural foundation. The second is making a rather sharp distinction between private and public morality, with higher norms expected for individuals than for groups. The best a

Christian can be expected to do in the area of public policy is to seek middle axioms, the provisional standards of behavior required of Christians at a given period and in a given circumstance. The third form of accommodation suggests that a Christian is a citizen of two worlds and as such has different standards and expectations on a dualistic level—the secular and the sacred, the temporal and the eternal, the kingdom of this world and the kingdom of God.

Yet another accommodationist viewpoint is the maintenance of both the relevance and transcendence of the Christian ethic. A Christian must recognize that he resides in an evil world and that if he is going to do anything about the conditions therein his choices will frequently be between relative evils. He should always seek to be identified with individuals and movements that are associated with the lesser rather than the greater evil. Of this approach, Maston says, "The greatest danger is that the Christian will not maintain in proper balance the relevance and the transcendence of the Christian ethic. The greatest danger seems to be that the sense of transcendence will be lost."

Transformation. Acknowledging that transformation might be viewed as a goal rather than as a strategy, Maston states that "it represents a strategy just as much as the withdrawal or identification strategies." He then sums up this approach by saying, "This strategy would not reject the world nor identify the Christian ethic with the ethic of the world but would transform the world into the likeness of the Christian ideal."

After positing the question about what the church's contribution to the transformation of the world should be, Maston answers his query thus: "It should certainly keep before society the ultimate Christian goals for society. It should not get involved, however, in the details or the methods to be used to attain those goals. It should apply the Christian spirit and ethic to the methods but not dictate the details of the methods to be used."

While Maston's approach to change would probably not satisfy today's social activists, even those within the walls of some churches, his pragmatism is remarkable as he asks about any strategy, "Is the strategy workable? Can it be used to carry the Christian spirit and Christian principles out into the life of the world? A strategy may sound good on paper, but if it will not work it is worse than worthless."[18]

Christianity and World Crisis

In his classes and in several of his published works, Maston gives considerable attention to the crisis in Western civilization and to the role Christianity, including its individual followers and the church, should play. In the preface to his *A World in Travail*,[19] Maston sums up his thoughts in the following fourteen statements:

1. The world is in the midst of the most serious crisis it has known since the days of the Renaissance and the Reformation.
2. The present period of chaos, confusion, and travail is symptomatic of the existing crisis and will continue until the world gets beyond the crisis period.
3. This crisis is particularly acute in Western civilization.
4. This crisis in Western civilization is most acute in Western Europe, which has . been the center of Western civilization and which has for various reasons experienced greater decay and collapse.
5. The crisis in the remainder of the world is related to and results from the crisis in Western civilization in some way and to some degree.
6. The contemporary crisis is so pervasive as to affect inevitably every phase of life.
7. A phenomenon of the proportions of the present crisis will have many contributing factors, both historical and contemporary. To attribute it to any one cause would be an oversimplification.
8. Although many factors have created the contemporary crisis, it is basically spiritual in its nature.
9. Since the cause of the crisis is basically spiritual, the remedy likewise must be primarily spiritual.
10. Simply stated, the contemporary crisis has resulted from the fact that man and his civilization have drifted away from God, and the only real remedy for it is for man and civilization to return to God and make him the integrating center of life.
11. This reintegration or reorientation of life must begin in the Christian church if the church is to be an effective instrument of God for the inner spiritual renewal of man and civilization.
12. Since God himself is the most determinative factor in the crisis, we should seek earnestly to discover the direction in which God is moving in our world.
13. The most important contribution we can make to the solution of the problems of the world is to pray for our world and for ourselves with an abiding faith that God is big enough to handle these problems and that his overall purpose in the world untimately will be accomplished.
14. With a strong faith in God we should seek to know and to do the will of God, knowing that nothing that we do for him will be lost.

The Individual's Orientation

Although Maston has spent his adult life as a teacher and author in the field of Christian social ethics, he has never lost sight of the individual and of the personal nature of Christianity. Even when relating the individual to great, revolutionary issues of the day and to an entire civilization in crisis, he does not minimize the individual and that persons's obligation to try to make the will of God the ruling principle in his life and the world. Perhaps the most fitting place to terminate a discussion of his thought about the church and the world is in a brief list of statements Maston gives in *The Christian, the Church, and Contemporary Problems* under the heading, "A Transcendent Orientation."

To be most effective the Christian citizen must not only be intelligent and cultivate a historical perspective, he must also maintain a transcendent orientation or point of reference. What does this mean and what will it do for him? If one has an abidingly transcendent point of reference:

1. He will believe that his God is active in the world and that He is on the side of the right, the good, the true.

2. He will attempt to sense the direction in which God is moving in our world and will seek to catch step with Him.

3. He will believe that all areas of his life and all phases of the life of his nation and the world must ultimately recognize their dependence on God and dedicate themselves to the service of God and mankind.

4. He will have an abiding faith in a sovereign God whose overall purpose will be triumphant in the world; he will believe that God will have the last word.

5. He will recognize that above the kingdom of this world is the kingdom or rule of God.

6. He will recognize that his supreme and final obedience belongs to God and not to the state or to the church.

7. He will seek to retain a constant sense of the eternal; he will make the eternal values supreme in his life.

If the Christian citizen can achieve and maintain such a transcendent, eternal orientation in his life, it will give to him a sense of purpose and patience, poise and perseverance as he follows what he considers to be the divine purpose of his life and the will of God for his world. Underneath the tensions of his life, which are the common lot of those who take seriously the demands of Christ, will be a peace that passeth understanding, a peace that comes only to those who are conscious of the presence of the Sovereign God who is our loving heavenly Father.[20]

T. B. Maston did not just write those lines—he has lived them.

Notes

1. T. B. Maston, *The Christian, the Church, and Contemporary Problems* (Waco: Word Books, 1968), p. 5.

2. Ibid., p. 6.   3. Ibid., p. 7.

4. T. B. Maston, *Christianity and World Issues* (New York: The Macmillan Company, 1957), p. 205.

5. Ibid., p. 206.   6. Ibid.

7. Ibid.   8. Ibid., p. 208.

9. Ibid., p. 210.   10. Ibid., pp. 211-212.

11. Ibid., p. 213.   12. Ibid., pp. 216-224.

13. Ibid., p. 223.   14. Ibid.

15. Ibid., p. 224.   16. Ibid.

17. Ibid., pp. 16-28.   18. Ibid., p. 27.

19. T. B. Maston, *A World in Travail* (Nashville: Broadman Press, 1954), pp. xiv-xvi.

20. Maston, *Christianity and World Issues*, p. 46.